The Internet Unplugged
Utilities & Techniques For Internet Productivity...Online And Off

DISCLAIMER OF LIABILITY

TRADEMARKS

COVER PHOTOGRAPHY BY PETER BAKER
COVER DESIGN BY MATT KORNHAAS

The Internet Unplugged
Utilities & Techniques For Internet
Productivity...Online And Off

Michael A. Banks

Edited by Donald R. Eamon

Wilton, CT
1997

 Printed on recycled paper.

With appreciation and affection, this book is for my mother, Sue Banks.

Contents

About Links to Sites and Staying Current

With new software tools and Web sites appearing (and disappearing) every day, the challenge for the author and publisher of *THE INTERNET UNPLUGGED* is to offer you a way to keep abreast of new resources and developments. Our mission is to provide you with a book that not only retains but actually *increases* its value as technology moves forward, unpredictably, in leaps and bounds. Today, the Internet—and specifically the World Wide Web—makes this possible.

At the Pemberton Press Web site, beginning in September 1997, we are publishing a regularly-updated **DIRECTORY OF INTERNET RESOURCES** that includes, wherever possible and practical, active links to sites (you must have an Internet connection and Web browser to utilize these links). The Directory is designed to help you find sites that offer specific types of information and software tools for Windows Internet users, and to keep you up-to-date on relevant trends and issues. It is being made available at no charge to you as a valued reader of *THE INTERNET UNPLUGGED*. Before using the Directory, please be sure to read the important disclaimer that appears at the bottom of this page.

To Access The **DIRECTORY OF INTERNET RESOURCES:**

1. Go to *THE INTERNET UNPLUGGED* Web page at:
www.onlineinc.com/pempress/unplugged

2. Click on the **DIRECTORY OF INTERNET RESOURCES** icon.
TIP: use your browser's bookmark feature to simplify reaching the Directory in the future

3. Note that the Directory is organized by chapter, reflecting the structure of the book (to effectively use the Directory, the publisher recommends that a copy of the book be on-hand). Read the descriptions of sites and resources, and visit those sites that interest you.

Please send feedback—including information about new or non-working Web sites and other resources—by E-mail to: *bookauthor@onlineinc.com.*

DISCLAIMER (please read carefully)
Neither publisher nor author make any claim as to the results that may be obtained through the use of the DIRECTORY OF INTERNET RESOURCES or any of the Internet sites it references. Neither publisher nor author will be held liable for any results, or lack thereof, obtained by the use of any links, for any third-party charges, or for any hardware, software or other problems that may occur as a result of using links. The DIRECTORY OF INTERNET RESOURCES is subject to change or discontinuation without notice at the discretion of the publisher.

Figures

CHAPTER 3
Browser Utilities, Shareware, and More   55

CHAPTER 4
Internet Support Software Basics   65

CHAPTER 9
Help for Your Web Site   139

Foreword

Each of us comes to the Internet from a different direction, with our own set of experiences and expectations. For some, it's an entirely new phenomenon, something we feel obligated, whether through professional demands, peer pressure or simple curiosity, to get a grip on, to "master" somehow. For others, the Net as a whole is an extension of work we've already been doing with computers or in one particular corner of the online universe. We may be fluent in the applications we use every day, perhaps even conversant with certain Internet protocols and resources, but we're hampered by tunnel-vision; we lack a coherent picture of the whole.

Nobody has "mastered" the Internet. That would be like mastering the world of music—all genres, all instruments, all eras—as a composer, a performer and a profoundly knowledgeable listener. Some of us strive for a broad understanding, acquiring a sense of the Net's history and architecture, how its various components evolved and fit together, and a general comprehension of how things work. Others go for depth, becoming fluent in specific protocols or the vernacular of a particular virtual neighborhood or Net subculture. Some of us—compulsive, overachieving or insatiably curious—try for both.

That's where *The Internet Unplugged* comes in. Michael Banks offers both the broad perspective and the detailed instruction necessary to become comfortable on the Net. He gives a comprehensive overview of what the Internet is and how it came to be that way, along with guidance on how to get online and what to do when you get there. He provides a solid introduction to the big issues, such as copyright, security, and assessing the quality and reliability of information on the Net. He covers the nitty-gritty of Web site design and hosting, the do's and don'ts of advertising and promotion, and other practical and technological considerations associated with the commercial use of the Net.

He also plunges fearlessly into what I call the Denial Zone, an assortment of Internet-related competencies and procedures that many of us have been muddling through cluelessly, executing by rote without understanding why, and avoiding outright wherever possible. He demystifies such pesky and problematic areas as graphics files and formats, the whys and wherefores of file compression and decompression, and the various flavors of E-mail attachments. He deconstructs the internal logic of a numeric Internet Protocol address, explains the difference between 7-bit and 8-bit encoding, distinguishes between browser plug-ins and helper apps, and conveys, throughout, a sense of why such apparent minutiae are important. He even manages to avoid that bane of technical discussions, the dreaded MEGO (My Eyes Glaze Over) effect.

Regardless of your own background or interest in the Net, Michael will fill in the blanks at both the broad-brush and the fine-detail level. He will bring you up to at least a minimal standard of competency in those areas that had been terra incognita for you. He will build your confidence where you've felt on shaky ground. And he will reinforce your expertise, and shore it up, if necessary, in the sectors of Net-literacy where you may not fully comprehend the tools and resources with which you're working. His approach is complete without being complex, simple without being condescending. For a sense of the scope of this book, take a look at Appendices B and C, which summarize all the significant readings, resources, and research aids, both basic and advanced, that are revealed and described throughout *The Internet Unplugged*.

I came to the Internet as an information specialist, a professional researcher. I was already conversant with Boolean search tools and heavy-duty online database services like DIALOG, Dow Jones News/Retrieval, and Lexis-Nexis (services that are now, incidentally, migrating to the Web). My learning curve, initially, involved brute-force protocols like archie, Telnet and FTP, along with the UNIX-based acronyms, switches and shortcuts required to use them effectively. Most of these arcane commands have since been subsumed, mercifully, into easy-to-use graphical client software or the "click here" comfort of the Web.

When the Web came along, it was a natural progression, for me, from text-only Internet resources like gopher sites and library OPACs (online public access catalogs), to their Web-based equivalents and the indexes and search engines needed to ferret them out. I was comfortable within my own area of expertise, locating information online, yet woefully underinformed about most other regions of the Internet. Terms like MIME, UUENCODE, Base 64, and BinHex were guaranteed to put me in a trance. Though I suspected that learning a bit about them would enrich my online experience, reduce stress, and contribute to my overall quality of life, everything not directly related to my research work went onto my mental "To Do Someday" list. It was all too much to absorb at once.

Like all good researchers and smart people in general, I am terminally curious. Once I got a taste of what the Internet was about, it began to exert a powerful pull. I wanted more context. I needed to know if I could do my job more efficiently. I wondered whether I was depriving myself of features and functionality with which I really should be conversant. I suspected that I was missing whole realms of experience, some tangential, some extremely germane. Once you've gotten in touch with your "inner geek," there's no turning back. You take joy in your expanding tech vocabulary; every step along the road to competence is thrilling. Knowledge, it turns out, *is* power.

Why "unplugged?" That's the component that makes this book unique. Despite the echoes of Eric Clapton et al, we're not talking about an acoustic

Internet (wooden computers; now there's a concept) or even a wireless one. The device we're unplugging is the telephone; it's the phone jack on the cover of this book, not a power plug, that's disengaged. The symbolism is clear. But isn't connectivity the essence of the Net? It is indeed, and yet there's a lot more to using the Net effectively than the process of spontaneous discovery, the real-time journey from site to site, or the 24-hour-a-day "cruise 'n schmooze" that the media love to depict. Your relationship with the Internet doesn't dissipate the moment your modem disconnects.

There's an entire constellation of tips, tools and techniques associated with the Net that you can utilize, offline, to augment and enhance the time you spend there. Michael Banks discusses virtually all of these—resources, both print and electronic, that will increase your basic understanding of the Internet, ideas and applications for archiving, manipulating and managing the information you find there, knowledge and protocols that will extend your use of E-mail as a communication and distribution channel, and browser add-ons and plug-ins that enable the Web to show off its entire repertoire of multimedia tricks.

The Web has made the Internet deceptively "easy" to use—so effortless, in fact, that some of us have become complacent, overconfident of our expertise and our ability to take advantage of everything it has to offer. Face it: you've been missing a lot. Techie or newbie, intrepid explorer or reluctant user, writer, researcher, software junkie, or afficionado of Web sites too mundane, bizarre, or numerous to mention—there are hidden dimensions to the Net that your browser hasn't yet begun to uncover. I can't tell you what they are because, like the fable of the blind men and the elephant, each of us is traveling with a different mental map of the Net. But, regardless of where you're starting from and where you want to go, Michael Banks is prepared to give you some massively useful clues. All you have to do is get yourself "unplugged."

Reva Basch
The Sea Ranch, California
15 July, 1997

(Publisher's Note: *WIRED Magazine* has called Reva Basch, "The Ultimate Intelligent Agent." Among her many other accomplishments, she is the author of *Secrets Of The Super Net Searchers: The Reflections, Revelations, And Hard-won Wisdom Of 35 Of The World's Top Internet Researchers.*)

Acknowledgments

An acknowledgments page usually carries names of people that almost no one reading the book knows. This one is no different. Or, maybe it is. Everyone listed here is an uncommon individual, the sort of person that anyone might feel privileged to know; the sort of person who was there at the right time during a certain period of disasters and accidents.

Dr. Raul David Alfaro de Alverez, Hiram Banks, Susanne & Mike Beeler, Chuck & Kate Berndt, Jack Cunkelman, Dr. Melvin Gale, George G. Gardner, Esq., Mike Getz, Larry Judy, John Kohus, Roger & Marj Krueger, Becky Lasater, Dr. Luis Pagani, Peter Prinz, Patrick Rose, and Dave Smith of AR. Thanks, too, to several unnamed physicians at Mercy Anderson and Clermont Mercy Hospitals in Cincinnati, and to Don Wilson for the offer of the drive to Belize.

Thanks to everyone at Online Inc. for their fine efforts, especially editorial manager Christine Watts, senior copyeditor Holly Pivor, production manager Sharon Peck, and art director Matt Kornhaas.

For input, suggestions, and corrections to the manuscript, thanks are due to Mary Ellen Bates, Paula Berinstein, Susanne Bjørner, Hillary Dietz, Nancy Garman, Drew Griffin, and Adam Pemberton. Thanks also to Paula Westwood for her feedback on the manuscript and for her fine work on *The Internet Unplugged* Web site.

Special thanks to my publisher, John Bryans, and my editor, Don Eamon, for their professional handling of this project.

Michael A. Banks
Oxford, Ohio

Introduction

It is safe to say that the Internet is the biggest thing to happen to the civilized world since the telephone. Millions of people use this worldwide network daily for business and personal communications, research, education, and entertainment. The Internet is constantly in the electronic news media, and major publications devote entire sections to this entity because it is recognized not only as a legitimate communications medium, but also as a source of news. All this for something that has existed for some thirty years, but didn't catch the public eye until just a few years ago.

Indeed, the Internet has gained popularity faster than any technological innovation in history. At the beginning of this decade, the Internet was the exclusive realm of "techies" and computer hobbyists. And a few of the "just curious" who, like me, hung around in case anything interesting and worth writing about happened. Actually, we were all techies, out of necessity; like it or not, being online even ten years ago often required that you knew how everything worked, almost down to the electron level!

Today, technical adepts are a minority on the Internet. The majority of Net denizens are computer *users*, who neither know all of the technical ins and outs, nor care to. And they don't have to, largely because PC hardware and software no longer require users to know how they work in order to use them. To "surf the Net" today, you need to know little more than how to log on to the Internet and fire up a Web browser.

In many ways, this easy access is a good thing. Being free of concerns about how to make something work lets us focus on putting it to use. In the case of the Internet, users are free to concentrate on the *content* of the Net, rather than how to get at that content.

At the same time, however, this ease of use has insulated users from some of the Internet's more interesting features, and some content. In short, you need to know a bit of the technical aspects of the Internet, your computer, and certain programs to fully access the Internet and all it has to offer. But, because you don't have to know much to use a Web browser in basic mode, you avoid picking up much of that knowledge.

So, if you want to enjoy all the benefits of Internet access, you must know more than how to make an Internet connection and use hyperlinks to move from one Web page to another (the limit of most Web surfers' knowledge). You can hyperlink from page to page all day, reading text and looking at graphics, and maybe downloading a file or two—but these are only the basics.

BEYOND THE BASICS

If you limit yourself to the basics of the Internet, you're missing more than a little. Anyone who's downloaded a very large file and found it completely unusable, or received a program or data file attached to an E-mail file and found that file totally useless, will vouch for this.

So, although you need know only the basics of using a browser to access the Internet, much of what the Internet offers requires you to go beyond these basics. You still need to know more than how to make an Internet connection and use hyperlinks.

Does this mean you have to become a techie or engineer to use the Internet efficiently? Not really. All you need to do is extend your knowledge of a few selected computer topics and put certain easy-to-use utilities to work.

Extending your knowledge is what this book is about. In these pages, you will learn what you need to know to use the Internet at full power. I'll also show you software—in the form of utilities and add-ons—that simplifies the most complex tasks of using the Internet and the data you gain thereby.

UTILITIES: SIMPLE AND VITAL

As you will learn, all kinds of utilities are necessary to get maximum efficiency from the Web (and, indeed, to even handle some basic tasks, like reading files that often are attached to E-mail).

Some of these utilities are vital; others are helpful but not vital, depending on your applications. Most have a common theme: they are not the kinds of programs the person who sold you your PC told you about; nor do the companies responsible for your operating system, Internet access, and other applications tell you about these important utilities and specialized applications.

Most of the time, Internet service providers don't offer a clue, either. But without the right support software—the utilities that you use offline, when the Internet is "unplugged" (as well as those you use while online)—you can be dead in the water, unable to do what you need to do. You may not even know what questions to ask.

The Internet Unplugged not only tells you which programs are needed, and why, but also where to find them. Many of the programs cited are shareware, which you can download from dozens of Web sites on the Internet, as well as from online service libraries.

WHAT YOU WILL FIND IN THIS BOOK

The first chapter is a basic guide to the Internet. You'll examine what the Internet is, what it is *not*, and a bit about how it works.

Chapter Two is for those of you who are new to the Web, as well as those who are wondering whether there's a better browser for you out there. This chapter also provides advice on choosing an Internet Service Provider.

Chapter Three is an introduction to the concepts of utilities and shareware, and discusses installing new software. This chapter will be of interest to those who would like to understand why some software is free—and why so much software that is thought of as "free" really isn't.

Chapter Four provides an overview of the categories of utility software known variously as "support software," "online helpers," "add-ons," and "plug-ins." That is, the programs you need to make your Internet experience complete—online or offline. Here you will find descriptions of utilities categorized by the sorts of tasks they involve—graphics, data conversion, archiving, and others.

The remaining chapters take you through all the categories of utilities and "helper" software you need to crank up the Internet, online or off: archiving software; graphics viewing, printing, and conversion software; data and text file conversion; MIME translation software; and more.

You'll also find some lasting references in the appendices. Appendix A is a glossary of terms. Appendix B provides cross-references of offline helper software by application and category. Appendix C lists additional sources of information—specifically, relevant Web sites mentioned in the book. Appendix D contains The ASCII Table.

Of special note is the fact that these appendices will be updated regularly at *The Internet Unplugged* Web site: **http://www.onlineinc.com/pempress/unplugged**.

And that pretty much tells you everything you can learn about the subject and contents of this book. But don't spend all your time reading. When you discover something interesting in a chapter, try it out! Go to a Web site, download a program under discussion, or try some of the tips. You'll learn more—and learn it faster—by putting knowledge to work as quickly as you can.

The Internet Defined: What It Is, What It Isn't, and What It Offers

Whether or not you've been on the Internet, you probably have quite a few questions about it. This chapter shows you a bit about what the Internet is, what it isn't, what it offers, and how to access it.

INTERNET BASICS

A simple description of the Internet might go like this: "Tens of thousands of computers at locations around the world, each interlinked with the other, providing access to all interlinked computers and their files to anyone who has access to any one of these computers." This description is accurate, but it's too quick, too easy. So, let's take a closer look at the basic structure of the Internet.

NOTE: If you are Internet-savvy, you may want to skip the rest of this chapter— although you may find the section on the history of the Internet of interest (see "A DESCRIPTIVE HISTORY OF THE INTERNET").

First, you need to understand that the Internet is no single entity, nor is it a consumer online service like America Online or CompuServe. For that matter, neither are online services the Internet. However, online services can connect with the Internet. I mention this because sometimes those new to the online world confuse online services and "the Internet," which is easy to do, because the Internet holds endless potential for confusion.

The Internet is particularly confusing if you are unfamiliar with the terminology used to discuss it. You won't be among that group by the time you finish reading this chapter; you'll know more about Internet terminology and the Internet itself. The glossary beginning on page 205 will also be helpful.

Basic Elements: Resources and Links

The Internet has two major elements—*resources* and *communications links*, which make the resources available to other computers.

There are several varieties of resources, the most important of which are *data resources*. Data resources consist of millions of data, text, and program files stored on tens of thousands of computers on the Internet worldwide. These resources are the main reason many computer users access the Internet. Data resources make up much of the surface content of the Internet—that is, what many perceive as being the Internet: text in Usenet newsgroups and/or the text and graphics displayed on screen as *Web pages*.

Not incidentally, Web pages are the result of data and program files being transmitted to your computer. See the following section, "The Internet: Bringing It All Together" for details.

Data resources may be stored in any of several ways on computers hosting Web sites—on hard drives, in RAM, or by other means. How the data is stored is immaterial; the important thing is that Internet data resources are available to anyone who has access to the Internet.

The storage media, along with the computers on which the data is stored, and associated communications hardware and software, represent still more resources. In this case, *hardware* and *software resources*.

After resources, the other major element of the Internet is its system of *communications links*. These links interconnect thousands of computers and help modem-equipped computer users access the data resources stored on those computers. Communications links consist of conventional telephone lines, high-speed data lines designed to carry only computer data, satellite and microwave relay links, modems, cable-TV links, and other components—including the computers on which Internet resources are stored.

These communications links provide a means whereby individual computers on the Internet are *networked*—simultaneously interconnected and sharing data resources—hence, the frequent reference to the Internet as a *network* of computers, any of which can be accessed at any time by any other computer on the network. In a sense, these communications links are resources, too.

(Interestingly, some computers linked to the Internet are themselves a part of networks, in the form of several PCs linked by a *local area network*, or LAN. Other computers that make up the Internet include mainframes, minicomputers, and individual PCs.)

Cumulatively then, data resources, the computers on which data is stored, and the links that interconnect the Internet's computers with other computers, *are* the Internet. Your perception of the data received from these resources completes the picture.

If the overall image here seems fuzzy, don't let it bother you; the Internet *is* more than a bit fuzzy both in concept and in reality. But the Internet is not incomprehensible.

The Internet: Bringing It All Together

To better visualize just how the Internet functions, consider what happens when you are connected with a remote computer system—an online service, for example, or a computer bulletin board system (BBS). When you dial up another system, you have varying access to and control over that system. The commands you issue to view messages, download files, and so on cause programs on the host machine to perform certain actions. (Defined in detail in the section headed "Clients, Servers, and Hosts" later in this chapter, a *host machine* is any computer you dial up and connect with via modem.)

In a sense, you are like a *remote terminal*, issuing commands and sending/receiving data—an extension of the online service or BBS computer to which you're connected. (A remote terminal is a device connected to a computer by direct lines or telephone lines. Sometimes called a "dumb terminal," a remote terminal may consist of a keyboard and monitor, and perhaps a printer or other peripheral, but it is not a computer. Rather, it is used to operate the computer to which it is connected, from a remote location. It performs no other functions, but using a remote terminal is like being at the main keyboard of the computer to which it is connected.)

Something similar happens when you connect with a computer on the Internet, although your access and the range of commands are comparatively limited. Basically, you can request to see certain files (text and graphics) and, in the case of *applets*, run programs. (Applets are mini-programs transmitted to your PC.)

You request files by telling your Web browser to "go to" or "open" a specific Web page, or by clicking on a *hyperlink*, which does the same thing. When you take either action, the remote computer—the one with the page you want to see—sends data to your computer. Your Web browser translates the data into images and text on your computer's screen.

The data sent to you—and your request for it—may be routed through a number of other computers on the Internet before you see it. However, as far as you and your computer are concerned, you are connected to and communicating with only one computer. Thus, the entire *web* of interconnected computers can be said to be "transparent." Not incidentally, because this web of interconnected computers is worldwide, it is often referred to as the *World Wide Web*, or *WWW*.

Now imagine this: tens of thousands of mainframe, mini-, and supercomputers around the world, all containing data and programs you can access. These computers, at a different location or *site*, are linked to all the other computers by an extended network of connections. Every site linked by this network is as accessible as every other site. Not only are all the sites connected, but they are connected in more than one way (in the web-like structure), and also relay information between other computer systems and sites.

What Is a Site?

I should note here that a *site* is a computer or group of computers accessible via the Internet. Somewhat confusingly, "site" is also used to refer to the set of resources on a computer at a particular location that is accessible via the Internet. For example, you can access Chrysler Corporation product and other information on the World Wide Web at: **http://www.chryslercorp.com/**. Collectively, the product and promotional information presented is known as Chrysler's "product information *site*." Thus, another way to think of a site is as a collection of related information files.

Each site has a unique "address," called an *URL* (pronounced "Earl"). The address (**http://www.chryslercorp.com**) in the preceding paragraph is an example of an URL. URL is short for "Uniform Resource Locator," which is the function of the addressing system of the Web. The name is appropriate because it provides a uniform protocol for locating resources (files) on the Web.

As you will learn in this chapter, all navigation on the Web is based on URLs. You'll take a closer look at URLs in a bit, but for now, consider an URL to be a site's address.

NOTE: Internet addresses are preceded by http, *which is short for "Hypertext Transport Protocol." This prefix may be thought of as a command to your Web browser to connect with the World Wide Web and see the location or "file" following "http." There are other prefixes, such as one that tells the browser to look for the file on your hard drive, discussed in the section headed, "URLs: The Key to Navigating the Web."*

Some sites *are* networks, and some sites are part of other networks, existing simultaneously on the Internet and other networks. (There *are* other networks, something worth mentioning in this context. In fact, connecting other networks to the Internet was a major source of growth for the Internet in the early 1990s. So, the Internet also is a "network of networks.")

THE WORLD WIDE WEB

This is the element of the Internet that the majority of newer modem users, as well as those who've never been online, think of as the Internet. This view is understandable because the Web gets the most media coverage. The coverage and the interest of new users is in turn understandable because the World Wide Web is the most "glamorous" of all Internet elements. (All elements that are real, that is; many misconceptions about what the Internet and the Web are and offer have been fostered by film, novels, and the more sensationalistic press.)

"Glamorous" is somewhat appropriate because—compared with other elements of the Internet—the Web offers glamour on several levels. There are Web sites that offer not only text, but text in colors, as well as graphics and photographs, sound, and even video, as well as the previously mentioned applets.

A Pragmatic Overview of the Web

There are many ways to look at the Web. Perhaps the most straightforward viewpoint is to consider the Web as made up of millions of computer files. Data and program files are the essence of the Web; all else is the means by which you locate and retrieve files.

These millions of files are accessible, but you must know how to get to them. Later in this section, you will look at how you can "navigate" the World Wide Web to find files.

Once transmitted to your computer, as described earlier in "The Internet: Bringing It All Together," Web files are put to use. If you have a Web browser capable of interpreting the files and presenting the result on your computer screen (and, in some instances, through your computer's speakers), your system presents the information contained in the Web-retrieved files as it was intended to appear.

Of course, you do not perceive all the chains of file search, retrieval, transmission, and interpretation. Rather, you see only the *information* that makes its way to your screen. And this is what the Web is all about—visual and audio information, in new forms and through new media and, sometimes, with new content.

Documents, Pages, Hypertext, and Hyperlinks

Files at Web sites are organized into documents, each of which has one or more pages. The usage of *document* derives from the fact that, on the early Web, documents in the form of text files were the most-commonly accessible files.

FIGURE 1.1

Online Inc.'s home page

The moniker stuck, and is used with reference to even today's Web pages, many of which have multimedia content. (Binary files—typically graphic or program files—also are often called "documents." For a more detailed discussion of binary data, please see Chapter Seven, "Computer/Internet Data Formats and Conversion.") Most references to the Web actually allude to these documents, or individual pages within documents.

Home Pages. Note that the terms "document" and "page" are often used interchangeably, with page most often used to mean document. The first page of a document is always referred to as a site's or document's *home page*. If you navigate to a site without specifying a page, the home page is displayed. This is the default or index page for that site, which Web surfers consider the "main" or opening page.

In common use today, however, the term home page is often taken to mean an entire document carried on behalf of an individual, commercial, or other entity at a Web site. Therefore, Online Inc.'s entire Web site (**http://www. onlineinc.com**) is often referred to as the corporation's home page. Figure 1.1 shows the opening page at that Web site. (You may notice that various elements of Netscape here and elsewhere are missing, such as the button bar. This is also true of Explorer in various illustrations. I turn off the button bar, and sometimes the location and other browser elements in order to display as much of the Web page as possible on the screen. So, don't be concerned if you don't see the exact same thing on your screen; it's just that we're running with different operating parameters.)

A given site on the Web usually contains more than one document or page. Plus, some Web sites are hosts to numerous clients who create their own sites (or have them created) for personal, business, or commercial reasons. The Online Inc. Web site, for example, contains many pages devoted to Online Inc. corporate matters and products. It also hosts the Web site for Pemberton

Press, the book publishing arm of Online Inc., at: **http://www.onlineinc. com/pempress/**, which itself has numerous pages.

Viewed another way, adding the **/pempress/** element of the URL **http://www.onlineinc.com/pempress/** is asking to access a subdirectory of the **onlineinc** server, named **/pempress**. Rather than a directory of that subdirectory, however, you see the default page (or home page) for Pemberton Press, as shown in Figure 1.2.

Page Sizes and Roles. However you may refer to them, Web *pages* vary by size (the number of kilobytes transmitted for a page) and display length (the number of computer screens required to display one page in its entirety). Depending on the layout and how much text or other material it contains, a page can require several computer screens to display. A Web page may be designed to scroll vertically or horizontally and Web browsers accommodate both designs.

Because of their inherent flexibility, Web sites may play many roles: data forms, E-mail, search tools and lists, file transfers, newsgroups, and even Telnet may be found at Web sites.

HTML: The Language of the Web. Web pages are written in a simple, high-level language that Web browsers can understand and process, known as *hypertext markup language* (or *HTML*). Because of this, Web pages are sometimes referred to as *hypertext pages*.

Typically, the first file transmitted to your computer when you open or go to a Web page is an HTML file. Your Web browser interprets the HTML commands contained in a page to display the data it contains and data from other files, if any, as a Web "page."

Text on a Web page is usually *embedded* (included) in the HTML document that makes up the

FIGURE 1.2

The Pemberton Press home page

page. Other data may be transmitted as separate files. This includes, but is not limited to, graphic images (typically binary .JPG or .GIF files), additional text, binary data for sound files or video, and mini-programs referred to as *applets*. (As mentioned earlier, binary files are often graphic image files. Since almost all images on Web pages are .JPG or .GIF format, these are the types of binary files you are most likely to encounter. For detailed information on graphics file types, see Chapter Six, "Offline Graphics Helpers." For a complete discussion of binary data and file types, see Chapter Seven, "Computer/Internet Data Formats and Conversion.")

Figure 1.3 shows a Web page (left), and the HTML code used to generate it (right).

FIGURE 1.3

A portion of a Web page, as displayed with a browser (left), and in its HTML form (right)

Typically, the initial HTML code or page is transmitted first, which causes your browser to display the embedded text as instructed by *formatting codes* included in the HTML page. (Formatting codes are contained within the greater-than/lesser-than symbols you see in the example in Figure 1.3. For example, <b> means, "display all the text following this symbol in boldface," and </b> means "stop displaying in boldface.") The coding system is like typesetting—at least where text display is concerned. HTML files are designated by the filename extensions .HTM or .HTML. Other codes specify additional layout elements, such as the location of graphics on the page, and special elements, like *links* to other pages.

Graphic images come next, transmitted as separate files. Commands embedded in the HTML document instruct your browser where and how to display images.

NOTE: For additional how-to and reference information about the HTML language and its applications, visit: **http://www.ncsa.uiuc.edu/General/Internet/ WWW/HTMLPrimer.html**.

This site is sponsored by the National Center for Supercomputer Applications. For more information, E-mail: **pubs@ncsa.uiuc.edu**.

Thus, a typical Web page is composed of several files. The text HTML file is the foundation of every Web page, the basic element. Other text or binary files may follow, depending on the page's content.

Hyperlinks. An important coding element in HTML documents is the *hyperlink*. A hyperlink is a means of linking the current document to another Web page, or to a binary file. Linked pages or files may be other documents at the current Web site, or they may be at another site entirely. The function of a hyperlink is to have another Web page, or a specific file, transmitted to your computer.

Hyperlinks may be textual or graphical in nature. A text hyperlink is usually distinguished by the fact that it is displayed as underlined, <u>like this</u>. A hyperlink may also be a different color from surrounding text, and hyperlinks you have already visited are usually another color still.

When you pass the mouse pointer or cursor over a hyperlink, the cursor becomes a pointing finger. Also, the URL to which the hyperlink connects is displayed in the browser's status line, at the lower left of the display.

A page connected by a hyperlink is accessed by clicking on the hyperlink. Therefore, it can be said that a hyperlink is a means by which a document page, or any element within a page, can be linked to other pages, files, or even other sites. The hyperlinked structure of the Web is the key to its magic; any one element of a Web site or page can be linked directly to literally any other element.

FIGURE 1.4

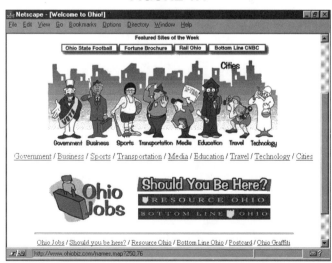

A World Wide Web page with hyperlinks and image maps

As implied a few lines back, some hyperlinks are embedded in graphic images (called clickable graphics or *image maps*), as shown in Figure 1.4. You can identify image maps by their labeling, and by the fact that the cursor becomes a pointing finger when passed over them, indicating a hyperlink. As with text hyperlinks, the URL to which an image map leads, or the coordinates of the image itself, is displayed in your browser's status line when the mouse cursor passes over the image map.

As previously stated, a hyperlink can be a continuation of the current Web page (another page or supplementary material such as images, sounds, and so forth), a page from a different document at the same site, or a page at a different site. For example, many Web sites contain reference lists, which are really links that connect to pages at other sites.

Hyperlinks to other sites are often creative, adding "features" to pages such as the current time from the U.S. Naval Observatory. (To do so, you add the URL: **http://tycho.usno.navy.mil:80/what.html** to a page as a hyperlink.)

Hyperlinks may also run programs on the host machine or at another remote computer. An example of running a program that's not a part of the Web page in question is the "Web counter," which tracks and displays the number of people who have accessed a Web page. This counter is actually a link to a program running on the host computer or another machine (not on your PC). The program actually tracks the number of "visits to" or "hits" on that Web page. It then transmits the results to a designated location on the Web page each time it is run.

Interestingly, the lists that Web search engines compile and present are also just lists of hyperlinks. The list is compiled by a search program that runs on the host computer, and the URLs, or addresses, are inserted as hyperlinks in the HTML document you receive.

Files for Images and Add-On Programs. As previously stated, graphic images come next, transmitted as separate files. Commands embedded in the HTML document tell your browser where and how to display images, which typically have extensions of .JPG or .GIF.

Following the HTML code and text files, and any graphics files, there may be binary files in any of several forms and formats. These files might include special image types, video or animation, sound and MIDI files, fonts, and specially formatted data (such as a spreadsheet). These kinds of data might be handled by your browser, but more often, they are handed over to *add-on programs*. Add-ons, a.k.a. *plug-ins* and *helper applications*, are programs stored on your hard disk that your browser can activate when it encounters specific types of data.

Knowing *when* to run such programs—also referred to as *spawning*—is your browser's job. A browser can recognize specific types of data by filename extensions and, based on the browser's setup, it then runs a specific program and "feeds" the incoming data to it. Everything else is either turned over to an add-on program, saved to disk, or canceled in the case of unrecognized file types.

Most browsers can be set up to use a specific add-on when it sees a particular type of data coming in. Audio files in the RealAudio format, for example, identified by the extensions .RA or .RAM, are played with the RealAudio player program—provided that you have the program on your hard drive, and your browser knows where to find it. Your browser also must know the extensions for RealAudio data. This is a setup item, specified from within your browser's Options or Preferences menu—about which you will learn more in Chapter Two, "Selecting a Browser and an ISP." Most browsers come set up to recognize most of the more popular add-on programs' data extensions.

It's worth noting here that you must obtain many of these add-ons—your browser probably doesn't come with add-ons. It has certain built-in capabilities, but these do not provide all the extra features that add-ons provide. Also, some add-ons may perform certain tasks better than your browser's built-in capabilities.

Fortunately, most add-ons either are free or are shareware, which you can download at a variety of Web sites or on online services, as discussed in Chapters Three, Four, Ten, and Appendix B.

A DESCRIPTIVE HISTORY OF THE INTERNET

The Internet's beginnings lie in a United States Department of Defense research program. The goal was to design computer networks that could survive a nuclear attack. Even in the 1960s, more than a little sensitive and critical data flowed through the nation's infant computer networks. The project was *ARPANET*, an acronym for the "Advanced Research Projects Agency Network." (ARPANET is sometimes referred to as DARPANET, an acronym that includes "Defense.")

Packet-switching networks were a major element of the Internet. A given data file or data group can be divided into many *packets*, or units of information, each containing a portion of the file. Each data packet also contained information as to its destination and how it fit with other packets. Data packets would be reassembled by the receiving system's communications program.

Along the way, data packets could be routed via available paths that included going *through* various computers on the Internet. This kind of routing required that each computer be able to communicate with every other computer on the network, at any time, which is how the network was designed: to provide, in effect, simultaneous links among all computers on the network.

Depending on whether a given computer site on the network was too busy (or, in the worst-case scenario, "taken out" by a nuclear strike), the same route might not be available for all the data packets. This was fine because the data packets did not have to use the same route; as long as the data packets carried information to their destination, any one route was the same as the next; no one path for data was *the* critical route. Any computer on the network could reroute data packets as required for them to arrive at their destination.

Also created by this project were certain basic network communications and control protocols, known as *Transmission Control Protocol / Internet Protocol*—or *TCP / IP*. You'll see TCP/IP bandied about quite a bit in references to the Internet, but you don't need to understand it. Just know that it refers to a set of rules by which computers linked to the Internet communicate and handle the data they're carrying. It also (in part) defines the Internet because a computer cannot be a part of the Internet unless it communicates by using these protocols.

NOTE: In case you are curious, TCP is the protocol in charge of making sure that data packets get to the appropriate destination. IP is the address protocol, used to assign a destination—or address—to data packets. Addresses from IP are used by TCP to route each data packet.

The ARPANET became immensely popular and, as more and more interconnections developed, the user base grew tremendously. Eventually, commercial computer sites began hooking into the network, in addition to the educational, scientific, and government computer sites that formed its base. As the network continued to grow and evolve, its military component became a separate entity, MILNET (for "MILitary NETwork"), and the Internet as we know it today began to take shape.

The National Science Foundation (NSF) promoted the growth of the civilian Internet throughout the 1980s, in part with its joining a network of supercomputers on the Internet. As the Internet continued to grow, international links using Internet communications protocols were forged. By the end of the decade, commercial as well as government, education, and scientific organizations were setting up sites on the Internet. For some time, commercial entities had been using the Internet for E-mail communication and for research. Today, the overwhelming majority of new sites on the Internet are commercial.

In 1989, researchers at the European Organization for Nuclear Research (or CERN, which is the acronym, in French, for the organization's name) created a worldwide network of several supercomputers, to facilitate access to data by physicists and other scientists, using the Internet. This network quickly evolved into the massive Internet adjunct, the *World Wide Web* (or, *WWW*). The Web is the sophisticated system previously described. Its page-oriented documents teem with hypertext links, and today's technology adds graphics, sound, and even video at some sites for a true multimedia network.

As noted previously, the World Wide Web *is* the Internet to many observers and users. But as you will learn, the Web is only one of many resources available on the Internet.

BUT, HOW DOES IT ALL WORK?

As noted, the Internet is a globe-spanning network, with a *backbone* of interlinks among some 40,000 computers. There is a structure to the sites and their interconnections, but it frequently changes—despite which, any computer on the Internet can communicate with any other computer on the "Net." The Internet is set up so that data is typically routed over the fastest links—which may or may not be the shortest geographical route.

The Internet's "geography" usually has little to do with physical locations. Instead, the Internet routes connections by using a dedicated address format. Specifically, each site has a 32-bit numeric address that tells all other systems on the Internet how to contact it. In human terms, these numeric addresses are the "*xxxxx*.com" or "*xxxxx*.edu," and similar addresses we use to navigate.

NOTE: A 32-bit address is known as an IP address *that looks like this:* **192.80.63.253**.

We deal with IP addresses in more meaningful human terms, thanks to *DNS* (Domain Name Service). DNS is a protocol used by computers on the Internet to translate IP addresses. Thus, a 32-bit address takes the form of a text address, like: **http://www.bix.com**. This address is a.k.a. *Fully Qualified Domain Name*.

Data packets transmitted from one computer to another are sent through the routes that are easiest to take, and eventually arrive at their intended destination. This process is transparent to you, the Internet user, thanks to Internet Protocol addressing and Transmission Control Protocol that routes the data.

URLs: The Key to Navigating the Web

I have referred to Web "addresses" a number of times, always in this format: **http://www.*xxxxxx*.com/**. This type of address is called an URL, as you know.

Consider the process of using an URL as analogous to directing your computer to a file on your hard disk. This, by the way, is something you can do, although the command to your Internet browser would be something like: **file:///c:/myfiles/chapter1.htm**.

Navigating the Web by using URLs is an expansion of finding a file on a disk. (Remember my discussion of the World Wide Web as a series of files on computers at various Internet sites?) The difference is that the file can exist on any computer on the Internet.

Many URLs include a filename, so you can go directly to a file. The addressing system follows UNIX conventions. (UNIX was an early computer operating system that still has its adherents today. It was used on all types of computers—mainframe, Apple, PC, minis, and so on—which is probably why so much of the Internet uses UNIX-based routing.) An address indicates the site (server/computer), any directories involved, and the file to retrieve. If no file is specified, you go to the site in question, and its home page or index page is retrieved and displayed.

You must direct your browser outside your machine to browse the Web by using a prefix to tell it to connect to the Internet. The special protocol you use is *http*, or *Hypertext Transport Protocol*. Hence, the prefix "http" in an URL.

The front-slashes in the address are, again, a UNIX convention. The name that follows **http://** is the site, followed by the name of the server, and the file path on the server in question.

The **http://** prefix tells your browser to find the URL on the World Wide Web. To find a file on your system, enter the **file://** prefix. To make a connection through an FTP server, you use the prefix **ftp://**. A Telnet connection is indicated by **telnet://**.

Putting all this together, if you wanted to retrieve a document named **pretend.html** in a directory named **fiction** at a fictional site called **ficcion**, you would use this URL: **http://www.ficcion.com/fiction/pretend.html**.

Note that you will find many, many documents with the filename extension **.html**; this is the extension of hypertext documents that use the HTML language. Your PC, being restricted to three-letter filename extensions, uses the extension **.htm** for HTML files. Some servers do the same.

By the way, the first part of the site name alludes to its network type. In our fictional example, **www** means this is a World Wide Web site.

Web-Browser Access to Usenet Newsgroups
To use your Web browser to access a Usenet newsgroup, in the Web page box, simply type: news: followed by the name of the newsgroup. (You do not need to include the http:// prefix.) Therefore, to view the rec.autos.antique newsgroup, you type: **news:rec.autos.antique**.

The actual computer name makes up the second part of the name. The final part is the *domain identifier* (sometimes called the *domain name*). This indicates the type of operation at that site. In this example, **com** means "commercial," which is one of six domain names:

.com—*Com*mercial site, operated by a company or corporation, such as: **compuserve.com** or **microsoft.com**

.gov—Sites sponsored by *gov*ernmental agencies. Examples: **whitehouse.gov** and **epa.gov**

.edu—*Edu*cational institutions, such as **muohio.edu**

.mil—*Mil*itary site, such the U.S. Naval Observatory mentioned previously

.org—*Org*anization, usually something that doesn't fit in another category

.sci—*Sci*entific or research site

Some sites carry geographical suffixes as a part of their domain name, like "uk" for a site in the United Kingdom. (These are sometimes used in the U.S., the suffix being "us".) There may also be a colon and a number (like this, **:80**) appended to some site names; this is merely a designator for a given port on the computer at that location.

Incidentally, if you have the numeric IP address for a computer on the Internet, you can use it as easily as you use the domain name. For example, rather than entering: **http://www.bix.com** to go to the BIX Web site, you can enter the IP address: **192.80.63.253** in place of bix.com

TIP

If you know the file or document you want to access from a Web site, you can add this to the address, preceded by a slash, as in the following example, where the fictional commercial server **zxrb.com** contains the file **mike.html** in its root directory: **http://www.zxrb.com/mike.html**. Typing this URL takes you directly to the page contained in mike.html, without having to view the main page of zxrb.com.

With all Internet sites linked full-time with all other computers on the Internet, moving data to a given address is no different than moving it to any other address on the Internet.

Clients, Servers, and Hosts

Before you get rolling with these applications, you'll encounter three important terms in nearly every discussion of Internet resources and applications. I mention them here because they are sometimes used in a way that can confuse their respective meanings. The terms are *client*, *server*, and *host*.

A *client* is, strictly speaking, a program that communicates with another computer to obtain access to files or programs. In the overall vernacular of the Internet, it has come to mean the computer that is communicating with another computer system to access resources.

A *server* is a computer system or program that provides resources on a network. A server is often referred to by the kind of resource it provides. Examples: mail server (accepts, sends, and receives mail), news server (carries Usenet newsgroups). "Web server" and "Internet server" are sometimes confusing usages; either can mean a system that offers access to the World Wide Web or the Internet, or a system that has Web or Internet resources (such as Web pages). The simple rule for servers is this: a server provides resources, and the client connects with the server to access those resources, be they files, hyperlinks, access to other systems, or other information.

The term *host* is often used synonymously with *server*. More often, however, it refers to any system you dial up for any reason. It is logical either way. If you are dialing into a system to use resources, it is your host. If the system is enabling your access to other systems, in the manner of an Internet Service Provider (or *ISP*), it is your host, enabling your activities on the Internet or wherever it may take you.

WHAT DOES THE INTERNET HAVE TO OFFER?

I previously described the Internet as "...a set of *resources*, in the form of millions of files and programs on tens of thousands of computers." This description is valid, but what exactly are these resources?

When you get to the bottom line, files and applications are the foundation of all computing. The uses to which they are put are the *real* resources. Internet resources are no different; there are several categories of applications that make up the major Internet resources:

- E-mail
- Usenet newsgroups
- The World Wide Web
- FTP (File Transfer Protocol)

- Telnet
- The Internet itself

The following sections explore each category of Internet resources. These resources reside on the computers at various sites. As you may imagine, millions upon millions of files reside on the computers at the more than 40,000 Internet sites that currently exist (with more being added daily!).

E-mail

Internet E-mail is something of a wonder, considering what can be done with it. Millions of Internet, online service, and BBS users at tens of thousands of sites worldwide can exchange unlimited messages, with the delivery of most mail taking place within hours, if not minutes, of sending it—all this, and at a very low price. The cost of sending a typical E-mail message of two screen pages ranges from nothing to perhaps fifty cents—that upper range is the cost of time spent online typing the message on a service with high per-minute rates.

E-mail was one of the first Internet elements to surface in "mainstream" telecomputing. E-mail among Internet sites has been available from the beginning, but Internet E-mail exchange with commercial online services and BBSs is relatively recent. Commercial online service users recognized the advantages of Internet E-mail access almost as soon as their respective services made it available. There was no charge beyond their online connect time (minimal with offline E-mail composition), and mail delivery was almost as fast as an online service's internal mail service.

Because E-mail could go to, as well as from, a commercial online service, users quickly discovered that they not only could stay in touch with Internet sites, but also with friends and associates on other commercial online services. (CompuServe pioneered this area, being the first commercial online service to offer Internet E-mail service, along with several other direct E-mail links, including MCI Mail, X.400 connections, and more.)

Today, all commercial online services—whether consumer, business, or specialty services—have Internet E-mail access.

Internet E-mail was most commercial online service users' first exposure to the Internet. Long before many had heard of Usenet newsgroups, Web pages, or other elements of today's Internet, they were using Internet E-mail to communicate with those on other services, and at Internet sites.

Internet E-mail is simple to send. The "address" consists of the recipient's user name and the name of the online service or Internet site where the recipient has an account, entered in a simple format. The Internet takes care of routing and delivering the message. Other than that, mail composition and actually sending it goes pretty much like sending internal E-mail. Internet mail that you receive appears in your E-mail inbox, just like E-mail from other sources. (Internet sites follow the naming conventions discussed in the preceding section, headed "BUT, HOW DOES IT ALL WORK?")

Depending on your Internet Service Provider—particularly if it is an online service—there may be special addressing protocols to follow for sending E-mail to other sites on the Internet. Refer to your ISP's online help or manual for more information.

It is also worth noting that many World Wide Web pages contain *mail hyperlinks*, which can be used to send mail. When you click a Web page's mail hyperlink, a form for an E-mail message pops up. The message is already addressed, with your and the sender's E-mail addresses. Type the message, press Send, and your mail is sent. (This is true if your Web browser is set up with a designated mail server, your user ID, and a return address.)

Such a link is often known as a *mailto* because it makes use of the HTML command: **mailto:*userid@system*.com** (where ***userid@system*.com** is the E-mail recipient's address).

Usenet Newsgroups

You probably heard about Usenet and newsgroups not long after you first encountered the Internet. Commercial online services such as CompuServe began carrying (providing) Usenet newsgroups early on because there was a large demand for them—particularly groups involving special interests.

What Is Usenet? Is it another network, like the Internet? Not at all. The name Usenet is an acronym for *User Network*, but Usenet is more a set of rules for—and a way to organize—newsgroups. It has no specific location, and it exists both on and off the Internet.

Newsgroups are just extended simple message bases that contain messages arranged by subject, and organized into *threads*. (Threads are messages that are linked, by subtopic and/or a chain of posts and replies.) Figure 1.5 shows some newsgroup listings.

Newsgroups are like the message bases or bulletin boards on computer BBSs and online services in that they contain messages grouped by subject and thread. However, the similarity ends here with most newsgroups because anyone can post anything they want in the majority of newsgroups. So, prepare to wade through a lot of extraneous commentary and personal diatribes.

The better newsgroups do not have this problem because they have moderators who track and weed out extraneous and irrelevant messages—and users. *Moderated* newsgroups, however, are in the minority.

FIGURE 1.5

```
15 comp.ai.philosophy
        Philosophical aspects of Artificial Intelligence.
16 comp.ai.shells
        Artificial intelligence applied to shells.
17 comp.ai.vision
        Artificial Intelligence Vision Research. (Moderated)
18 comp.answers
        Repository for periodic USENET articles. (Moderated)
19 comp.apps.spreadsheets
        Spreadsheets on various platforms.
20 comp.arch
        Computer architecture.
21 comp.arch.arithmetic
        Implementing arithmetic on computers/digital systems.
22 comp.arch.bus.vmebus
        Hardware and software for VMEbus Systems.
23 comp.arch.embedded
        Embedded computer systems topics.
24 comp.arch.fpga
        Field Programmable Gate Array based computing systems.
25 comp.arch.storage
        Storage system issues, both hardware and software.
26 comp.archives
        Descriptions of public access archives. (Moderated)
27 comp.archives.admin
        Issues relating to computer archive administration.
```

A typical listing of Usenet newsgroups

All newsgroup messages are referred to as *articles*. So, when a system menu that presents Usenet newsgroups refers to articles, it means messages.

Most ISPs (whether they are independent ISPs or commercial online services) offer all public newsgroups. (A few newsgroups, such as those devoted to a specific system and its users, are available only if you are a user on the system in question.)

In practice, you determine which newsgroups to read, and your ISP's newsreader system takes care of bringing in new messages in those newsgroups, displaying them on demand, and tracking which messages you've already read.

The typical Usenet newsgroup server copies in all messages frequently, and distributes replies and new messages posted to newsgroups to all other newsgroup servers. The whole concept is not unlike an open-ended chain letter.

Usenet newsgroups are organized into broad subject categories, with endless subcategories. These categories are worth exploring, and you will quickly learn which newsgroups have content worthwhile to you (typically, the moderated ones). The range of subject matter covers literally *everything*!

The basic subject categories for newsgroups available worldwide are: alt, bionet, bit, biz, comp, control, decus, general, gnu, ieee, junk, k12, misc, news, rec, sci, soc, talk, to, and vmsnet.

Among these categories, the most popular are:

biz—Discussions of business topics

comp—Discussions of computer-related subjects

misc—Topics that don't quite fit anywhere else

news—Topics having to do with newsgroups

rec—Recreation and related subjects

sci—Science, from archaeology to zoology

soc—Social subjects, including cultural mishmashes

talk—Discussions/debates/argument on controversial themes

Newsgroups branch into subcategories and specific topics and subtopics, which are readily identified by their names. For example, a newsgroup named: **alt.autos.antique** contains discussions about antique cars. The newsgroup is in the **alt** (alternative) category, under the subject of **autos**, and focuses on the topic of **antique**. The material covered by one newsgroup may overlap another newsgroup. For example, **alt.autos.antique** has some similarity to **rec.autos.antique**.

There are also introductory, regional, special, and local newsgroups (such as **compuserve** on CompuServe, **aol** on America Online, and **netcom** on NETCOM)—not to mention some foreign (especially German) newsgroups. In all, there are nearly 20,000 newsgroups.

Coded Transmissions and Binary Files Via Usenet. The majority of newsgroups carry text only, but some newsgroups are used to provide binary files for transfer. These files require that you use special software, which translates files that contain token 7-bit *ASCII* characters into their original binary form. (ASCII, an abbreviation for American Standard for Computer Information Interchange, is a standard electronic format for textual data. ASCII format guarantees that characters—letters, numerals, and symbols— are represented within computers and during data transmission and storage in an agreed-upon electronic format called the ASCII code. This enables computers to exchange data. I discuss this and related data format elements in detail in Chapter Seven, "Computer/Internet Data Formats and Conversion.")

This tokenizing, or *encoding*, of files is necessary because 8-bit files cannot be carried in Usenet's text-only messages.

NOTE: 7-bit ASCII characters are those generated by your keyboard's typewriter keys. That is, the letters of the alphabet, numerals, and punctuation marks commonly used in communication. These are called 7-bit because the groups of electronic impulses used to represent a given character in transmission or storage requires only 7 data bits. There are 128 of these 7-bit ASCII characters.

8-bit characters—a.k.a. binary characters—*are the control, graphic, and other characters used internally by your computer to store programs and certain types of data. As you might guess, they are 8-bit because 8 data bits are required to represent one of these characters.*

Again, see Chapter Seven for in-depth explanations of data formats.

This capability means that images, PKZIP files, and other 8-bit data files can be transmitted via newsgroup messages. Because there is an upper limit to newsgroup message size (50K in all cases), more than one message is often used to transmit a file. When this is the case, headers are included in the messages containing the file, which the "decoding" software uses to put the message contents together.

Among the better programs of this type is Wincode. This program handles both encoding and decoding files for transmission via Usenet newsgroups, using what is known as a *MIME* (or *Multipurpose Internet Mail Extension*) type of encoding.

As detailed in Chapter Seven, MIME is a process of encoding data files (most often 8-bit data files). The characters that comprise the data are replaced by token 7-bit characters, which are the only sorts of characters that can be handled by Usenet. They are then transmitted as 7-bit messages. Software takes care of the encoding and decoding for you.

Such programs also can be used to E-mail binary files as 7-bit ASCII text files. WinZip is also a fine tool for decoding binary newsgroup and E-mail files.

Some online services, including AOL and CompuServe, provide Usenet front ends. Among other things, these front ends can decode certain ASCII-coded binary files transmitted as Usenet newsgroup messages. This feature saves you the trouble of decoding or translating an ASCII-coded binary file; the front end decodes and stores the file in its original format for you.

FTP

FTP is an acronym for *File Transfer Protocol*, which in turn refers to the Internet's special File Transfer Protocol. As with other areas involving the Internet, special protocols are involved in transferring files (text or binary), and special software is required.

Special sites are required for FTP, as well. You can access FTP through almost any site that offers it, but it must be open to you. Most FTP sites allow you to sign on as an "anonymous" user, with a standard ID and password, which is given to you before you sign on, and means that you do not need an account with the site in question. Many FTP sites do not require a password. However, because

FTP sites are frequently busy, they may have restricted hours of access, or may be available to only a certain number of users at a time.

File offerings at FTP sites vary. Sites offer everything that can be put into

FIGURE 1.6

Netscape - [Directory of /1]				

le Edit View Go Bookmarks Options Directory Window Help

Current directory is /1

Up to higher level directory

	winzip95.exe	486 Kb	Tue Apr 30 00:00:00 1996 Binary Executable
	wz16v61.exe	421 Kb	Thu May 02 00:00:00 1996 Binary Executable
	wz32v61.exe	486 Kb	Tue Apr 30 00:00:00 1996 Binary Executable
	wzptch16.exe	481 Kb	Tue Apr 30 00:00:00 1996 Binary Executable
	wzptch32.exe	573 Kb	Tue Apr 30 00:00:00 1996 Binary Executable

An example of FTP site directories

a file: text, graphic images, photos, data files, and on and on.

When you log on at an FTP site, you see directory and file listings, as shown in Figure 1.6.

These listings represent files available for download. Select the file(s) you want to download, and they will be transmitted to you over the Internet, using Internet File Transfer Protocol.

HTML pages can be made to deliver files—which they do by transferring a file whenever a graphic, for example, is included in a Web page. Pages also can be set up to access a site via FTP, eliminating the need to enter the FTP address or to go through a complex selection process. This is how File Transfer Protocol is made available at some World Wide Web sites. This is the case with the WinZip site, winzip.com (**http://www.winzip.com**). Figure 1.7 shows you what this kind of resource offering at a Web site looks like.

With these kinds of Web pages, you simply click a download button or other hypertext link to receive a file. Your Web browser software and the Web server take care of the rest. In time, file transfer via HTML front ends at Web sites may well supersede FTP as a separate entity.

TIP

To get to an FTP site by using a Web browser, you enter: **ftp://** followed by ftp and the name of the site, like: **ftp://ftp.cdrom.com**, or you enter it like this for a numeric IP address: **ftp://123.456.7.890**. (Alternately, you can use **file://** rather than **ftp://** at the beginning of the URL.) If you know the directory and filename you want to reach, you can add these, using slashes to separate directory names.

Telnet

The Internet's major function is to transfer data, and it does this well. So well, in fact, that you can sign on to certain computers on the Internet (those that are accessible in this way) by using the Internet in the manner of a packet-switching network like Tymnet. This is done using Telnet, which is a terminal-emulation communications protocol.

You must know the site's Telnet address, which, when entered, takes you to the service's log-on prompt. From here, you normally must have an account with the service, so you can supply your user ID and password.

Using Telnet is convenient at times (you don't have to hang up and make a new connection if you want to check in with your account on an online service or other computer). It also may cost less than using a commercial packet-switching network (some online services charge less for access via Telnet than via packet-switching networks). On the other hand, money that you save may be negated by your ISP's rates for Telnet use.

Note that a Telnet connection can handle any online activities the online service provides—reading online text, transferring files, sending and receiving E-mail on the service to which you are connected, real-time conversation, and so on. However, you must sign on in standard terminal mode. Also, because you are putting a long and involved chain of connections between you and the Telnet connection, you will notice a distinct slowdown in response time and service.

You can also use Telnet with a Web browser, provided that it is properly configured. The URL format is **telnet://**, followed by the site's address in numeric or plain English. Examples: **telnet://site.name;** or **telnet//123.456.7.890**.

FIGURE 1.7

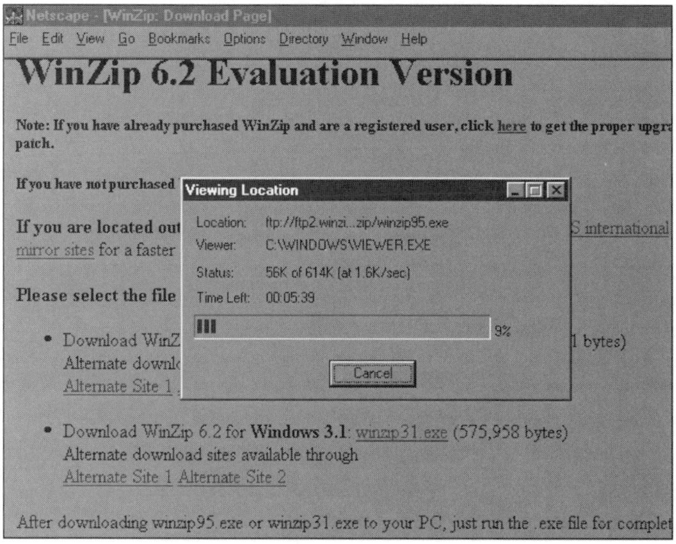

A file transfer in progress at an FTP WWW site

The Internet as a Resource

The Internet itself is a resource. The physical Internet of computers, connections, and support hardware, along with the software that maintains the connections and handles data, actually *is* the Internet. What I have just discussed are applications for the Internet.

But, in a roundabout way, the Internet is also its own application. File storage, and data transmission and reception are elements without which neither the Internet nor the other Internet applications could exist.

The Internet's viability as a resource depends in large part on its capability to carry data from one point to another—which it was designed to do even under the most adverse conditions, and which it will always be able to do.

SUMMARY

This too-brief introduction to the Internet has been to help you learn what the Internet is and how it works, with a slight emphasis on the World Wide Web, that being the most popular element of the Internet.

You should now have a better understanding of the various elements of the Internet and how to access many of its resources by using your Web browser. You should also have a solid feel for what the Internet is, in terms of its structure and resources. It would be very surprising if you have completely understood *everything* covered in Chapter 1, so if you haven't, don't worry. As you read ahead, keep in mind that it is not necessary for you to memorize every new term introduced, or to fully grasp every concept—time and practice will take care of that, so relax!

Now, on to Chapter Two, "Selecting a Browser and an ISP." There, we review the core of Internet applications—the Web browser—and your gateway to the Internet, the Internet Service Provider.

Selecting a Browser
and an ISP

The purpose of this chapter is to acquaint you with the factors that affect your choice of the most important of Internet tools—a *Web browser* and an *Internet Service Provider* (ISP).

Now, I'm certain that most of you already have a Web browser and an ISP. But, are your browser and ISP providing optimum functionality and service for your online applications? Maybe, or maybe not. This chapter helps you evaluate each.

The first part of this chapter focuses on Web browsers—mainly Netscape Navigator and Microsoft Internet Explorer. As you will learn, these two browsers are not the only viable choices available, but they are the most practical.

The second part of this chapter provides information about ISPs. It is intended to help you decide whether you want to use an online service (like AOL or CompuServe) to access the Internet, or a dedicated Internet access service (like Mindspring or NETCOM).

The intent in both sections is to provide the information you need to make intelligent choices for the most important Internet tools. These choices, of course, should be based on *your* preferences, needs, and working habits.

Even if you already have a Web browser and an ISP, don't skip this chapter: you may find something that works better than your current setup. Approach this chapter with an open mind, and don't worry about what is labeled as "best" by other users, co-workers, or magazines. Those sources can't tell you what's best for your needs because there is *no* absolute best. There is only what works for you, and what doesn't work for you. So, if something here looks interesting, try it out.

WEB BROWSERS: AN OVERVIEW

Web browsers didn't exist before the advent of the World Wide Web. They weren't needed. But, while they are a fairly new type of software, Web browsers are far from primitive. Competition and the general state of computer technology makes it possible for Web browsers to enjoy a much faster evolution than most kinds of software.

In addition, the demand for better browsers and the ever-increasing extension of Web capabilities made it necessary for browsers to reach a high state of sophistication quickly.

Interpreting HTML code was the main function of early Web browsers. Most browser features existed to support this function—the capability to connect with and navigate the World Wide Web included.

It wasn't long before other features were suddenly necessary, or at least convenient. These features include "bookmark" files to store commands to navigate to specific sites, more sophisticated file-handing capabilities, and a lot of other features that are standard in today's browsers.

The most important of these additional features were mail composition, sending, and delivery; Usenet newsgroup access; and FTP capabilities. Some features were previously handled by other programs, as was dialing up and connecting with an Internet link. (Dialing and connecting is still accomplished by a separate dialer program in most instances, and mail chores are often handled more elegantly by E-mail programs, such as Eudora and Pegasus, which Chapter Eight examines.)

Demand and competition resulted in these and many other features and capabilities being added to various Web browsers—thus, the evolution of Web browser programs began. This evolution continues today, with new capabilities being added to keep pace with Internet technology.

Obviously, which browser you use is a vital consideration. This is also the first of the "Two Great Internet Debates." Deciding which browser is best has become an emotionally charged pastime for many on the Web. The overwhelming majority of Internet users are polarized on the subject, but each has the same opinion: the "best" browser is the one he or she uses.

Ironically, however, there are only two good choices among all the browsers available for Windows users—Netscape Navigator and Microsoft Internet Explorer. I'll explain why this is so in a few pages, but first, look at some Web browser basics.

Browser Functions

All browsers have certain basic functions in common. These functions include the following:

- Connecting with the Web through Point-to-Point Protocol (PPP) and/or Single Line Internet Protocol (SLIP) connections

- Navigating the Web and your system via http, FTP, and local system file-retrieval operations, as well as links on retrieved Web pages

- Translating/interpreting HTML codes, to display pages appropriately (It is important, of course, that your browser handle the latest version of HTML.)

- Displaying GIF and JPG images

These functions—Web connection, navigation, and page and image display—are the primary reason Web browsers exist. All browsers have these functions. *How* a browser presents itself, and the degree of refinement and sophistication of its user interface, are the main differences between one browser and another...

...until you start looking at features that are tied to the way other people use the Web. Specifically, the user interface and certain features that are often termed "bells and whistles."

Browser Features: The Extras

The better Web browsers feature a number of extra features. Some simplify the Web. Others enhance it. Here's a listing of the more important browser features, not in order of importance:

- Additional "local navigation controls" that let you move through a list of Web pages you've already accessed during a given online session; these include "backward" and "forward" buttons and a cumulative list of pages visited during the current session, which you can use to navigate back to those pages.

- A file-access system that lets you open local files (on your hard drive), and save files from the Web—including HTML pages, image files, and other types of files.

- A "helper program" feature that starts a specified program when/if a certain file type is received from the Web. (For example, if a .WAV file is transmitted from a Web site, your browser should be able to start a program that can play .WAV files.) You should be able to specify programs to be used beyond what is already set up, and be able to add new file types and applications to the list. (More on these kinds of programs are discussed in Chapter Three, "Browser Utilities, Shareware, and More.")

- The capability to use plug-in programs (utilities that extend a browser's capabilities, about which Chapter Three has more to say). Ideally, a browser should be able to use plug-ins designed for a competing browser, but this is not always true.

- If you need it, multiple language support—the ability to handle special characters you will find at some foreign language Web sites (for example, Kanji characters at Japanese-language sites).

- Again if you have a need for this, a foreign language version of the browser (all the menus, prompts, and so on are in the language of choice).

- A changeable list of frequently visited Web sites that you can use to navigate to Web sites quickly. (This feature is often referred to as a *bookmark*, or a *hotlist*.)

- User-specifiable sizes for the RAM and disk caches used to store elements of Web pages you've visited. These caches store pages and elements of pages so they can be quickly reloaded from your disk if you re-visit them, rather than having to wait for them to be transmitted again.

- E-mail capability (enabling you to send messages to other users while online with the browser), including specifying the system to handle your E-mail (typically, the SMTP server), your return E-mail address, and so on.

- Usenet newsgroup retrieval and posting capability (includes allowing you to specify the server that will handle newsgroup traffic for you).

- FTP and Telnet capability (with servers, as specified by you).

- Flexibility in changing operating parameters, such as whether or not graphic images are loaded with a Web page (important when speed is a consideration), fonts used to display text, and so on.

- The capability to run programs in the Java, JavaScript, VB Script, and/or ActiveX languages. These programs are the development tools/languages responsible for the ubiquitous "applets" found on so many Web sites. This feature is either built-in to your browser, or may be added with plug-ins.

- Controllable security features, including those described in a few paragraphs, in the section, "Special Notes on Security Features."

Additional features include full compliance with the current version of HTML (normally built into the latest version of every browser); special HTML extensions to permit the viewing of additional content and/or format at a Web site; and special Web sites that support and enhance the browser in question.

Beyond all this, you will want a user interface that you find efficient and pleasing. You

FIGURE 2.1

The anatomy of a Web browser

will also probably want a user interface that you can alter. (Being able to turn toolbars, buttons, and windows on or off is helpful.) Figure 2.1 shows the major elements of a browser user interface, along with other elements.

Special Notes on Security Features. The biggest concern for most users on the Web today is security. There are several approaches to Web security, including the following:

- Protecting data you send over the Internet from being intercepted and observed—and/or tampered with—by a third party. This is accomplished on more than one level. The simplest protection is a warning dialog that appears when you opt to send text data to a Web site that is not secure. More complex protection techniques involve *certificates* (which are described in a few paragraphs).

- Using a certificate to ensure that you are communicating with a specific Web site and not an "impostor." This procedure can also verify or authenticate a Web site's security, or lack of security.

- Identifying yourself to a Web site with a certificate. This approach protects against anyone else accessing data at that site that is specific to you.

- Protecting yourself against virus-infected software or data files, and/or other unwanted data. This can be accomplished by restricting the sorts of software that can be downloaded from a Web site and run on your computer.

- The capability to restrict access to Web sites with specific content.

- Password protection, to restrict access to a browser.

- Control over whether or not your browser accepts *cookies*, either on an ask-first or a yes/no basis. (Cookies are information that some Web sites store on your disk, and which others can retrieve later. You can use this feature to help identify you to a Web site, as well as to gather information about your Web activities, and more.) For additional information on security features, see Chapter Seven, "Computer/Internet Data Formats and Conversion."

Notes on IRC and Telnet. One feature that few browsers support directly is *Internet Relay Chat*, or *IRC*. IRC is chatting real time via the Internet, kind of like talking on the telephone, but you type and read rather than speak and listen. You almost always have to obtain additional software for IRC. You will learn more about this software in later chapters.

Telnet is another Internet feature that you will probably have to go beyond your Web browser to implement. Unless you use CompuServe or NETCOM, which at present are the only commercial online services that provide built-in Telnet access, you may find it necessary to add a program known as a *Telnet Client* to your collection of Internet software.

Which Browser Should I Use?

As I noted previously, there are two viable choices in PC Web browsers, both available as Windows programs, of course. These are Microsoft Internet Explorer (better known simply as "Explorer"), and Netscape Navigator (a.k.a. "Netscape"). Your choices boil down to these two, not so much because they are the best products available, but rather, the market—Internet users and Web page developers—more than any other factor, decided which browsers "almost everyone" is using.

Note that a few ISPs provide you with a browser. However, you do not necessarily have to use that browser. Given that a PPP link exists once you sign on to an ISP (be it an independent ISP or an online service), most browsers can link up with the Internet, no problem. So, you are not confined to one Web browser, even when using an ISP that gives you a browser.

Browser Wars. How, you may wonder, did it come down to a choice between Netscape and Explorer? Mainly by word-of-mouth, and force of numbers.

(It also helps that Microsoft gives away Explorer for free, figuring to profit by sales of add-ons and support. This sales technique is similar to the late 19th century strategy of King C. Gillette, who gave away his new invention, the safety razor, knowing that those who had the razor would buy his blades.)

In the earliest days of the Web, most were using NCSA (National Center for Supercomputing Applications) Mosaic, or some knock-off thereof. (This is the original WWW browser for the PC-using masses. It is available for download at: **http://www.ncsa.uiuc.edu/SDG/Software/WinMosaic/index.html**.)

When other browsers began to appear, Internet users had choices. And, as often happens with software in a competitive environment—even free software—one browser gained a "word-of-mouth" edge over the others.

This browser is Netscape Navigator. If you have browsed the Web for any length of time, you have noticed that many Web pages are labeled, "Netscape-Enhanced" and carry the Netscape logo. These pages take advantage of certain Netscape features that extend HTML and enable additional display elements. When viewed with a browser other than Netscape, those additional page elements aren't visible. Worse, text and graphics that are visible may not look "right." Columns and other blocks of text, for example, may be run-on.

Today, there are similarly enhanced pages for Explorer. Although it is a relative latecomer, Explorer has managed to capture a good portion of the market for various reasons. And, like Netscape, it has a great deal of word-of-mouth support, largely because it is from Microsoft. (Of course, there are those who do *not* use Explorer simply because it is a Microsoft product.)

Also, competition has resulted in quite a bit of evolution of the products and supporting technologies. The latter include the *Java* programming language and applets for Netscape, and a similar development system called *ActiveX* for programs that can run within Explorer Web pages.

Other factors affect the popularity of each browser, as you will learn in a few pages. But, you may wonder, which browser has the most users and supporters? This question is easy to answer: Navigator has the clear edge. As of second quarter 1997, Netscape Navigator was used by around 70% of all Windows-based Internet users. However, Explorer is gaining fast, with perhaps half the number of users enjoyed by Netscape.

The numbers of users for both browsers are increased by the fact that AOL, CompuServe, and others give away special versions of one or the other with their front end software.

Which Browser Is Best? Even with the field narrowed down to two choices, it's not easy to answer the question, "Which is the best Web browser?" Or, more properly, "Which is the better of the two?"

As previously implied, "best" is a relative term. You will certainly prefer one over the other, for several personal reasons. And you will probably like some of the features of your second choice, and wish they were included in the browser you prefer.

As for which browser you will prefer, the answer probably is the first one you used. Computer users tend to regard the first program they use for any length of time as the one to which all others must measure up. This is true of any type of application, and even of online services and other ISPs.

Of course, the real issue here is not so much how many people use which browser, but the number of Web sites optimized or enhanced for use with one browser or the other. A related consideration is exactly how much you miss not using a browser that "fits" a given Web site. Both of those considerations are variable.

At present, Netscape-enhanced Web pages seem to outnumber those dedicated to Internet Explorer. However, Netscape and Explorer each accommodate more of the other's features with every new version. Explorer's version 3, for example, offered compatibility with Netscape Navigator's proprietary plug-in technology. Version 4 (the latest versions for both browsers) saw even more duplicated features. So, the days of Web sites completely dedicated to either browser may eventually end.

What will remain important are each browser's control, command, and menu structures; how specific features (like bookmarks) are set up; and other elements endemic to each, including their respective "look and feel." More than anything else, these aspects are what determine most users' choice in a browser.

To a lesser extent, Web sites that enhance a browser have some effect on decisions—but you normally do not know about these sites unless you have the browser in question. If you are curious about these, read on—and visit both the Netscape and the Explorer Web sites. (The respective URLs are **http://home. netscape.com**; and **http://www.microsoft.com/ie/download**.)

The overview descriptions of Netscape and Explorer that follow may help you evaluate each, and decide which will be your primary browser.

Meanwhile, you may want to do as I do: Use both! While I spend much more time online with Netscape, I have found it expedient to use Explorer to visit Microsoft Web sites, and other Explorer-enhanced Web sites. (Also, because I use both CompuServe and AOL, it is good to have some knowledge of Explorer, since both commercial online services offer it as their default, or primary, Web browser. The same is true of the Prodigy Internet Service.)

In the end, you may choose one browser over the other simply because you like it.

Netscape Navigator

Before Netscape, browsers were fairly basic. You could connect with the Internet, call files, and interpret HTML commands, display graphics, and handle other basic tasks. By the time Netscape came along, HTML itself had not advanced much further than enabling browsers to fetch and display HTML files and a few images, anyway.

Netscape's big attractions included—but weren't limited to—new HTML capabilities that were exclusive to Navigator, that they could be obtained for free or with a price that wasn't bad for the registered version, and that it was a fresh alternative to what little else was available.

Mostly, however, Netscape's early success was a case of coming along at just the right time. Merely offering an alternative to what was then available was as much to Netscape's benefit as anything. Hundreds of thousands of Internet users jumped on the Netscape Navigator bandwagon in a very short time.

With so many users enamored of Navigator, it wasn't long before a new phenomenon hit the Web. Netscape Navigator users who had Web sites made sure that their sites supported special Netscape features that extended beyond the HTML standard. Before long, a near-majority of Web sites were custom-tailored for optimal viewing using Navigator. (You still see this today, of course—the Netscape logo on a Web site's first page, along with a statement that the site is "Netscape enhanced" or "optimized for Netscape.")

This enhancing meant that the Web site wouldn't look "right" unless you used Netscape Navigator. The difference might be as simple as not being able to see certain text formatting (created by using text-format commands unique to Navigator), or as complex as not being able to access several pages at once by virtue of the use of Navigator's "frames" feature. Indeed, some browsers still crash when they hit a Web page that's enhanced for Netscape Navigator, even older versions. To be fair, the same crash can happen with pages that are optimized for Explorer. At the least, you may miss some important features, such as using forms.

As Netscape progressed (as previously stated, Navigator is now up to version 4, the version bundled with Netscape Communicator), more and more new features were added, and it is now at a point where you cannot view some Web sites at all unless you use Netscape—the latest version! (Never mind that this limitation may reduce the potential audience for such a Web site; the majority of folks who create Web sites that are "Netscape-only" either don't know any better, or are for reasons of their own determined that Netscape is the absolute *best* for everyone.)

One of the biggest of these kinds of "lockouts" that Netscape used was the Java programming

FIGURE 2.2

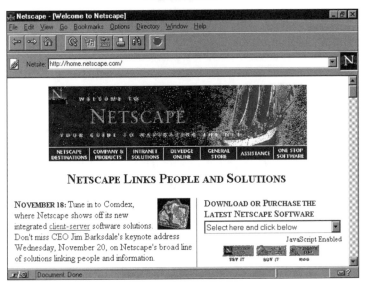

The Netscape Navigator Web browser

language. This language creates "mini-applications," a.k.a. "applets," which can run within an HTML Web page. *JavaScript* is a simpler approach to the same thing; both have in common the fact that they take some of the load off a Web site server by running on the client who is receiving the host Web page. They also have in common their basis in enabling the user and page elements, actions, and events to interact. That is, if you select an object (image, hyperlink, color, or whatever) on a Web page, certain things may happen (such as a sound or video file being played) that would not happen otherwise. Such an event may in turn lead to other events or bring other objects to the page.

These are programs that, originally, only Netscape Navigator could interpret and run. So, if you wanted to run Java applets found at various Web sites, you had to have Navigator—or a browser that was at least somewhat compatible with them. (Some applets have been known to lock up or crash browsers.) Fortunately for many, Explorer introduced the capability to run Java and JavaScript applets. (Also fortunately, the advent of Java resulted in the competitive development of Explorer's ActiveX technology.)

Finally, Netscape has worked to have ISPs offer or adopt Navigator as their official Web browser. This usually means that the ISP makes it easier to set up Navigator with their service—and may bundle it for new members, and/or design their Web sites for optimal viewing when using Navigator. They may also offer technical support for Navigator, but not for other browsers.

Netscape Navigator Features: An Overview. As shown in Figure 2.2, Navigator presents a fairly uncomplicated face to the world.

However, the uncomplicated theme isn't echoed by its features. Navigator offers almost everything you might want in a browser, and some features that you may not know you want until you try them.

For example, take a look at the user interface. All the most-frequently used controls are right in front of you, on the toolbar. The same goes for information about the current URL. The bottom-of-the-screen status bar provides information about in-progress activities (like connecting with and downloading a Web page), the URL associated with a hyperlink when the mouse cursor passes over it, and even a one-line text message from properly set up Web pages.

Fortunately, you can turn off most of these displays to show more of a Web page. This feature is handy because, unfortunately, Navigator doesn't offer what is sometimes known as a "kiosk mode." Kiosk is a display mode that fills the entire screen with a Web page—no borders, no controls, or anything else from the browser. It's a great feature, particularly when you are dealing with long pages that have large graphics or image maps. In kiosk mode, you can put the maximum portion of a page on your screen, reducing the need to scroll up and down. (As in Figure 1.1 in Chapter One, I have turned off certain of the Web browser's features—display elements—in order to better display the Web page.)

Otherwise, Netscape Navigator offers most of the browser features discussed previously, although it tends to be a bit lighter on security features than Explorer. Navigator provides simple warnings when you are about to send data to a server that is not secure (with or without a form) and when you are entering or leaving a secure server. Navigator also offers passwords and personal and site certificates for authenticating purposes. It supports security protocols SS2 and SS3, but not PCT, an emerging protocol. Navigator also can warn you when a Web site is about to pass you a *cookie* and gives you the option of accepting or rejecting it. (As detailed in an earlier section, "Special Notes on Security Features," a cookie is information written to your hard drive by a Web site. Among other purposes, this is used to identify you on later visits.)

To run ActiveX and Shockwave applications, you have to add *plug-ins*. (This capability could become a built-in Navigator feature in the near future.)

Speaking of plug-ins, one of Navigator's more interesting features is its "Installed plug-ins" registry. This registry makes it extremely easy to quickly survey which plug-ins you have. Select **About plug-ins** on Navigator's Help menu, and you see a list of plug-ins, complete with information as to type and so on, and their drive/directory locations. (For more detailed information about plug-ins, see Chapters Four and Ten.)

Some additional bells and whistles include a drag-and-drop feature that makes it quick and easy to store or add the current URL to your bookmark list; a bookmark list that you can customize; and a command and menu structure that makes more sense to me than Explorer's.

Netscape, of course, originated *frames*, which is the ability to display several more or less mini-Web pages within one

FIGURE 2.3

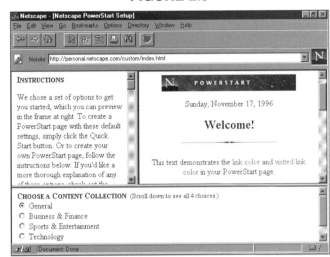

Netscape frames on a Web page

page. (Figure 2.3 illustrates this.) So, as you might expect, it does an excellent job of handling pages with frames.

Although frames initially slowed down Web page loading tremendously for most users, the latest version of Navigator seems to have eliminated this problem.

Figure 2.3 also shows another Netscape Navigator feature, one of Navigator's several online enhancements. This particular enhancement, called a "PowerStart page," lets you set up an online home page with your choice of a number of categorized links. The PowerStart page can be set as your default personal home page, which is the page to which your browser goes first when you link with the Internet. Link categories include general news, sports, technology news, weather, finance, reference, and more, including your own list of personal links. (There's even an optional notepad, which stays "live" on your home page whenever you're online. You can save the contents to disk and access them next time you're online. Other options include a calendar and a calculator.)

This is a great enhancement to Navigator, and it's probably the best of its type.

Additional enhancements for Navigator include a download page for plug-ins, and free trial access to some pay Web sites (mainly publications and information services). The latter is for those who register their copies of Netscape Navigator online. Select **Registration Information** on Navigator's Help menu.

Navigator gets a downcheck in the area of online help. Its online help is *literally* online, meaning you have to go to Netscape's Web site to view help. A fairly comprehensive (but at times obtuse) online manual, release notes, FAQs, and more are available via the Help menu, which enters the requisite URL to get to the help feature of your choice. It would be far better to have duplicated all this offline. A megabyte or so of standard Windows Help files wouldn't have hurt a bit. (I suspect that some of the Netscape folks were perhaps overly enamored of the cuteness of having *all* the online help for a Web browser on the Web. It sure makes getting help difficult—especially if you need help on how to get online!)

Navigator's mail and Usenet newsgroup features are a bit easier to use and slightly more powerful than Explorer's, largely because Netscape has had more experience with these applications. However, Explorer's "do it different from Netscape" approach figures here, too.

That's the quick look at Netscape Navigator features. I strongly recommend that you try it for yourself. To get more info on Navigator features, visit **http://home.netscape.com**, download a copy, and take it for a test drive. Or, you can buy Netscape from almost any software retailer. (If you sign up with CompuServe, DELPHI, Prodigy, or any of a number of independent ISPs, you may receive Netscape at no cost.)

Microsoft Internet Explorer

Originally designed for use only with Microsoft's online service, The Microsoft Network (MSN), Microsoft Internet Explorer began life as a fairly simple Web browser. Explorer had no really new and exciting features when it was introduced, but it didn't have to because it was intended for one market— MSN members.

Things changed rapidly late in 1995, though, as the market's focus left online services and zoomed in on the Internet. It wasn't long before the decision had been made to put Explorer out as direct competition for Netscape and other browsers.

This step required drastic improvements to Explorer. At the same time the program was undergoing improvement, Microsoft began pushing it as the browser to have. Quite a few Internet users went along with this idea, thanks to Microsoft's reputation. Microsoft was able to get it included with certain products. Eventually, Explorer reached the point where it was the Number Two browser. And that's where it remains; as of late 1997, Netscape pretty much dominates the market, with Explorer second.

Obviously, Microsoft brought its Internet Explorer to the game rather late, but the company is making up for lost time in two ways. First, it's following Netscape's strategy of adding features exclusive to their own browser. There are many add-on programs and utilities (ActiveX, mainly) that work only with Internet Explorer. Indeed, Microsoft's main tactic in this area is to develop plug-ins that work better—or only—with Internet Explorer.

Microsoft's second strategy is to put their Internet Explorer in the hands of as many people as possible. This strategy was easily accomplished by adding it to Windows 95, where it is a part of the newer interlinking of applications and the Web. But Microsoft hasn't stopped there. Many ISPs and some online services (including AOL, CompuServe, The Microsoft Network, and Prodigy Internet) feature Explorer as their browser-of-choice. That means the ISPs make Internet Explorer easier to use with their services. The ISPs provide extensive support for Explorer, design their Web sites to work best with Explorer, and last, but certainly not least, they include Explorer with the software they give to new members.

Not all the major ISPs are going with Explorer. CompuServe and Prodigy Internet, while favoring Internet Explorer in its front end software, allow users to choose between Internet Explorer and Netscape. Another major online service, DELPHI, provides Netscape, along with a suite of Internet software. Some larger national ISPs provide Netscape to new users, as do smaller regional and local ISPs.

NOTE: Not incidentally, the embracing of one browser or another by online services and ISPs does not mean you are locked into that browser. You usually can run a second browser easily enough; simply start it after you log into your ISP. As I write this, I am running three browsers: I'm logged into AOL, which comes with a built-in version of Explorer, and I have that running. To better investigate some Explorer updates, I started Explorer and it latched on to the PPP connection provided by AOL, and navigated as I directed it. A few minutes later, I wanted to compare Netscape with its Explorer counterpart, so I started Netscape. It, too, hooked up with the Net via AOL's PPP connection.

(This took up well over 8MB of memory. So, don't try this at home unless you have 16 megabytes of RAM or more!)

Still, Explorer may catch up. Marketing, rather than word-of-mouth brought it farther faster than Netscape. Its new technology is sure to take advantage of Explorer's existing momentum and take it still farther. ActiveX and the built-in capabilities to handle Shockwave and Java have helped Explorer claim market territory that Netscape had not previously considered.

Microsoft Internet Explorer Features: An Overview

As was said for Netscape, Explorer (see Figure 2.4) boasts all the major features discussed previously in this chapter. However, its user interface seems a little less friendly to me. (Perhaps you find it otherwise, which is fine; such judgments are largely a matter of taste.)

Explorer really came into its own, feature-wise, with version 3.0. Introduced late in 1996, this version rolled out ActiveX and Java capabilities, and the ability to handle Netscape frames (albeit noticeably slower than Netscape).

FIGURE 2.4

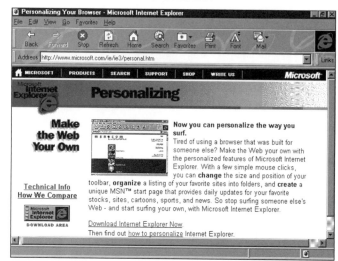

The Microsoft Internet Explorer Web browser

ActiveX has generated the most excitement. This language caught everyone off guard, at a time when Java was the hottest thing going as far as the Internet was concerned.

Another plus is the fact that Explorer originated the semiautomatic downloads of necessary applications from Web sites. (Go to a site that offers features that require a plug-in, and you're queried as to whether you want to download that tool.)

Explorer 3.0 scooped Netscape in two other feature areas—Security and Help.

Explorer has security features and options galore. The typical setups for certificates are there—personal and site—and there's an additional certificate category called "Publishers." Cryptography protocols are supported, and you have the option to tell Explorer to not save secure pages to disk. Password protection of some settings is also available. Some of these security elements are difficult to find (a symptom of what I feel is Explorer's relatively poorly-designed user interface).

SSL2, SSL3, and PCT security protocols are supported, and you can disable downloading and running "active content," ActiveX, and Java programs.

As with Netscape, you can have Explorer warn you before accepting cookies (giving you the option of whether or not to do so), and provide other warnings regarding the state of security of a site.

Explorer has a unique feature known as "Content Advisor" that lets you lock out access to Web sites based on language, nudity, sex, or violence. In addition to locking out children from questionable sites, it can be used to ensure that co-workers don't spend all their online time exploring the more salacious corners of the Web. (Look for this feature to appear in other browsers, and to grow more elaborate as the Internet evolves.)

As for Explorer's Help features, many are "online" in the traditional sense of Windows Help files, as well as online at Microsoft's Web site. This is an improvement over Netscape's approach to online help. The Windows Help is well-written, and misses very few areas where you would have questions. The only weak areas involve when the Help authors obviously assume that you know more than you really do—such as when they refer to MIME program types.

On-the-Internet help focuses on online support and on a special interactive "Web Tutorial" that provides introductory and intermediate information about the Internet. The only improvement on this help system would be to duplicate the Web Tutorial in Windows Help files. (It would go faster that way.) Online and on-the-Internet help features are all on the browser's Help menu, along with some Microsoft sites, including a gateway to several search engines.

Another online enhancement is the "Microsoft Custom Page." This is tied to MSN, and is a means of setting up a personal home page as the first page you go to when you link to the Internet, with links of your choice. As with Netscape's "PowerStart page," the Microsoft Custom Page is entirely user-defined, and features links by category and a set of personal links. Microsoft also provides a download page for Explorer plug-ins.

Finally in the realm of online add-ons and enhancements, registered users get free-trial access to value-added services and publications.

Explorer's mail and newsgroup applications, as indicated in previous sections, are not on a par with Netscape's. They *will* get the job done, however.

The rest of Explorer's features match up with Netscape's fairly well. The only other area in which Explorer lags behind Netscape is a seemingly minor matter—but one important to those of us who have used browsers for any length of time. This is Microsoft's insistence on referring to hyperlinks as "shortcuts." This is more than annoying, actually; it runs counter to accepted and common usage, and will create a lot of confusion on the part of both new users and old hands. No doubt, this comes from Microsoft's insistence on doing it their own way. (The term harks back to Windows 95, where it originated as another name for a startup command.)

Its few downchecks and my opinion of the user interface aside, I do recommend that you give Internet Explorer a try. You can download it at: **http://www.microsoft.com/ie/download**.

Explorer is, after all, completely free. A special version of Explorer is an integral part of AOL, CompuServe, and Prodigy Internet software, and a number of independent ISPs provide Explorer to new members, as well. And of course the full version is supplied to members of the Microsoft Network (MSN).

A FEW OF THE REST

As you might imagine, there are relatively few other browsers worth considering. As Netscape Navigator and Microsoft Internet Explorer continue to compete, one will always best the other in some small feature or other. However, in terms of important features, I expect both will give you what you need.

A discussion of Web browsers would not be complete without pointing out some additional browsers that are worth your consideration.

Back Where It All Began...

NCSA Mosaic (shown in Figure 2.5) is always worth trying if you are interested in examining alternate browsers. The National Center for Supercomputer Applications (original devel-

FIGURE 2.5

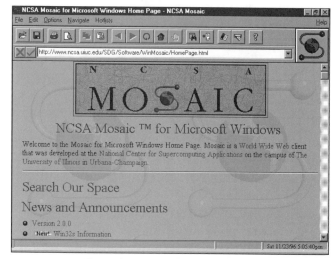

The NCSA Mosaic Web browser

oper of Mosaic) continues to evolve the program, and it is interesting to see where it is going.

You will find the latest version of NCSA Mosaic, along with all the information you can use about it, plus support software, at the NCSA Mosaic home page. The URL is: **http://www.ncsa.uiuc.edu/SDG/Software/WinMosaic/index.html**. Mosaic is free.

Other Commercial Web Browsers

Although NCSA Mosaic and Microsoft Internet Explorer are free and you can at least try Netscape for free (as a fully functional version), there are other commercial Web browsers. Most offer little for the additional cost (they are typically double Netscape's price).

However, there is one commercial Web browser worth a look. It is the browser included with PROCOMM PLUS for Windows. Nicknamed "Web Zeppelin," it seems to provide the widest support for HTML page layout features of *any* browser, period. Figure 2.6 shows Web Zeppelin in action.

FIGURE 2.6

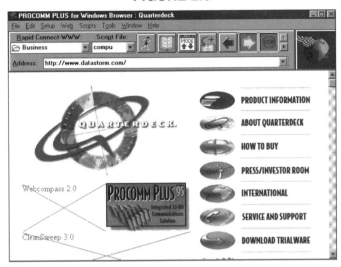

The PROCOMM PLUS for Windows Web Zeppelin browser

The browser is but one element of a full-featured communications program. You may already know PROCOMM, and PROCOMM PLUS for Windows. The program is, of course, the latest incarnation of the ever popular PROCOMM PC communications software, which started as a shareware program early last decade. PROCOMM PLUS for Windows is the latest iteration of this program, and a commercial application. As might be expected, this is a *total* computer communications package. In addition to all existing dial-up communications features, and the Web browser, PROCOMM PLUS for Windows offers an incoming and outgoing Fax, a newsreader, superior E-mail tools, and even front ends for popular online services.

Almost all the program's components are interconnected. For example, you can E-mail or Fax a Web page you're viewing with just a few mouse clicks, and ditto for newsgroup postings.

PROCOMM PLUS for Windows can also dial up and connect with your ISP in Web browser or newsgroup mode. FTP and Telnet features are included.

The list of features goes on. PROCOMM PLUS for Windows is highly recommended for use as both a dial-up communications program and an Internet tool. To check it out, visit this URL: **http://www.procomm.com**.

ISP-Specific Web Browsers

A few ISPs provide their own Web browsers. Most of these are commercial online services, which were integrating Internet services into their offerings several years ago. They quickly moved to add Web browsers and the PPP connections to support them. A few, like AOL, started with browsers of their own design. Today, online services offer Netscape and/or Explorer as their Web browser. (In the case of Explorer, a special limited version is incorporated into some online services' front end software.)

Independent ISPs are in much the same situation. Almost none provide Web browsers of their own design, however; most offer Netscape or Explorer, and a very few offer other browsers.

NETCOM's NetCruiser. Most notable among browsers in the ISP-specific category is NETCOM, which offers NetCruiser, shown in Figure 2.7.

As you can see, NetCruiser's design is visually bold. The icons on the control buttons are easy to understand, and make it ideal for beginners. Browser help is well-written, even though most users rarely need to consult it.

The one major drawback you're likely to find in NetCruiser has to do with Java and ActiveX. If you want to take advantage of applets on the Internet, you may have to go to Netscape or Explorer—unless a future version of NetCruiser can handle them.

Otherwise, NetCruiser is a decent Web browser. Plus, NETCOM offers some integrated features for NetCruiser, one of which is "SurfWatch," a service that lets you block access to objectionable material on the Net. NetCruiser also supports IRC, so you do not have to obtain an additional add-on or plug-in to use IRC. There is also a gopher tool (for Web-wide research) included. Additionally, there is an interface for "finger," a utility used to get information about Internet users based on their E-mail addresses. (See Chapter Eleven for more about such tools.)

E-mail and newsgroup access are likewise integrated, which makes the NETCOM/NetCruiser combination a good value and an easy way to get started on the Internet.

FIGURE 2.7

NETCOM's Web browser, NetCruiser

AOL's Web Browser. AOL's original Web browser was one of their own design. It wasn't bad, but it wasn't the best. Today, AOL offers a special version of Microsoft Internet Explorer. Like all earlier AOL Web browsers, it is an integral part of the AOL front end software.

It is somewhat limited in functions, as shown in Figure 2.8, but not as limited as you might think.

As you can see, Explorer's familiar toolbar is missing. So are some Explorer features, but a surprising number are included, belying the simple-looking interface. As for the buttons that are there, there are the standard navigation buttons, and one labeled "Search" which has a "hardwired" URL that takes you to AOL's Web search site. "Home" goes to an AOL site, too. The "Prefs" button goes to browser options for setup.

FIGURE 2.8

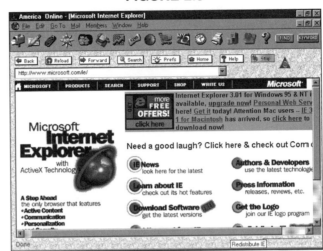

The AOL version of Internet Explorer

Available Explorer features include all standard browser operations, ActiveX and Java capability, full security features (including certificates and cookies), content advisor, and standard controls for graphics, sound, and which programs can be downloaded and run from the Web.

There's also a favorite places list (a.k.a. "bookmark list"), and a means to navigate to sites already visited during a session.

Finally, some sites will download add-ons for Explorer to the AOL browser, and set them up. You have the option to accept or reject such downloads.

This is not a bad browser for getting into the Internet. If you use AOL for your ISP, though, you will eventually want to switch to using Netscape or the full version of Explorer.

AOL also offers browser-independent access to Usenet newsgroups, FTP, and gopher services.

CompuServe and the Internet. CompuServe's built-in version of Microsoft Internet Explorer is a little more limited in some ways than that used by AOL. A quick tour of its features will explain what I mean.

FIGURE 2.9

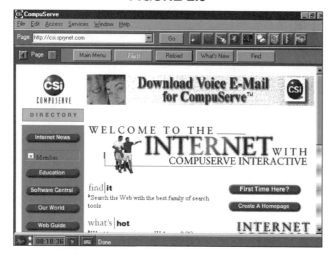

CompuServe's version of Internet Explorer

Referring to Figure 2.9, the buttons at the top of the browser window are more for CompuServe than the Web. Three are for navigation: the left and right arrows for backward and forward, and the Reload/ Stop button. (The latter is shown as "Reload" here, but when a page is loading it changes to "Stop.")

The "Main Menu" and "What's New" buttons are for CompuServe services. The "Find" button brings up a dialog that you can use to search CompuServe or the Internet. The "Page" window beneath the menu labels at top left acts both as a location display and as a means of revisiting pages. It drops down to display a list of all URLs recently visited, from which you can select an URL to open. The "Go" button allows you to enter the URL of a Web site or CompuServe area to visit.

A "Favorite Places" feature allows you to bookmark not only CompuServe products and services, but also URLs.

Setup features are limited, almost nonexistent. So, you won't be able to set security levels, toggle pictures and sounds off and on, and so forth.

The operation of this version of Explorer is not quite seamless, but smooth enough. Here again, the goal is to give the user the impression that Compu-Serve and the Internet are all one big entity.

Like AOL, CompuServe offers browser-independent Internet services, including FTP, Usenet newsgroups, and Telnet.

Browsing the Web with Prodigy Internet. Prodigy Internet (an offshoot of the Prodigy online service) offers a special version of Internet Explorer, as well.

Unlike CompuServe and AOL, Prodigy Internet did not limit their version of Explorer. It is a bit more like the standalone version.

INFORMATION SERVICE PROVIDERS

If you are reading this book, you may already have an ISP. However, there may be a better ISP than the one you currently use. For that reason, as well as for those who are just considering the benefits of Internet access, this section of the chapter provides information you can use to select and judge ISPs.

In the "old days" (less than a decade ago), Internet users depended upon connections with educational institutions or government entities for Internet links. There were virtually no Internet Service Providers. There was insufficient demand to make providing links a commercially viable proposition. Also, there were vague injunctions against anything commercial touching the Net.

That was before the World Wide Web, and before the Internet was drafted as a mass E-mail carrier. The majority of the online world used commercial online services. As the Web evolved and online services began offering Internet E-mail links, awareness of the Internet grew. With this awareness came a demand for the Internet.

At first, the primary demand was for Usenet, with E-mail links to existing Internet sites not far behind. Most commercial online services were able to satisfy the demand. Usenet "feeds" were set up, and each tied into the Internet for E-mail.

There was still the Web, though. At first, a near-abstract element of "the Net," the Web almost overnight became something of a famous entity, thanks in large part to publicity in the computer and mainstream media.

All the attention focused on the Web generated a greater demand for full Internet access. As is common, consumer demand was met by commercial entities. Thus were commercial ISPs born.

The first ISPs were independent—that is, they were created for the sole purpose of providing Internet and World Wide Web access. Unlike commercial online services, they did not provide "content" in the form of information services.

Commercial online services were fairly quick to recognize the demand for Internet connections. They met this first with the aforementioned E-mail and Usenet links. But it was not long before they recognized that they could provide the Internet and the Web in their entirety to their members. After all, what were those entities but still more online content? So, online services became ISPs.

Today we have two flavors of ISPs. The first is the independent Internet Service Provider, existing solely to provide Internet connections. Well, not exactly; many independent ISPs now offer content of their own, in one way or another. It's a way of competing against other independent ISPs and the commercial online services. Examples include NETCOM, SpryNet, GNN, and Earthlink.

The second flavor of ISP is the commercial online service. These are a rather small group, consisting of AOL, CompuServe, DELPHI Internet

Services, MSN, and Prodigy Internet. Each of these services is becoming increasingly involved in the Internet. All have added Internet information services (Forums, reference and research tools, and the like) to their range of products and services. In addition, most of the online services have evolved front ends that attempt to make their existing services a part of the Internet, and vice-versa.

If this seems like an identity crisis, that's because it is. Independent ISPs and online services exist in a highly competitive market. To stay competitive, each has been forced to take on some attributes of the other. Look for this trend to continue; in a few years, the major ISPs will be online services that have succeeded in blending and melding their conventional services with the Internet, and independent ISPs that have successfully mixed value-added information content with Internet access.

This brings us to the second of the "Two Great Internet Debates"—independent ISP or online service.

Independent ISP or Online Service?

As with Web browsers, which ISP you "should" use is the subject of intense emotional debate between permanently polarized viewpoints. One view is that online services should not be ISPs, and that independent ISPs are somehow "better." The other perspective is that it doesn't matter; use the flavor of ISP (and the specific ISP) that best meets your needs.

My viewpoint is the latter. As with anything, you should use what works best for you.

If your online applications do not extend beyond sending and receiving E-mail, browsing Web sites, and accessing Usenet newsgroups, an independent ISP will work for you.

If you have other needs or expectations about being online, you need to compare the content offered by online services with the content of the Internet at large. Which service truly meets your needs? Also, which service do you find easiest to use?

This question is not easy to answer. As noted previously, independent ISPs provide some content, but they offer nowhere near the content of the online services, which have been building their offerings for many years.

Content, Content, and More Content. What is "content?" On online services, content consists of information resources, ranging from encyclopedias to magazines to reference works and directories; people resources, in the form of special interest groups and Forums; news, weather, and financial information from trusted sources; online shopping services; magazines; exclusive columnists, consultants, and entertainment features.

There is also online product support—that is, manufacturer support for computer hardware and software products. Online services are a better choice over ISPs when it comes to product support services, at least in rapidity of response and file resources.

Most categories of online service content are available to some extent on the Web. And, unlike online services, the Web doesn't charge for access.

But, what form does the Web content take, and how far does it go? Just how reliable is information on the Internet?

In my experience, some of the Web's content is not as reliable as we want because so much of the Web is put up by amateurs who do it for no direct return. As a result, many Web site developers have no incentive to make the effort to get things right. Find an error in online information and point it out, and you're as likely to get "What do you expect for free?" as, "Thanks, I'll change that" in reply.

Commercial Web sites tend to provide better information. They exist as a part of a commercial enterprise and are anything but a hobby. They are either promoting or directly selling products, and the information provided can be construed as reflecting the quality of their products, or at least their image. Commercial sites have the incentive—and the means—to provide accurate information, most of the time. (One way to judge the probable accuracy of a Web site's information is to see when it was last updated. If this information is not placed on the site's home page, try viewing the source code with your browser, to see if a date is embedded there.)

Now, take a look at *who* is providing information on the Web. You see Web sites for many well-known corporations and publishers, as well as government agencies, but just as many Web sites in a given category are put together by amateurs.

In contrast, some information products on online services are constructed and offered as products for sale. Others are included with the online services' normal charges. Either way, the emphasis is on quality because, unlike the Web, online services are delivering products for a price.

Because of this, information on commercial online services is likely to be more complete, more accurate, and more in-depth. This isn't always true, but it is true enough to matter.

So, in choosing whether the Web's content or what a commercial online service offers is better for your needs, you must judge by the type of information you seek.

Also, you will find that online services offer information products and services that are not available on the Web. These include things like CompuServe's Phone*File and Biz*File directories, and its Dun & Bradstreet databases, and service-specific forums, publications, and reference works found on AOL, CompuServe, DELPHI, MSN, and Prodigy.

Also, regarding the relative quality of information on online services and the Web, consider this: it is time-consuming and costly to compile information. Few people or organizations do so in order to give away the information; in fact, the "information industry" comprises a large segment of our economy. Therefore, you will often find the more valuable information where you must pay for it (whether it's on an online service or at a Web site that requires you to pay).

Special Services. There is another service category where online services shine more than the Internet. I call this the "special services" category. Special services on online services include E-mail features, real-time conversation (or "chatting"), and such things as outgoing Fax and hardcopy mail.

If you have heavy and complex E-mail requirements, CompuServe and AOL are perhaps your best bets. However, with such add-on programs as Eudora or Pegasus (see Chapter Eight), you can have almost all the features that online service E-mail offers.

Real-time communication is a bit more difficult for the Internet to match. While Internet Relay Chat (IRC) is growing in popularity thanks to its general addictiveness, the technology is relatively poor—relative to that offered by the online services, that is. With online service chat areas, you have one less layer of communications links between you and others. Communication is routed from you to the online service's host computers, then directly to others in the conversations. IRC communication goes through another entire link—the Internet—after leaving your Internet host. So, it's usually faster, less "clunky," and cleaner to use an online service for real-time conversation.

Specialty E-mail services, including sending E-mail to Fax addresses, and even having it printed out and mailed to recipients for you, are other classes of services you will not find for free on the Internet—not with any consistency. Like gathering and offering quality information, these services are costly, and must be paid for by the consumer.

Remember, too, that many online services offer special Internet services. AOL has a decent interface for Usenet newsgroups that enables searching, reading, and posting. AOL also has FTP capability built into its software.

CompuServe also offers Usenet and FTP services. Moreover, it has a really good Telnet service.

DELPHI includes among its offerings Usenet newsgroups, placed among its Special Interest Groups (SIGs) as appropriate by topic.

Finally, remember that all online services offer Internet E-mail, and Internet support and information services.

Cost. Cost of service is the element about which the proponents of independent ISPs argue the loudest. Coming from a time when just dialing into an online service cost as much as 30 cents per minute, I don't see what all the fuss is about. *Everything* online looks like a bargain to me. Still, cost is an important element, and we'll examine it here.

In recent history, independent ISPs have traditionally charged a flat monthly rate for unlimited access. Online services at the same time were charging X for Y hours access per month, with additional hours billed at a couple of dollars each. And, a few premium products on the online services (business information, primarily) incur additional charges.

Today, the price structures are leveling out. The extra charges for premium information services remain, but online services are meeting the demand for economical Internet access by offering Internet access at a competitive rate. Some charge separately for access to their traditional services, and some don't.

No matter how the billing goes, the best value in the online world is the perceived value—if you have no need for the extra products and services provided by online services, you will perceive no value in their availability. Therefore, you should go for the more straightforward and conventional Internet access offered by an independent ISP.

If, however, you need access to those online service "extras," the value of using an online service increases. The value-added elements of those extras would probably make the online service seem like a bargain.

Ease of Access and Connectivity. It is a given that you want to use a local telephone number to access the Internet. You do not want to have to dial long-distance to access the Internet; access should be free of extra cost and free of interference.

From the viewpoint of telephone connections for your computer and modem, there are three approaches to linking up with the Internet that don't involve long-distance connections. These are local ISPs, public packet-switching networks, and private packet-switching networks. There are varying potential effects on the speed and quality of your connection with each.

Dealing with a local ISP is simple enough. You dial a local number, your modem talks to their modem, and you're on, using the ISP's PPP or SLIP connection to the Internet. The quality of the connection between you and the ISP is good. However, smaller ISPs may not have as high a quality of links with the Internet as do large, national ISPs. Thus, a local ISP with a heavy load can bog down, and slow down. You may even encounter a situation where all dial-in ports are busy, and you can't log on.

With national or regional online service providers—either commercial online services or independent ISPs—packet-switching networks come into play.

Simply described, a packet-switching network is a special kind of data link between your computer and the ISP's computers. You dial a local number, and data is routed through a network of computers and data link equipment to its destination. As with the Internet, packet-switching networks use more than one path to deliver data.

Without packet-switching networks, which use leased-line telephone connections that aren't charged a per-minute rate, you would not be able to dial locally into an ISP that was not in your area. There is a cost for network service, but it is relatively small per user, and it is built into an ISP's charges. Therefore, packet-switching networks are "invisible" to us in terms of how they make connections and in their cost.

There are two kinds of packet-switching networks—public and private. Public networks are those used by anyone; Tymnet and SprintNet are the largest. Private packet-switching networks are those used exclusively by the ISPs they serve. AOL, NETCOM, and CompuServe operate private networks. (You can access AOL and CompuServe via a public network if there is no local number for their private networks.)

What's the difference? Quality! Private networks are set up for one purpose, and they do their job well. Public networks, on the other hand, carry traffic for hundreds of different customers in addition to the ISP you may be using a public network to access. This traffic can mean delays in routing data, which translates into slower connections for you. The number of users on a public network also can affect the speed.

All of these factors come down to the following guidelines:
- If a local ISP has a reliable and high-quality connection with the Internet, go with it.

- If the local ISP's connections are not the best, go with a large national or regional provider.

- If you go with a large provider, choose one that offers its own private packet-switching network over one that uses a public packet-switching network.

NOTE: The ISPs which provide software are those most likely to offer the greatest ease in connectivity. They will have set up all of their systems to work best with the software they provide.

Software. The software an ISP provides, or the lack of it, may be an important consideration in choosing an ISP.

Most of the larger ISPs—independent and online services alike—provide Netscape Navigator or Internet Explorer to new members. Some ISPs, DELPHI is an example, provide a suite of software which includes a browser like Netscape, E-mail software like Eudora, and a group of utilities and add-ons, all quite useful. Be sure to find out what software is offered, keeping in mind that the ISP will normally offer technical service and help for that software.

Several of the online services—AOL, CompuServe, MSN (for Windows 95 users only), and Prodigy—provide software front ends that you must use to access their services. It's a good idea to learn as much about these as possible. Better yet, give them a trial run by taking advantage of free trial membership offers. You will have to use their software to dial up and connect with them, before you link up with the Internet. So, it's a good idea to sign up with a service that provides software you can live with. (CompuServe is the only service among these that offers more than one front end.)

A very few independent ISPs offer custom software. Earthlink has a special Netscape setup. NETCOM has NetCruiser, described previously. Here again, you want to consider the software before making a final decision.

Putting It All Together

As you have undoubtedly gathered, choosing an ISP is not the simplest thing in the world. There are no hard-and-fast rules because so many subjective requirements—and tastes—are involved.

Because this is the case, I suggest that you eliminate as many potential ISPs as possible on the basis of content and services (or lack of same), ease of use and connectivity, cost, and software. Check out the remaining ISPs by taking advantage of free trial memberships. It is possible to get a good feel for a service in just a couple of hours, and the process of trying different services will help you determine your needs.

If you're already online, you are in an excellent position to evaluate ISPs. You already know what you want and need, and you know what's possible. Go for it!

SOFTWARE AND INFORMATION SOURCES

■ Web Browsers

Microsoft Internet Explorer
http://www.microsoft.com/ie/download

NCSA Mosaic
http://www.ncsa.uiuc.edu/SDG/Software/WinMosaic/index.html

Netscape
http://home.netscape.com

PROCOMM PLUS for Windows
http://www.procomm.com

■ Independent ISPs

Earthlink
http://www.earthlink.com

GNN
http://www.gnn.com

Mindspring
http://www.mindspring.com

NETCOM
http://www.netcom.com

SpryNet
http://www.sprynet.com

■ Online Services

America Online
http://www.aol.com

CompuServe
http://www.compuserve.com

DELPHI Internet Services
http://www.delphi.com

The Microsoft Network (requires Future Splash Animator Plug-in)
http://www.msn.com

Prodigy
http://www.prodigy.com

Browser Utilities, Shareware, and More

I n this chapter I'll acquaint you with some important concepts. Specifically, I'll define several important categories of software used with browsers and introduce you to the concept of shareware. You'll also look at considerations involved in installing Internet software. If you are a long-time PC user, you may find some of the information in this chapter familiar. So, you may want to skip the section "MORE CATEGORIES: COMMERCIAL SOFTWARE, FREEWARE, AND SHAREWARE." However, I do urge you to read the discussion of copyright and fair use that leads off each section.

You should also look over the section "GETTING THE WORDS RIGHT" and "UTILITY PROGRAMS." This will help ensure that you have a good working knowledge of the terms and concepts used to describe various types of application and utility software.

Finally, even if you have installed your share of new software, at least scan the section, "SOFTWARE INSTALLATION AND SETUP."

GETTING THE WORDS RIGHT

Computing has always had a problem with words. Computer professionals and users alike tend to throw around words indiscriminately, certain that you'll know what they mean. For example, software goes by several names. There is, of course, "software," and "programs," and even "software programs," which is redundant. And do not forget the currently popular "applications."

All that's probably simple enough, but how about "utilities?" For a full discussion of utilities, read on.

UTILITY PROGRAMS

Many people think of a utility as a program that performs functions in DOS, or which debugs or analyzes code for programmers, but this view is too narrow. (Although utilities do exist for DOS and for programmers.) If you consider a utility to be any small, specialized program, you are on the right track. Today's utilities aren't necessarily small, but a good working definition of a utility might be a specialized program.

Utility Software Defined

More accurately, a *utility* is a specialized program that helps or enhances another program. Depending on the tasks required, a utility may perform its job while the program for which it works is running, or the utility may run on its own.

Examples of utilities that perform specific functions while running in concert with another program are spelling checkers—especially those that check spelling as you type. Also in this category of co-running utilities are *components* that can be added to browsers: the Java "applets," Netscape "plug-ins," and ActiveX "controls" mentioned in Chapter Two, "Selecting a Browser and an ISP," and covered in more detail in Chapter Four, "Internet Support Software Basics."

The Helper applications examined in Chapter Four are also examples of utilities that run at the same time as the programs they serve.

Utilities that add to, enhance, or perform functions for another program without the other program running are sometimes called "standalone utilities." These utilities most often alter or enhance data files so they can be used by another program. Utilities that run "unplugged" from the Internet, such as those that convert data from one format to another (graphics, or text), fit the bill here, as do the archiving programs (PKZIP, ARC, and so on) discussed in Chapter Five, "Archiving Software."

MORE CATEGORIES: COMMERCIAL SOFTWARE, FREEWARE, AND SHAREWARE

This section addresses still more computer nomenclature. Specifically, the terms used to describe how software is distributed: *commercial software*, *freeware*, *demoware*, and *shareware*.

There are also some important notes on copyright and about staying on the legal side of software distribution.

Commercial Software

In conventional software marketing, you purchase a program from a publisher or a retailer. A licensing agreement among the packaging clearly spells out your rights and limitations for using the software, and you're in business, agreeing to the terms of use by default. You get to use the software as long as you want, under these terms.

But this is not the only way software is marketed. A surprisingly large number of the most important PC utilities (and applications) are marketed under terms of temporary, extendible licensing. Still other software is provided completely free of cost, but only if you agree to specific terms of use.

These approaches to marketing are known as shareware and freely licensed software (or "freeware"), respectively. If you have doubts as to the meaning of either, or think that free software is free to do with as you desire, read on.

Freeware

Very little software labeled "free" is completely free. Although free software costs nothing, some restrictions apply. The licenses for individual programs detail (often in the extreme) what you may and may not do with the program.

The basic restrictions are simple: although you can use a free program as you want for its intended purpose, you cannot alter it in any way, nor can you sell it or include it with other items for sale. The creator/provider of the program retains complete ownership of all copies in use. Other restrictions may or may not involve copying and sharing the program.

In all, you can't really complain about these restrictions because they don't really limit your personal use of the program, and it costs you nothing (other than the cost of downloading). The restrictions protect the owner's copyright and ensure that they get credit for the program's creation.

And what does the software creator get in return?—credit for the program, for one thing. Also, some free programs exist to support commercial Web sites. Such Web sites may sell products or promote products that require the use of the program in question (as is the case with some Netscape plug-ins).

Still other free programs introduce and support other products. Microsoft Internet Explorer exists largely for this purpose. So do many plug-ins for Netscape.

As you can see, this is a great way to market other products. Give the user a program that lets him use other programs, for which you charge.

Whatever the return for the software creator, you are granted the right to use the software all you want—but only if you agree to and abide by the terms and restrictions the copyright holder places on you.

Basically, you are "safe" if you download or otherwise obtain and use the software from the copyright holder—anything beyond that is outside the terms of the user agreement. This limitation includes selling the software on disk, offering it for download at a Web site without permission, altering it with a promotional message and distributing it that way, or anything else not specified in the agreement.

"Free" software costs nothing, and you can use it all you want. Now, look at another type of software that might be construed as free, but isn't.

Taking a Test Drive with Demoware. A popular approach to marketing anything is to put the product in the hands of the consumer. Software publishers have used this approach since the mid-1980s with what is known as *demoware*. A demoware program is a partially functioning version of an application (a word processor that doesn't print or save files, for example). These are typically provided free, by download or on disk. The theory is that if the user likes the demo so much, he or she will buy the program.

A different approach to giving the user a test drive is to give him the complete, fully functional program for a limited time. Along with this approach comes a licensing agreement that binds the user to paying for the program if he wishes to continue using it.

Netscape Navigator is distributed on this basis. You are granted a temporary license to use the program for 30 days. After that, you must register the program by paying a license fee (unless you meet Netscape's criteria for a free license).

This concept is somewhat similar to shareware, explained in the following section, but the software is not made available in the same way, indiscriminately distributed online, on disk, by mail, hand-to-hand, and so on. Netscape controls how the Navigator program is distributed, including the licensing of "official download sites" for Navigator.

Netscape Navigator was distributed in this way, along with commercial packaged versions that contain the same product. This approach was unique, and it proved tremendously successful for Netscape. Few programs, however, use this technique.

Shareware

Shareware is a way to try software before you buy it. It is both a marketing method and means of distribution. The term *shareware* derives from the fact that anyone who has the program is encouraged to "share" it with friends. This, along with placement of the software for download, ensures the largest possible distribution.

As a sales method, shareware is best described as an honor system. You use shareware at no initial cost. However, it is expected that you send a user fee to the author if you then use the software on a regular basis. (Paying for the program is euphemistically known as *registering*.)

"On a regular basis" usually means using a program beyond a trial period of thirty days. The user fee is sometimes referred to as a "donation," but the idea is the same: to compensate the author for his or her work.

Why Shareware? Why do programmers market their work in this way? Shareware authors quite often cite the "try before you buy" benefit as the main reason. This approach gives them an edge over higher-priced software from high-powered companies, who can afford to get your attention with expensive advertising. In most instances, they also enjoy worldwide distribution.

Many programmers further cite the success of shareware companies such as DataStorm or Nico Mak Computing (whose WinZip is a major success story) as examples of what they're emulating.

I suspect that most shareware is published as such because the authors can't get their programs distributed by established commercial publishers. This isn't surprising; there is a glut of good software out there—too much, in fact, to be marketed by commercial publishers.

Other programmers don't *want* their products handled by commercial publishers. They may feel they can make more money by publishing their work themselves, and/or want total control over their creative work.

Fortunately for these authors, the ease of copying files to disk and the vast network represented by commercial online services and the Internet gives them access to a powerful distribution network.

Shareware Quality. All of this by no means implies that shareware is intrinsically of poor quality. Publishing shareware is similar to self-publishing a book. Unlike many self-published books, most shareware programs are of some quality. Many shareware products are of superior quality when compared to their commercial counterparts, and many shareware products have no commercial counterparts. (WinZip—discussed in Chapter Five and elsewhere, where applicable in this book—is a prime example of a superior-quality program published as shareware.)

SOFTWARE INSTALLATION AND SETUP

Whether you're dealing with utilities, applications, or anything in between, installing Internet software differs little from installing other kinds of software.

In recent years, few Windows programs—whether commercial, freeware, or shareware—arrive without an installation element. The few programs that require manual installation almost always come with detailed instructions. The "readme" file (given a **READ.ME**, **README.TXT**, or similar name) that comes with almost all shareware programs usually contains all the information you need to install and get started. So, you should have no problems with the actual installation. The potential problem areas are related to preparing for installation, and properly setting up a program. These areas are briefly examined here.

Disk or Download?

From the viewpoint of installation, the major difference between most Internet software and other types of software is that you rarely install

Internet software from a CD-ROM or floppy disk because most Internet applications and utilities are available for download at Web sites. A few publishers of Internet applications and utilities make disks available on request, but if you are like most Internet users, you will prefer downloads to waiting for the U.S. Mail service.

So, unless you copy downloaded software programs to floppy disks—which, because of their large size, cannot be done easily with all Internet applications—you probably will install them from one directory in your hard drive to another. With this in mind, what follows are considerations to remember when downloading and installing Internet software.

Stay in Control of Your Drive. Always try to keep your hard drive and its files under control. It's easy to lose a quarter, a third, or even more of a hard drive's space to old program versions, installation files of one sort or another, forgotten data files, and so on.

Because most of today's programs are megabyte-eating hogs, you really want to conserve as much hard drive space as possible, even if you have a gigabyte or more of free space.

One important way to keep disk space free is to properly "clean up" after installing downloaded programs. As you may already know, a browser download can be several megabytes in size, even when compressed. Internet utilities aren't quite as big, but when "unpacked," they are larger than they seem. (For more information about file compression and unpacking in relation to downloads, see Chapter Five, "Archiving Software.")

Be Prepared. Proper preparation makes the cleanup process easy. When you download a program from the Internet or an online service, it will reside in the directory specified by the program that you use to download it. If you're not sure where it is, check your browser or communications program's setup parameters, as appropriate. Or, start a download; your program will ask where you want to save the download. Downloads usually go into a program subdirectory named \DOWNLOAD, which is fine. Just keep track of where your downloads go.

And track what's in this directory. If you have downloaded more than a couple of times, it is likely that you have a bunch of leftover files in your download directory. These file are wasting space that your system can use for other purposes. (So, delete them—and follow the procedures discussed here so you won't have this problem again.)

Now, *before* you install a downloaded program, put it in a special directory that you use only to hold programs you plan to install. Keep only one program in it at a time (I'll explain why directly). I use a directory named \INSTALL; the name and purpose are easy to remember.

Your program installation directory should be empty, except when you are preparing to install a program. When you are ready to install a download, copy the file from the download directory to the installation directory. (This makes two copies of the download, but don't worry; you'll remedy this duplication after you complete the installation process.)

There are good reasons for installing a downloaded program file from a copy in a separate directory. If something goes wrong, you still have the original download. After the program is installed, you know where to go to delete the download (both copies). If you are likely to wait to do the deletion, checking this installation directory reminds you what to delete (there, and in the download directory). It's a built-in reminder service.

If the download is a .ZIP, .ARC, .ARJ file, or self-extracting archive, also unpack the contents to the installation directory. (Again, see Chapter Five for more information on these files.) This keeps all the files from the archive in a convenient spot for simple, one-command deletion. If, however, you unpack an archives file in the \DOWNLOAD directory, you could end up playing hell on a tin fiddle figuring out what files came from the archive.

A final tip on installation: if, when you install a program, you are asked to name a destination drive and directory, you should probably use the default names provided. Even if you change the drive (for example, from C: to D:), retain the directory name. There usually is no reason to change the directory name, and you'll find that doing so can leave you confused when you read documentation or help files, which assume that you are using the default names.

Also, if you install a newer version of an existing program, changing the name of the directory can result in *two* full copies of the installed program on your disk, one old and one new. (Concerning this, it is a good idea to make backup copies of any program data files—such as a browser's bookmark file—before you install the new version. This backing up is protection against something going wrong, and protection against a program that may overwrite existing data files when it installs a new version.)

During Installation

The installation process for most programs is pretty much automatic. Some do ask whether you want to perform a "full" installation, as opposed to a "minimum" or "optimal" (a.k.a. "common") installation. You don't have to think too long about this one; just decide if you have the extra hard drive space to accommodate files that you will rarely use—which is what you will need if you select the "full" installation. (These files typically include extra printer or video drivers, and other things the program's creator included to accommodate unusual hardware setups or other personal requirements.)

If you don't have space to waste, "optimal" or "common" is usually the best choice. With this installation option you get help and/or tutorial files, and other files that do not come with the minimum installation. (If you are already familiar with the program, you won't need these files, so "minimum" would be your best choice.)

After the Installation

Most programs do not require setup after installation. Usually, setup options are established during the installation either by default or as the result of questions the installation program asks you.

If the program is a standalone utility, such as browser helper applications or, for example, a graphics viewer program, it's a good idea to run it before you need it. Most applications come with example files; load these files to test the application. Note where the program's data files are located, and any defaults it uses for things such as file types (opening or saving), and so on. There should be defaults for every variable; if not, you are given the opportunity to set them now. If any defaults do not fit your way of working, change them.

When installing a helper application, it's a good idea to check your browser's setup for assigning files of various types to given programs. Make

sure that the browser knows the application exists (if so, the application name will appear in a list the browser keeps).

The browser should also know to which file types the application should be linked. This is determined by the MIME type settings in the browser's setup. (See Chapter Seven, "Computer/ Internet Data Formats and Conversion," for more information about MIME.) To check this in Netscape

FIGURE 3.1

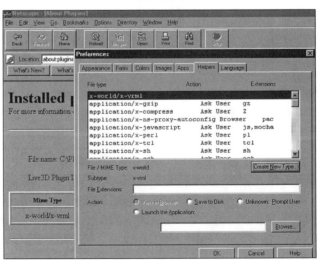

Netscape's list of helper application assignments

Navigator, select General Preferences...on the Options menu, and then select the Helpers tab. You will see the screen shown in Figure 3.1.

With Explorer, select Options... on the View menu and select the Programs tab, followed by the File Types...button. The screen in Figure 3.2 is displayed.

This chapter is only intended to cover the basics of Internet utility files. The chapters that follow give you more detailed information about utilities and other support files, including helper applications, add-ons, and more.

FIGURE 3.2

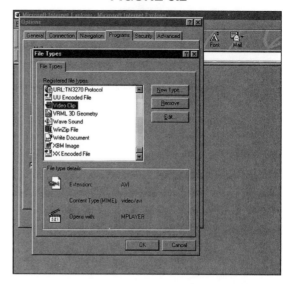

Internet Explorer's File Types listing

Shareware Links

The sites listed here offer thousands of programs, add-ons, upgrades, data files, and other kinds of freeware and shareware. All offer "best of" collections, as well as browsable lists of software by category. Most also provide search tools, so you can find the files that interest you with a keyword search. All are free.

CNET Online's searchable PC shareware site, with browsable categories, feature stories, and more
http://www.download.com

Another CNET Online site—a shareware repository (reviews and downloads—browse or search)
http://www.shareware.com

Jumbo Shareware and Freeware Download Site
http://www.jumbo.com

Windows95.com Shareware Collection
http://www.windows95.com/apps/

ZDNet's Software Library
http://www.hotfiles.com/

Internet Support Software Basics

WHAT IS SUPPORT SOFTWARE?

n Chapter Three, you learned about utilities—programs that perform functions on behalf of other programs. In this chapter, you look at two kinds of Web browser utilities. These utilities are *add-ons*, which work within your browser, and *helper programs*, which work outside your browser to extend its Internet capabilities.

ADD-ONS, PLUG-INS, AND CONTROLS

Add-ons are perhaps the most important and definitely the most universal of browser utilities. You may have seen references to add-ons in computing magazines and online. Also known as *plug-ins* or *plug-in modules* or even *controls*, *add-ons* are programs that add to a browser's capabilities. The concept of add-ons for a browser is similar to a Photoshop plug-in or a Quark Xpress extension. In all cases, the creator of the application (Adobe or Quark) has published a document (API) that explains how other programmers can "extend" the basic functionality of an application. This strategy is brilliant, both from a marketing and from a performance point of view.

Add-ons can give a browser new capabilities, or they can greatly enhance existing capabilities. Getting an add-on is almost like getting a newer version of a browser program, with new features added.

More Words About Words

The term "plug-in" usually applies only to Netscape Navigator, not to Microsoft Internet Explorer. Microsoft, in typical fashion, decided that add-ons for Explorer should have a name of its own choosing, so it came up with *ActiveX controls* (*controls* for short).

Therefore, in this chapter and ensuing chapters, you see the three terms in use at different times and as appropriate. Just remember that:

plug-in = Netscape
control = Explorer
add-on = both!

What Can Add-Ons Do for Me?

Add-ons are utilities that add capabilities to your browser. For example, if you download the Quick-Time for Windows movie player plug-in for Netscape, you add the capability to play video. Then, if a site sends a data file with the filename extensions .MOV and .MPG, you can view the video file within Netscape, as demonstrated in Figure 4.1.

FIGURE 4.1

The QuickTime Movie add-on, playing video in Netscape

Similarly, if you have the RealAudio player/control for Explorer, you can listen to audio sound clips in real time. (Interestingly, if you have the RealAudio helper program—discussed in a later section of this chapter—you can use it with Explorer to hear sound clips.)

Other add-ons let you view 3-D images, view animation within Web pages, enjoy two-way audio and video communication, and much more.

The range of plug-ins is seemingly endless, and the majority of them are free. Many, of course, support other products, which are not free. AutoDesk MapGuide, a Netscape plug-in, is an example of a plug-in in this supporting role. The free plug-in interprets and displays vector-based maps within Netscape. The map development tools, however, are not free.

Many plug-ins support Web sites, too. An excellent example of this is the PointCast Network. PointCast, the first worldwide Internet news network, broadcasts news and other information to Internet users who visit their site. (PointCast is located at: **http://www.pointcast.com/**.) PointCast is advertiser-supported, but you must download the free PointCast Network plug-in to access it.

Another important plug-in is Macromedia's Shockwave. A vital addition to many Internet users' browsers, Shockwave is a plug-in that plays movies created with Shockwave Director and incorporated into Web pages. This is probably the most popular multimedia application going at present, even though you must prepare to wait lengthy periods to transfer data when you select a Web page with Shockwave data.

FIGURE 4.2

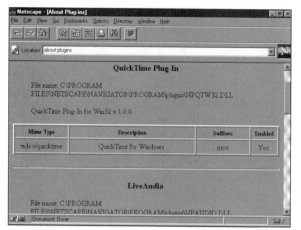

Netscape's installed plug-ins listing

Look for Shockwave to remain one of the "must-haves" for some time—although I suspect it will eventually get aced out by other programs that aren't trying to be everything to everyone.

Shockwave is available as a Netscape plug-in, as well as an ActiveX control for Explorer.

Netscape Plug-Ins. Netscape users have ample reason to take advantage of plug-ins. Netscape has actively encouraged the development of plug-in add-ons by third parties. The number of available plug-ins for Netscape runs into the scores. Netscape makes available its Live3D (a 3-D graphics viewer) and CoolTalk plug-ins (an Internet phone application) and others at its Web site.

Third-party plug-ins cover audio and video applications, image viewing, animation and 3-D, presentation and other business software, and utilities of various flavors. The range of plug-ins is seemingly endless, and most of them are free.

The bottom line here is that, thanks to its head start in the business and an aggressive marketing attitude, there are more sites using Netscape plug-ins than Microsoft ActiveX controls.

You can get a good idea of the kinds of Netscape plug-ins you need by watching the kind of data that gets sent to you by various Web sites. If you encounter a data type more than once, odds are you need to get the plug-in that supports it. (The data type—and the plug-in required to use it—is often provided by the Web site.)

You must, of course, download the plug-ins you need. Most Web sites that make use of Netscape plug-ins have a provision on their home page for downloading required plug-ins.

You can learn quite a bit about which Netscape plug-ins are available by visiting Netscape's plug-in download and information page at: **http://home. netscape.com/comprod/mirror/navcomponents_download.html**. Also, see Chapter Ten.

Netscape has an interesting feature that allows you to see the plug-ins currently installed. Click "About Plug-ins" on Netscape's Help menu, and you see a screen similar to Figure 4.2.

As you can see, this is a handy tool that tells you not only what plug-ins are installed, but also where each plug-in keeps its files.

Java, JavaScript, and VBScript

The section on Java is placed here, between Netscape and Explorer, because this is where it resides in reality. Java can be run with both Netscape and Explorer, and under many operating systems other than DOS/Windows.

Developed by Sun Microsystems, Java was created as a universal programming language to create applications that would be portable among most computer types and operating systems.

In the online world, Java is viewed as adding *active content* or *interactive content* to the Web. In reality, Java is less than interactive, but definitely active.

The most prevalent application for Java is to create small programs that are included within Web pages. These are dubbed *applets* because they tend to be very small.

In practice—and this is the major appeal of Java on the Web—a Java applet doesn't run on the computer hosting the Web page that contains the applet. Instead, it is transmitted to the computer that is connected to the Web page, and then interpreted and run by the receiving system's Web browser.

As you may imagine, this has tremendous appeal for Web designers and programmers. Suddenly, much more data can be transmitted, and in different ways, than previously possible. Java enables interactive, multimedia Web experiences that are at times even more intensive than video. Animation is a snap, and everything from graphic games and crossword puzzles, to word processors can be implemented with Java.

Some Java applets you encounter tend to be slightly disappointing, due to lack of smoothness in operation, lockups, or not being 100% compatible with the Java implementation of a given browser. (And it sometimes happens that an amateur programmer's experiments or lack of expertise can affect Java pages.)

Also, transfer times for Java applets, as with everything on the Web, can be slow. As Internet technology progresses, you can count on seeing more efficient implementations of Java, with correspondingly greater speed of transfer and operation.

Although Java capability is built into Netscape and Explorer, you probably will find that you need some updates or add-ons to Java itself. Web sites that use "extended" versions of Java usually inform you of what you need.

Several companies have built up standard PC applications that run within a browser Window, using Java. Among the more interesting are a word processor and spreadsheet developed by Cooper & Peters (**http://www.cooper-peters.**

com/**cpwp.html**), and an entire office suite for intranet and Internet applications from Corel (**http://www.corel.com/**).

When you load a Web page that contains a Java application, you will usually see some notification that a Java applet is being transmitted. After the applet starts, you may notice a delay before you see the results, but your browser usually notifies you that a Java applet is running. An example of this can be seen in Figure 4.3.

The applet in this example shows a blimp, cruising across the upper part of the Web page. The blimp contains a horizontally scrolling message.

Of course, you won't see motion on this printed page, but I simulated motion with multiple copies of the applet segment of the screen. Note, too, the browser's message about the applet in the status line at the bottom of the screen.

Java was the first approach to putting active content in Web pages, by sending a program for the receiving machine to run within a page. Java proved immensely popular—popular enough to spawn more of the same.

Most notable among Java's follow-ons is JavaScript. Created by Netscape and Sun, JavaScript is a simpler approach to writing programs that run within a Web page. It is a descendent of Netscape's "LiveScript," which was the first Internet scripting language. The idea with JavaScript is to put a tool for programming active Web page content in the hands of non-programmers. Like Java, JavaScript can run with Explorer as well as Netscape.

Visual Basic Script (a.k.a. *VBScript*) is a relative newcomer to the realm of interactivity tools for the Internet. This Microsoft-developed scripting language is a direct competitor for JavaScript in creating active content in HTML pages—and is, not surprisingly, designed expressly for Microsoft Internet Explorer. Netscape users do not find VBScript apps embedded in Web pages at all friendly.

FIGURE 4.3

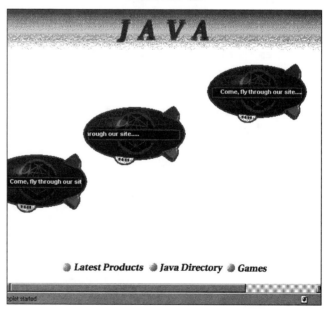

A Java applet, running within a Web page

Finally, as you may already know, Microsoft's ActiveX controls were created almost as a direct result of the existence of Java, to make Explorer more competitive.

ActiveX Controls for Explorer

As noted earlier, Microsoft calls its add-ons "controls." They are based on the ActiveX language, developed by Microsoft (and, not incidentally, the basis of many links between Windows 95 applications and the Internet).

More ActiveX controls for Explorer are oriented toward active content within a Web page. In this respect, controls are Explorer's counterpart of the Java development system. Still, some controls run applets within Explorer in the same way Netscape plug-ins do, so controls are somewhere between Netscape plug-ins and Java applets.

Note that, while Microsoft initially created ActiveX for Explorer, it's possible that you can look for Netscape to adapt to accommodate ActiveX Controls in the near future (with, perhaps, Microsoft helping behind the scenes in the next version of ActiveX).

Most ActiveX controls are easy to obtain and use because you do not have to first find and then download them. Rather, when you use Explorer to access a Web site where ActiveX controls are present, Explorer checks to see if you have the requisite control(s). If not, the controls download. This is true even with some limited versions of Explorer, such as AOL's Explorer-based browser.

Additionally, I have found that more than a few controls required by various Web sites are already built into Explorer.

I have found an interesting range of ActiveX controls on the Web, among them, drop-down menus (which give you a menu bar within a Web page), notepads, multimedia viewers, and more.

For the lowdown on ActiveX controls, start at this URL: **http://www.microsoft.com/ie/ie3/activex.htm**.

HELPER PROGRAMS

Now, you should consider the other browser utility category—*Helper applications* (a.k.a. *helper apps* or *helper programs*). Software in this category performs tasks handed off to it from another program. Unlike some types of utilities, helper programs are typically complex applications that perform a variety of tasks.

Helper programs have an additional defining element: their work (typically playing sounds or displaying image or video files) is not displayed inside the browser's window.

This is an important distinction because browser utilities known as add-ons *do* work within the browser window.

Another contrasting element between add-ons and helper apps is that add-ons are not normally browser-specific. That is, a helper that works with Netscape usually works with Explorer. Netscape plug-ins and ActiveX controls for Explorer, on the other hand, are exclusive to their respective browsers.

FIGURE 4.4

The RealAudio player, a helper app

Step-by-Step: A Helper Program in Action

An example of a helper application is the player for the immensely popular RealAudio real-time audio player. If you have visited sites such as ABC, NPR, MSNBC, and any of hundreds of others, you found RealAudio clips much in evidence.

If you have RealAudio installed, visit one of the sites named, click on a link that sends a RealAudio recording file to your system, and you'll see the RealAudio player start. It typically overlays the browser, as in Figure 4.4, so you can access its controls. (However, it does just as well in the background. I clicked over to WORD for Windows after starting the audio data stream, and the RealAudio player went happily along, playing the commentary from MSNBC.COM.)

The audio file being received causes the browser to start the helper. Click on the RealAudio file link, and here's what happens:

- Your browser recognizes the file as RealAudio by the filename extension **.RA**, and then checks its operating setup to see whether it should call a helper program to handle this kind of file.

- If the browser is properly set up, it "knows" to start the program **RAPLAYER.EXE**. (This is the RealAudio player.)

- The browser holds the incoming .RA file momentarily as the player program starts. After RAPLAYER.EXE starts, the browser lets it have the data, and the incoming audio stream plays through your PC's speakers.

Helper Programs and Your Browser

By now you may be wondering how exactly your browser knows to start a helper program when a given data file type comes in from the Internet.

Your browser can handle a number of file types by itself, including but not limited to .HTML, .JPG, .GIF, and many others, based on built-in capabilities. When a browser encounters a file type that it cannot handle,

FIGURE 4.5

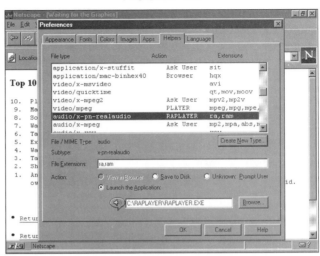

The Netscape Preferences dialog box

the browser consults a list of file types and associated helper programs. If a helper program is listed for this file type, the browser runs the associated program and shunts the data to the program.

If no program is specified for a given file type, the browser asks you what you want to do with the file. Your options then include specifying a program to run, saving the file to disk, or canceling the incoming file.

You can see a list of file types and associated helper programs via your browser's Setup, Preferences, or Options menu. Two examples follow.

With Netscape, select General Preferences...on the Options menu, then press the Helpers tab. You then see the dialog box in Figure 4.5.

With Explorer, select Options...on the View menu, and press the Programs tab, followed by the File Types...button. Explorer displays the dialog shown in Figure 4.6.

In each instance, you can see a list of file types, with "RealAudio" highlighted, along with information about the types of files played, and the program used to play it. Here is where the browser knows what program to run in the RealAudio example.

Browsers sometimes, but not always, work with the help of Windows registration files to link helper programs to file types. So, you must often link the helper program with its file types manually.

Not all helper programs are recognized by all browsers. Additionally, a browser will often take a specific program to handle a given file type, rather than an alternate program you have installed. Solving either problem is

FIGURE 4.6

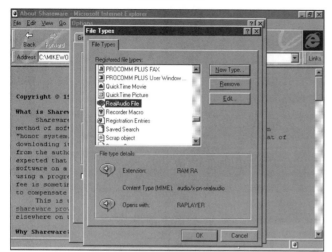

The Explorer File Types dialog

straightforward enough. Just go into the appropriate setup dialog and tell the browser it should use the program you want it to use.

VISUAL BASIC AND THREE FILES YOU *MUST* HAVE

Several years ago, Microsoft introduced *Visual Basic* (or *VB*), a programming language for creating applications in Windows. VB's immediate popularity among developers spawned thousands of shareware programs.

As with the many versions of the BASIC language with which some of us old-timers are familiar, there is a special file you must have to run the programs. With BASIC in DOS, the BASIC.EXE program served as an interpreter and actually ran the BASIC programs. The counterpart for Visual Basic is the *Visual Basic Runtime* (or *VBRUN*). The Visual Basic Runtime is a *Dynamic Link Library* (or *DLL*) file. (DLL files are usually characterized by the filename extension **.DLL**.)

The proper version of this file must be present in your \WINDOWS\SYSTEM directory before you can run a Visual Basic program. Moreover, you must have the version of the Visual Basic Runtime that matches the version of Visual Basic used to create the program you want to run.

The descriptions of most Visual Basic programs note which version of the Visual Basic Runtime you need, which is useful information, but checking to see if you have the right version when you go to download a Visual Basic program can get involved. So, I suggest that you download all versions now.

Each Visual Basic Runtime filename begins with **VBRUN** or **VB**. The filenames of the versions currently available (which go with Visual Basic versions 1 through 4) are:

VBRUN100.DLL for programs written with Visual Basic version 1

VBRUN200.DLL for Visual Basic version 2

VBRUN300.DLL   for Visual Basic version 3

VB40016.DLL   for 16-bit programs written with Visual Basic version 4

VB40032.DLL   for 32-bit programs written with Visual Basic version 4

If you're on AOL, CompuServe, or DELPHI, the .DLL file for each version of Visual Basic is easy to find. Go to the appropriate download area and search by using "Visual Basic," "runtime," and/or "DLL."

On the Internet, these files are even easier to find. Go to the SoftSeek Web site's "vbrun files" download area (**http://www.softseek.com/Utilities/VBRUN_Files/index.html**). Here you will find all the versions of Visual Basic Runtime DLL files.

You can also find the Visual Basic Runtime versions at: **http://www.shareware.com**. Use the keyword "vbrun" with the site's search feature to find the files.

You should download all of the VBRUN files at the earliest opportunity. In this way, you will be able to run any Visual Basic programs that you may download.

In obtaining all of the Runtime files, you also will realize an advantage when downloading. Many shareware authors make available two versions of program downloads: one with the required Visual Basic Runtime, and one without. With all existing Runtimes in your \WINDOWS\SYSTEM directory, you will always be able to download the smaller version, without the Visual Basic Runtimes included.

This chapter has covered Web browser add-ons and helper programs. Next, check out one of the most important categories of *offline* utilities: archiving/de-archiving software.

SOFTWARE & INFORMATION SOURCES

▪ Download Links & Info for Plug-Ins and Helper Apps in General

Each of these sites has information and links on plug-ins and/or helper applications for Netscape and Explorer.

"Recommended Plug-In Resources" (Links)
http://www.intouch.bc.ca/internetstore/utilities/plugins.html

Plug-Ins Today
http://www.hitznet.com/isocket/

I-World Internet News
http://www.iworld.com/

Plug-In Plaza
http://browserwatch.iworld.com/plug-in.html

■ Netscape Navigator Add-Ons

The following URLs are all found at Netscape's Web site. They offer extensive information on available plug-ins and helper apps, plus background and technical information on add-on components.

Inline Plug-Ins Page
http://home.netscape.com/comprod/products/navigator/version_2.0/plugins/ index.html

Download Netscape Navigator Components
http://home.netscape.com/comprod/mirror/navcomponents_download.html

Netscape Helper Applications
http://home.netscape.com/assist/helper_apps/

■ Microsoft Internet Explorer Add-Ons

The following URLs comprise "information central" for ActiveX controls for Explorer.

ActiveX Controls
http://www.microsoft.com/ie/download/ieadd.htm

http://www.microsoft.com/activex/controls/

http://www.mninc.com/tools/

General Info on ActiveX
http://www.microsoft.com/ie/ie3/activex.htm

ActiveX Downloads and Info
http://www.activex.com

■ Java Info and Links

Sun Microsystems' Java Page
http://java.sun.com/

Netscape's Java Page
**http://www.netscape.com/comprod/products/navigator/version_2.0/java_
applets/index.html**

Gamelon Official Directory Site for Java
http://www.gamelan.com/

Some Sites that Use Java:

CNET Online
http://www.cnet.com

ServoNet's Java Site
http://java.servonet.com/

EarthWeb
http://www.earthweb.com/java/

■ Specific Products

AutoDesk MapGuide
http://www.mapguide.com

Corel Office for Java
http://www.corel.com/

Cooper & Peters
http://www.cooper-peters.com/cpwp.html

Sun Microsystems' Java
http://java.sun.com/

PointCast Network
http://www.pointcast.com/

QuickTime for Windows
http://quicktime.apple.com/

Macromedia Shockwave Director
http://www.macromedia.com

Visual Basic Script
http://musicm.mcgill.ca/~simone/HTTP/webvb.html

Visual Basic Runtime Versions
http://www.softseek.com/Utilities/VBRUN_Files/index.html

http://www.shareware.com

Archiving Software

Suppose that you find an interesting file on the Internet or on one of the online services. The filename has a .ZIP, .ARC, or .ARJ extension, and you notice in the file description that the file is an "archive." You download the file and try to run it, but nothing happens. Slightly confused, you try to open it with a word processor, but your word processor refuses to deal with the file; or you can open the file, but its contents are totally meaningless.

Has this ever happened to you? If so, you are not in a minority. File archiving and compression is only one of the many areas of computing that no one tells you about—unless you know to ask. And you usually don't know to ask until you've wasted a lot of time and suffered more frustration than you need. When you do ask, you usually get an answer like, "Get PKUNZIP or WinZip," which you then have to find and then figure out how to use.

I know how it is—as a Forum Sysop (system manager) on several major online services, what to do with a file that has the file extension .ZIP or .ARC leads the list of new users' questions.

Part of the reason for the confusion is that, as important and ubiquitous as file archiving is, you don't find it discussed in your hardware and software manuals. Nor do you find information about archived files posted in many file download areas. Finally, archiving software just isn't among the application types bundled with your PC.

This omission in the PC world occurs because archiving software is traditionally shareware, and only the author makes money from shareware. So, there's no incentive to bundle it with other software, and it gets little attention otherwise. The result is that you are expected to either know to ask or to learn about archives on your own.

The overwhelming majority of data, application, text, and graphics files available for download at Web sites and in databases and libraries on online services are in archives. This is because many files are so large that if they weren't compressed in archives, it would take hours to download them. So, if you intend to do much downloading, you need to have at least one, and perhaps two or more, of the more popular archiving programs used with MS-DOS computers. The same is true if you will be uploading files. (Not surprisingly, archives are excellent tools for creating archival or backup copies of data to store on floppy disks.)

Therefore, you need to know how to access compressed files in archives, and you need to know a little about how archiving programs work. This chapter helps you understand the nature of archives and examines the software you need to handle them.

WHAT IS AN ARCHIVE?

An *archive* is a special kind of binary file that contains one or more files, in compressed form. Archive files created by the most commonly used archiving software end in .ARC, .ARJ, or .ZIP. There are also archives for Macintosh files—some of which can be useful to PC users, as described in the following section,"COMMON ARCHIVING PROGRAMS." These have the filename extension .SIT.

Files of any type—programs, text, graphics, or binary data—may be found in what are known as archived or *compressed* files, or just archives. (There are also archives that end in .COM or .EXE, and which actually run. These files are known as *self-extracting archives*, and I'll explain these shortly.)

As implied, an archive is much smaller than the actual size of the file or files it contains. Compression is achieved by use of one or more techniques, including—but not limited to—replacing long strings of repetitious data in a file with token characters. When archived, a file can be reduced in size as much as 90 percent, depending on the type of data it contains.

(A very few types of files, including .GIF graphic files, cannot be compressed; they only can be stored in an archive. This is because they already are compressed in file form; they are decompressed when used, then compressed again when you close them.)

A given archive may contain one or more files. Thus, archives not only reduce the size of the files they contain, they also present the contained files in an organized fashion. (In this respect, archives might be compared to file folders that contain multiple sheets of paper—each "sheet" in this metaphorical example being a computer data file.)

A special kind of utility software is required to place files into an archive. The same program—or, in a few cases, an accompanying program—is needed to remove or "unpack" files from an archive (except the previously mentioned self-extracting archives). These programs are referred to as *archiving software*.

What Is Archiving Software?

Sometimes called *compression* or *library* software, archiving software is a boon to modem file transfer. An excellent file management tool, an archiving program also serves as a way to speed up and organize downloads.

Operating offline as a utility, whether running under DOS or from Windows, an archiving program performs the following basic tasks, as necessary:

- Compresses files to their smallest possible size

- Combines several files into one file, reduced in size

- Allows you to view the contents of an archive

- Decompresses, or unpacks, files from an archive by creating copies of the files (Note that the archive is *not* deleted during this process.)

Figure 5.1 shows a typical archive's contents.

The program illustrated in Figure 5.1, PKZIP, provides quite a bit of information on the files in the archive. As you see, the files are much smaller than they would be if they weren't compressed—a glance at the file sizes and the percentage of reduction listings tells you this. The files' names and date/time stamps also are provided, along with information on the file types. Other archiving programs provide similar information when you view the contents of an archive that you create with them.

Why Use Archiving Utilities?

There are several benefits of storing and transferring archives. Because a file is smaller after compression, you can transfer it in much less time than it takes to transfer an uncompressed version. If several files are placed in one archive, only one file transfer operation is required. In either case, there is less risk of errors during file transmission

FIGURE 5.1

```
PKZIP (R)   FAST!   Create/Update Utility   Version 2.04g   02-01-93
Copr. 1989-1993 PKWARE Inc.   All Rights Reserved.   Shareware Version
PKZIP Reg. U.S. Pat. and Tm. Off.   Patent No. 5,051,745

þ 80486 CPU detected.
þ EMS version 4.00 detected.
þ XMS version 3.00 detected.
þ DPMI version 0.90 detected.

Searching ZIP: /ZIP/ZAB21.ZIP

Length  Method   Size  Ratio   Date    Time   CRC-32   Attr  Name
------  ------   ----  -----   ----    ----   ------   ----  ----
    22  Stored     22    0%  02-01-96  19:51  381150e2  --w-  A.BAT
    18  Stored     18    0%  02-01-96  19:51  9d40de0f  --w-  U.BAT
    19  Stored     19    0%  02-01-96  19:51  8b3fe410  --w-  V.BAT
    19  Stored     19    0%  02-01-96  19:51  0055ee73  --w-  AA.BAT
    16  Stored     16    0%  02-01-96  19:51  e2a8c78f  --w-  UA.BAT
    16  Stored     16    0%  02-01-96  19:51  b297bcd2  --w-  VA.BAT
    19  Stored     19    0%  02-01-96  19:51  4087da3c  --w-  AR.BAT
    16  Stored     16    0%  02-01-96  19:51  c99e7b3c  --w-  UR.BAT
    16  Stored     16    0%  02-01-96  19:51  99a10061  --w-  UR.BAT
 16967  DeflatN   5676   67%  02-01-96  19:51  d1f80619  --w-  READ.ME
------           ----   ---                                   -------
 17128           5837   66%                                        10
```

A file listing from an archive

because transfers take less time, and—in the case of multiple files in an archive—the number of transfers is reduced. With online services and ISPs that charge on a per-minute or per-hour basis, transferring compressed files saves you both time *and* money.

Any of several available compression, packing, archiving, shrinking, or stuffing programs can reduce files to as little as 40 percent of their original size (or even less—like 3 percent). I will leave the technical details for another book—it's enough to know that these programs work well.

Most archiving utilities can perform specialized operations on archives, in addition to their basic functions. Besides displaying a directory of the contents of an archive (refer to Figure 5.1), you may be able to use the archiving utility to display or run a file from an archive, add files to an archive, and delete or copy files in an archive. Some archiving programs can also handle archive files created by other archiving programs.

Self-Extracting Archives

Before looking at the individual archive programs, you should know something about *self-extracting archives*. These special types of archives are .EXE or .COM files that, when run, unpack the files they contain.

Any archiving program you download will be in the form of a self-extracting archive, rather than a "conventional" archive. Otherwise, you would have to download the many files that make up an archive program, or you may be faced with the irony of downloading an archive in archive format, but not being able to use it because you don't have the working archive program to unpack it.

A self-extracting archive is larger than a conventional archive that contains the same files because it includes a dedicated program that unpacks the archive. However, a self-extracting archive is still smaller than the total size of the files it contains.

As noted, when you run a self-extracting archive, it unpacks all its files. In doing so, it doesn't delete itself; it merely makes "full-size" copies of the files it contains. Therefore, you may want to delete the self-extracting archive after running it or, better yet, make a backup copy on a floppy disk.

The description of any self-extracting archive available for download should include a reference to its being a self-extracting archive so that you won't be surprised when you run the file and find a couple dozen new files on your hard disk.

Also note that self-extracting archives occasionally contain archived files. This gets confusing in the description, but it's not really the mess it may seem.

All you need to do is have on-hand the program required to unpack/unzip/de-archive the archived files in question (more on these programs soon), and unpack them.

If you are interested in creating self-extracting archives, you can approach this task in a couple of ways. You can use WinZip's (as seen later in this chapter) built-in facility for creating self-extracting archives. You can also use the program ZIP2EXE.EXE. This DOS application is provided with PKZIP, the original ZIP program.

COMMON ARCHIVING PROGRAMS

Most, but not all, archive/file compression programs in common use are shareware programs, with a couple public domain or freeware programs in the mix. Here is a rundown of the most frequently used archiving programs in the MS-DOS world.

The first three programs are "must-haves." If you have all three programs, you can handle just about every type of PC archive available online:

- PKZIP/PKUNZIP. More popularly known as "PKZIP" or just "ZIP," with this pair of DOS programs from PKWare, you can create, view, unpack and otherwise manipulate archives. (PKZIP programs operate only on archives created with PKZIP, identified by the file extension .ZIP.) Several programs and support files come with the package: PKZIP.EXE for creating, adding to, and viewing archives; PKUNZIP.EXE for unpacking archives; ZIP2EXE.EXE, a program that creates self-extracting archives; and PKZIPFIX.EXE, which repairs damaged archives. A Windows counterpart, PKZIP for Windows, is also available. As described later in this chapter, PKZIP for Windows offers the same features as the DOS version, but with a Windows interface.

- ARC. ARC, a product of System Enhancement Associates (a.k.a. Seaware), is among the oldest archiving programs, dating from the mid-1980s. It remains very popular and is rather efficient in that you need only the main program, ARC.EXE, to create, view, add to, and unpack archives. (ARC works only with archives created with ARC, identified by the file extension .ARC.) Several other programs are included in the ARC package, including ARCE, a simplified packing/unpacking program for handling ARC files.

- ARJ. Created by Robert K. Jung, ARJ is a relative newcomer among archiving programs. In some ways, it is superior to PKZIP. The ARJ package includes ARJ.EXE, for creating, viewing, and adding to archives, and UNARJ.EXE, for unpacking programs (the latter can be downloaded separately). ARJ files are identified by the extension .ARJ. In addition to other files, ARJ also comes with a program to convert archives in other formats (ARC, ZIP, ZOO, etc.) to ARJ format.

- LHA. LHA, by Haruyasu Yoshizaki, creates files with the extension .LZH, as well as self-extracting archives. It is free, and slowly gaining worldwide popularity.

- UNSIT and UNSTUFF. These programs are designed to read and unpack archives created with the Macintosh archiving program, StuffIt. StuffIt is the most popular Mac archiving program, and although you (as a PC user) cannot use Macintosh programs from StuffIt files, you will find text files, graphics files, and certain data files, which may be in StuffIt formats, that you *can* use. StuffIt archives are identified by the file extension .SIT.

There are a number of other archiving/library/file compression programs. I won't list them all because most are obsolete or just are not used enough to be of interest. (At least one of these programs does nothing more than collect several files into one without compressing them. Many PC users are wild about this program. I can't figure out why.)

The short list of such archiving programs is: LIB, LU.EXE, SQ.COM and USQ.COM, and ZOO. There's also LHARC (a.k.a. "LHA File Compression Program," by the author of the LHA program mentioned previously). LHARC creates self-extracting archives. You may find this one useful if you need to create self-extracting archives; it is very popular, largely because it works well and because it is a public domain (free) program.

USING DOS ARCHIVING PROGRAMS

As implied in previous sections, you have to "unpack" or remove the files in an archive before you can use them. You do this by using the program that created the archive, or, if you want, one of several independent programs designed to unpack and view the files within an archive.

NOTE: DOS instructions are here for two reasons. First, to show you how to use them—these instructions are far simpler than the instructions you get from the programs! Second, I want to show you just how cumbersome the DOS programs are, so that you'll be sure to go get WinZip, for example, rather than PKZIP/DOS (and some are DOS-only applications). You are likely to have the

DOS applications first because many of the online Forum moderators and other computer-literates simply advise new users to "get PKZIP."

With the exception of PKZIP for Windows, each major archiving program has one drawback—a rather primitive command structure that uses MS-DOS commands. To circumvent this, developers have written *archive management programs*. These programs not only simplify the commands, they also totally streamline the process of creating, viewing, and unpacking archives.

I'll discuss these management programs later, but first, look at how to use the basic archiving programs. (After you review this information, you probably will be more than ready for an archive management program or front end, if only for their ease-of-use.)

How-To: Archive Commands

I won't go into *all* the commands used by the major DOS archiving programs here—ARC, ARJ, and PKZIP—because these commands are diverse and get rather complex. But, the basic commands are simple enough that, with a little effort, you can learn how to use all of these applications.

Viewing an Archive's Contents. All the major archiving programs allow you to view their archives' contents. (Self-extracting archives' contents usually are not viewable, but they can be viewed with certain archive management programs, such as WinZip.) You may want to do so to make sure that all the required files are in an archive, to check the dates and sizes of the files, or just out of curiosity.

You must use the set of commands peculiar to the archiving program in question. Usually, you type the program name, followed by the viewing command and the location of the archive. Here are examples (where ARC runs ARC.EXE, ARJ runs ARJ.EXE, and PKZIP runs PKZIP.EXE):

ARC
ARC v \DIRECTORY\FILENAME

ARJ
ARJ v \DIRECTORY\FILENAME

PKZIP
PKZIP -v \DIRECTORY\FILENAME

As you see, the archiving program must be in the current directory (or a system PATH directory), and you must tell it how to locate the archive file. Alternatively, you can type the entire command string, prefaced by the location of the program, like this example, where ARJ.EXE is located in the directory \UTIL: \UTIL\ARC v *DIRECTORY\FILENAME*.

The "v" or "-v" is the command to view.

Incidentally, using this command with PKZIP results in the kind of display shown previously, in Figure 5.1.

Unpacking an Archive's Contents. The procedure for unpacking an archive is similar to viewing an archive's contents. Depending on the type of archive, you may have to use a special unpacking program, or you may need to merely substitute an unpacking command for the viewing command.

Here are the unpacking commands for each of the three major MS-DOS archiving programs:

ARC
ARC x *DIRECTORY\FILENAME*

ARJ
ARJ x *DIRECTORY\FILENAME*
(or)
UNARJ *DIRECTORY\FILENAME*

PKZIP
PKUNZIP *DIRECTORY\FILENAME*

Note that ARJ and PKUNZIP use a separate program for unpacking an archive (this is optional with ARJ).

Again, the command structure in these examples assumes that you are logged into the same directory as the archiving program that you're using. If you're not in this directory, you must precede the entire command with the location of the archiving program.

Unpacking a Self-Extracting Archive. Unpacking a self-extracting archive involves little more than running a program—the program being the self-extracting archive. For example, to unpack a self-extracting archive named GRAPHS.EXE or GRAPHS.COM, you type: **GRAPHS**.

Where to Unpack Archives, and Why. The question of *where* to unpack conventional archives (archive files ending in .ZIP, .ARC, .ARJ, or the extension used by the archiving program in question) can be complex.

To simplify matters, it's best to issue commands from the disk or directory into which you want the archive files unpacked. The standard command syntax in DOS is to type the unpacking command for the archiving program, then the location and name of the archive file. You also may have to precede all this information with the location of the archiving program's location.

If, for example, you want to unpack an archive named GRAPHS.ZIP located in the directory C:\DOWNLOADS, into a directory named C:\TEMP, and you are logged into the DOWNLOADS directory, type: **\ZIP\PKUNZIPGRAPHS C:\TEMP.** (Note: This command assumes that you have PKUNZIP.EXE in the directory \ZIP.)

It's easier to log into the directory \TEMP, copy GRAPHS.ZIP to \TEMP, and then type: **\ZIP\PKUNZIP GRAPHS**.

At any rate, an archive should be unpacked so that its contents are placed in a directory that contains no other files. This is true of both self-extracting archives and normal archives. A given archive can contain dozens, even scores, of files—or it may contain just one file. Certainly, you don't want to unpack a large number of files in just any directory; if you do, you will have trouble sorting them out when or if you want to delete them. So, I recommend unpacking an archive's files to a floppy disk (space permitting) or to a directory created for this purpose.

Sorting Out Viruses

The technique of unpacking the contents of an archive into a temporary, empty directory is helpful in avoiding viruses. When you unpack an archive into an empty directory, you isolate its contents. You can see the entire contents of the archive and examine the files without having to sort them out from other, unrelated files.

Reading the READ.ME or README.TXT, or any .DOC files, should give you an idea of what files should have been included in the archive. Some shareware developers even include a "packing list" with their files. This list, contained in one of these "readme" files, or in a file named PACKING.LST, or similar, consists of a directory listing that shows the names, file sizes, and date/timestamps of the files as originally put into the archive. Any variation in a file's name, size, or date/timestamp is an indication that tampering may have occurred with the file—there's a good chance that it or another file in the archive carries a virus. If you see this kind of change, both the files and the archive should be deleted.

You decide where to place an archive's files. I often create a directory specifically for an archive I unpack, but I also keep an empty directory on drive C, named \UNPACK, for unpacking files from an archive.

The simplest choice may be to download or copy an archive or self-extracting archive to the special directory, and unpack it there. However, I recommend that you keep the original archive or self-extracting archive in a separate drive or directory, and unpack its files to your special disk or directory because you may want to keep the archive for another purpose, or you may want to unpack it to yet another disk or directory.

With conventional archives, unpacking is easily done by using the archive management tools I'll discuss later. With a self-extracting archive, you log on to the drive/directory where you want the files to go, then you type the drive/directory name where the self-extracting archive resides, followed by a backslash and the program's name. The following example unpacks the self-extracting archive BONEHEAD.EXE in the directory \DOWNLOAD on the current disk, while you are logged on to another directory: **\DOWNLOAD\ BONEHEAD.**

After you unpack an archive, its files are usually ready to use. If the archive has a READ.ME, README.TXT, or similarly named file, read the file with a word processor or NotePad before you do anything with the files from the archive.

*NOTE: **Archives within Archives**...Some archives have archived files within them. That is, after you run a self-extracting archive, or unpack a conventional archive, you find one or more files with the extension .ZIP, .ARC, or .ARJ.*

If you use PKZIP, ARC, and/or ARJ regularly, I urge you to register the programs with their authors by paying the requested fee. There are a number of benefits to registering the programs, not the least of which is encouraging the authors to make improvements on them.

Creating or Adding to an Archive. You may need to create an archive—something you may not have considered until you began using archiving software. The applications are obvious—space-saving storage and file organization. You may want to save old data files on floppy disk, which is what happens to the files for this book when it's finished, and what happens to all my tax records, and other types of files. With an archiving program, you save a lot of disk space, and you can have groups of related files stored in one convenient spot, as well as two sets of duplicate files stored separately for safety.

Another benefit is that files in an archive have less of a tendency to "degenerate," or lose data. Conventional files on floppy disk sometimes become unreadable after a few years, this happened to many of my files, but rarely have I been unable to retrieve data from an archive file. This is because archived data is stored across fewer disk tracks, which means there's less chance of a track or block of the archived data going bad.

Creating an archive with a program requires a command syntax similar to the syntax needed for unpacking or viewing an archive. You type the program's command to "add" or "pack" files to an archive, followed by the name of the archive file and the files to be added to it. (Depending on which archiving program you use, the latter two elements may be reversed.) You can use wildcards for the files to be added. Optional command elements include the locations of the archiving program, the archive file, and the files to be added to the archive file.

In addition to creating an archive, you can add files to an existing archive, using the same process as described for creating an archive.

ARCHIVE MANAGEMENT TOOLS

Now that you've seen how difficult using archiving programs can be, I'll show you how to make it easy, with readily available management tools.

"But," you may wonder, "if there are easier ways to use archiving programs, why did you show me the hard way first?" The answer is simple: so you would understand how these programs approach their tasks—what they actually do with files. As you may recall, I made the point previously in this book that understanding how a thing works often makes life easier—and that understanding definitely applies to archiving programs.

Now, before you log on to download a Windows (or DOS) archive front end or management program you saw at a Web site, keep in mind that you don't want just any random program. In theory, archive management and front end programs let you bypass the often-difficult command structures associated with archiving programs. But most of these programs seem to make using archiving programs more difficult! Bulky, cumbersome, and overloaded with features, they are horribly complex. Fortunately, two Windows utilities do work wonderfully—WinZip and PKZIP for Windows. Also, a handy DOS application named ZABTOOLS (see the section, "Doing It from DOS, with Style") can streamline using ZIP, ARC, and ARJ programs.

WinZip

WinZip is the ideal Windows front end for *all* DOS archive programs. If you do not have it, go to the WinZip Web site and download it—right now—it's that good. (The URL for WinZip is: **http://www.winzip.com/**.)

As shown in Figure 5.2, WinZip offers an attractive, easy-to-use interface, and it is as simple or as feature-laden as you might want. WinZip's features include the capability to view, unpack, create, add files to, and delete files from archives. The types of archives WinZip handles are ZIP, ARC, ARJ, and LZH. It also handles the Internet file formats TAR, gzip,

FIGURE 5.2

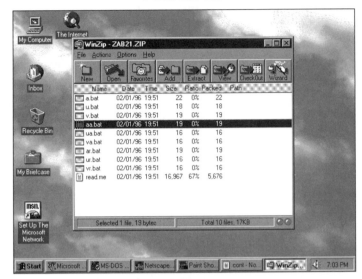

The WinZip screen

and UNIX compress. (TAR, gzip, and UNIX compress are older file-archiving formats used on the Internet. You may never encounter files stored and/or compressed in these formats, but if you do, WinZip can handle them.)

You must have copies of ARC, ARJ, and LHA (for LZH) software packages to use WinZip with archives created by these programs, but these are the only extras required. WinZip has built-in capability to handle ZIP, TAR, gzip, and UNIX compress, which means that you don't have to keep as many programs on file. (Note that if you want to create password-protected ZIP files, and/or create ZIP files that span more than one floppy disk, you still need the DOS version of PKZIP/PKUNZIP on your hard drive.)

Both 16-bit and 32-bit versions are available (for Windows 3.x and Windows 95/NT, respectively).

Additional WinZip features include:

- Virus scanning support, which allows you to link WinZip to a virus-scanning program so that you can check for viruses *before* you open a downloaded file

- Excellent context-sensitive help

- Full support for the Windows drag and drop interface, which means you can extract or add archive files by click and hold, and then moving them to/from the WinZip window

- The capability to try a program without manually unpacking and installing it; WinZip sets up the program for a trial run and lets you decide whether to keep it installed

- The capability to view or run any file in an archive, again without unpacking it

- Reasonably priced shareware, WinZip may be the only archive management tool you'll ever need. I strongly urge you to try it!

PKZIP for Windows

As you may be aware, more than 80 percent of conventional archives are in PKZIP format (with the extension .ZIP). You probably will work with ZIP files more than any other type and, *this* being the case, you really should have PKZIP and PKUNZIP on hand, in addition to WinZip.

Better yet, you may want to go for the Windows version of PKZIP named, appropriately, PKZIP for Windows. Using this program keeps it all in the family.

As shown in Figure 5.3, PKZIP for Windows has a streamlined, icon-based interface.

The emphasis with PKZIP for Windows is on simplicity. You have access to all the basic ZIP functions and operations, but nothing fancy. I recommend PKZIP for Windows if the only archives you deal with are ZIP files.

PKZIP for Windows is shareware, available at PKWare's Web site: **http://www.pkware.com**.

FIGURE 5.3

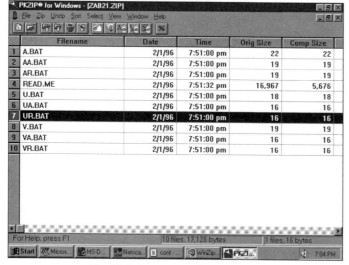

The PKZIP for Windows front end

Doing It from DOS, with Style

If you like getting your hands dirty in DOS, you may appreciate a batch-file-based front end for ZIP, ARC, and ARJ programs named ZABTOOLS.

ZABTOOLS is little more than a set of batch files (with instructions) that translate simple one-letter commands into the lengthy command strings required to use the previously mentioned archiving programs in DOS. For example, to unpack an archive named COMPLEX.ZIP, a ZABTOOLS batch file lets you type: **UA COMPLEX** rather than typing \ARC\ARC x COMPLEX. The batch files, of course, may be run from DOS or Windows.

Available on CompuServe and AOL, as well as selected Web sites, ZABTOOLS is low-priced shareware.

SOFTWARE SOURCES

This listing shows where to get information on the Internet about (and, in most cases, download) the programs discussed in this chapter. You can also download these programs on AOL, CompuServe, and other online services, as well as at Internet download sites, such as **http://www.shareware.com**.

ARC
http://www.shadow.net/~seaware/

ARJ
http://www.dunkel.de/ARJ/

LHA
http://www.shareware.com

LHARC
http://www.shareware.com

PKZIP/PKUNZIP and PKZIP for Windows
http://www.pkware.com

UNSIT/UNSTUFF
http:// www.shareware.com

WinZip
http://www.winzip.com/

ZABTOOLS
http://w3.one.net/~banks/zabtools.htm

Offline Graphics Helpers

D rawing, "painting," and design programs have been around for nearly two decades. Until recently, however, computer technology severely limited these graphics capabilities. As a result, the graphics field has only recently come into its own, particularly regarding PCs.

For the first few years of its existence, it seemed as though Macintosh would be *the* system for handling graphics and desktop publishing, even though it didn't have a color display. However, thanks to improvements in PC display technology and the clever use of existing and new technology, high-end MS-DOS computers with appropriate peripherals pretty much match the capabilities of Macintosh-based graphics/desktop publishing systems.

The same is true of display/presentation graphics, and certainly so of multimedia and Internet graphics.

To take full advantage of all the graphics available on the Web, you need some help. Although your Web browser can display GIF and JPG images, and save them to disk, you may find that you need to do more than use these simple view-and-save capabilities.

Depending on your applications, you may want to convert images from one *format* to another, resize them, change from color to gray scale, or otherwise alter images. These capabilities are particularly important if you create Web sites with graphics. Likewise, cropping or extracting one element from a picture are worthwhile capabilities.

This chapter reviews some useful tools for viewing, altering, and storing graphics.

GRAPHICS TERMS, CONVENTIONS, AND FORMATS

Before looking at graphics tools, you may need some background on computer graphics—specifically, basic graphics terminology and conventions, along with information on how graphics are handled by your computer. (If you are already versed in these basics, skip ahead to the next section.)

NOTE: For a comprehensive look at online computer graphics, read Finding Images Online, *by Paula Berinstein, available from Pemberton Press.*

For more information about this fine book, check out: ***http://www.onlineinc. com/pempress/images/****.*

Basic PC Graphics Terminology

An important term you see frequently used with reference to graphics files is "format." A *graphics file format* is a set of parameters that determines how an image is stored and, in many cases, how it is displayed. I'll discuss here some of the file formats you're likely to encounter, both on and offline.

There are also terms for the color composition of a graphic *image*. (An *image* can be a photograph, a line drawing, color or gray scale artwork, and/or text—or any combination of these.) For example, if the image is only black-and-white, it is referred to as *monochrome*. (Or, *black-and-white* or *B&W*. As you see, you're getting into the multiple-words-for-everything mode again.)

Color images usually are called *color* and are distinguished by the number of colors they contain. Depending on the system you use, a color image may have from 2 colors to 16 million colors, with any one of the colors being something other than black or white.

An intermediary composition is *gray scale*, which is distinguished from monochrome in that it uses not only black and white, but also shades of gray. As with color images, gray scale images use up to 16 million "colors" (here, shades of gray), although in practice, the number is far smaller. The shades are achieved by placing black dots in patterns, and varying the density of black dots in an area to produce a specific shade. (These dots are a.k.a. *pixels*, as explained in a couple of pages. Note, too, that when an image is printed, shading is sometimes achieved by having dots overlay one another.)

Other terminology that you may encounter in the realm of graphics are described in the following list:

- *Pixel.* Verbal shorthand for *picture element*. The smallest possible element of a picture, a pixel is basically a tiny square on the screen. A pixel can have several states—on or off, bright or normal intensity, and one color or another.

- *Bit-mapped graphics.* Bit-mapped graphics create an image by setting each of thousands of specific pixels to a certain color or intensity. The graphic is created as a series of locations in video memory. Each bit has an identity in terms of color and intensity, and each bit has a specific location in the memory map. A data file that contains a bit-mapped image has information about each screen location of the image, including color and intensity. Bit-mapped graphics are far more pleasing to the eye than graphics created by using the IBM extended character set (lines, double lines, corners of boxes, and so on). The familiar GIF and JPG/JPEG file formats are examples of bit-mapped image formats.

- *Dithering.* A process whereby colors are converted to shades of gray. Reds and yellows, for example, typically are converted to dark and light shades of gray, respectively. Gray scale *scanners* use dithering to convert color images.

- *Scanning.* The process of "reading" an image (photo, drawing, painting, or a printed page) from paper for storage in a computer file, using a device known as a *scanner*. A scanner can reproduce, depending on its features, color or monochrome/gray scale. Most scanners are either handheld (where the width of a scanned image is limited to four inches or so) or flatbed (for scanning images the size of a full-sized sheet of paper).

- *Digitizing.* The process of converting the analog data provided by a scanner (or a digital camera) into a digital representation of the image. Digitizing is achieved by creating data files that store patterns of color or black and white dots that approximate the patterns of the original image. The patterns are displayed on your computer screen by a program that reads the data file and converts the information into an image. Each pixel of the image is stored as a series of data bits that make up a code that defines various elements (location, color, and so on).

- *Contrast.* The difference between colors or shades of colors or gray. It can be the difference between two shades of red, or the difference between light gray and dark gray. To a point, greater contrast means a higher-quality image, with all elements easier to distinguish. Too much difference in contrast between colors or gray shades, however, can eliminate some colors or shades and remove a lot of the image's detail.

- *Resolution.* Resolution refers not only to an image's clarity and quality, but also to the contrast between colors or gray shades, and to the relative *density* (the number of pixels per row and column, which can be used to calculate the number of pixels per square screen inch) of the image. Generally, the greater the number of pixels, the better the resolution, which in turn makes an image "look" sharper or clearer.

Contrast between colors and gray shades also makes an image look sharper. "High-resolution" generally alludes to images that use more pixels. Resolution is limited by the display you use. A typical high-resolution VGA

(Variable Graphics Array) display can display 640 pixels across by 480 pixels vertically. A Super VGA (SVGA) display supports images of 800 by 600 pixels, or even 1,024 by 768 pixels. In contrast, a CGA (Color Graphics Array) display might have a resolution of 320 by 200, while an EGA (Enhanced Graphics Array) display usually offers resolutions of 640 by 350 and 640 by 200.

Graphics "Standards"

A major problem for those who write graphics programs (not to mention users of these programs) is that no single standard exists for computer graphics format. This is not unusual for anything to do with computers.

Therefore, you will find graphics available in many dissimilar file formats. Some formats are designed for specific programs—scanner software, for example, or a desktop publishing program. Other formats are attempts at providing a standard for graphics interchange among different programs and computers, but they may not be supported by all programs.

I leave the more technical ins and outs of file formats to other references, but you should know that the dimensions of graphic images are often expressed in three parameters: the number of pixels in each row, the number of pixels in each column, and the number of colors or gray scale shades. You find this information displayed about an image by a graphics program in the following fashion:

Width   Height   Colors (or Shades)

Therefore, a graphic 640 pixels wide by 480 pixels high, with 256 colors or shades, would be expressed as follows:

640 x 480 x 256

Moving to formats, you should know that the preceding information is not a defining factor for any graphics format. Any image can be described as width x height x colors, no matter what its graphics format.

Rather, the preceding helps define the relative resolution and color density of an image. These are important conventions—particularly the width and height elements, if you want your online graphic image to be as portable as possible.

Some Major Graphics Formats

The graphics world is a veritable Tower of Babel. Some file formats are supposedly "better" than others for particular applications or hardware setups (CGA, EGA, VGA, and so on). Variables in a file format's configuration include the number of pixels it uses to display an image on-screen or to print it, and the number of bits used to store each pixel); whether and how it compresses files on disk or during transmission; how the file is decompressed for viewing; whether color, monochrome, gray scale—or all three—are supported; and the number of possible color shades or, with gray scale images, gray shades.

Each of these elements, and others, vary from one graphic file format to another. So do the techniques by which they are saved in files. Rather than know the precise elements that define each graphical format, it is better that you be aware of which format a given image is saved in. A graphic image's filename extension usually tells you the format in use. Knowing this and just a little about a given format will enable you do a great deal with just about any image and format.

Here is a list of the major (and some minor) graphics file formats used by PCs:

- *BMP* (filename extension: .BMP). "BMP" represents *bit-mapped*, which is the sort of graphic stored in a BMP file. Of the several existing BMP subformats, Windows BMP is by far the most common, and the format supported by most graphics programs. A familiar application for BMP files is the wallpaper background displayed on the Windows desktop. BMP graphics can be monochrome or color (up to 256 colors in 16-bit mode, or several million in 32-bit mode), but usually cannot be compressed when written to a file. Microsoft Paint, a Windows 95 accessory, is primarily oriented toward the BMP format. This is why you will find BMP files used by so many Windows owners.

- *EPS* (filename extension: .EPS). Files in the PostScript laser printer format. EPS is an acronym for "encapsulated PostScript." Not all programs that can handle PostScript files can read EPS files. EPS files are often rather large because they carry information for printing.

- *GIF* (filename extension: .GIF). GIF is an acronym for "Graphic Interchange Format." This format was promoted by CompuServe beginning in the early 1980s as a means of providing online and downloadable graphics for a number of applications. Because CompuServe has always had such a large number of users, the file format caught on quickly. GIF graphics range from monochrome to 256-color or gray scale images. GIF images are stored in compressed files, and were for a long time the most popular form of downloadable and online graphics. Legal and technical issues paved the way for the *JPEG format* (a.k.a. JPG) to become as ubiquitous as GIF. Today, you will find almost all graphic files used on Web pages to be GIF or JPG.

- *JPEG* (filename extension: .JPG). JPEG is an acronym for Joint Photographics Experts Group (the name alludes to the group that devised this standard). JPEG images are ideal among other formats for use with the Web, for several reasons. The most important reason is that the file size of a JPEG image is often much smaller than a GIF or BMP counterpart. This means faster transfer of image files on a Web page, and thus faster loading for the page. JPEG has better on-disk compression than GIF, too, which means that JPEG files will take up less space on your hard drive.

- *MAC* (filename extension: .MAC). MAC files are, as you might expect, Macintosh files. Most are created with the MacPaint program. Graphics in the shareware and PD (public domain) software realm first appeared in large quantities in the MAC format, largely because of the aforementioned early popularity of the Macintosh among those with graphics applications. Clip art for use in desktop publishing, scanned photos, original screen art, and replacements for startup screens abound. MAC graphics aren't limited to use by Macintosh owners. Many PC programs will read MAC files. Because the first Macintosh computers could display only black-and-white graphics, MAC graphics are monochrome.

- *PCX* (filename extension: .PCX). PCX originated with Zsoft's PC Paintbrush program. It is almost a standard, thanks to the popularity of Paintbrush and its flexibility in handling color, monochrome, and gray scale images. (Versions 5 and later can handle up to 16 million colors.)

- *TIFF* (filename extension: .TIF). TIFF files come in many variations. TIFF is a "sort-of" accepted standard, in that it sometimes uses techniques based on recommended international standards set by the same organization that sets modem and Fax standards. TIFF is very flexible, but not as widely supported as GIF or PCX. One reason for this is the fact that, because it is so flexible in how it accommodates various images' content, it may save an image in any of a number of formats—some of which a particular graphics program may not know how to handle. TIFF supports monochrome, gray scale, and color graphics (up to 16.7 million colors or shades of gray), and saves graphics in compressed or uncompressed format. (This gives you the option of using less disk space for an image, or loading the image faster.) Corel Draw, among other programs, uses the TIFF format.

Your Browser and Graphic Formats

With respect to graphics, a Web browser's primary job is to display images. This includes images transmitted from the Web, and images stored in disk files. Browsers can also save graphics to disk. There are some limitations in how browsers perform these functions, as following sections of this chapter will explain.

Most browsers are set up to display two or maybe three graphics formats. All handle GIF and JPG files because these formats are the graphic image and file types you most often find online (be it at Web sites or in online service databases). A few browsers handle BMP files, although there aren't many BMP files on the Web.

You can view graphic files in the context of their Web pages, or you can view them separately by selecting "View" or a similar command from the menu that pops up when you left-click on a displayed image or its icon. Either way, the relative quality of browser graphics displays varies.

Netscape's display quality is slightly better than Explorer's. At present, no Web browser gives you the quality of a good graphics viewer. This is so because with browsers, there's a tradeoff between quality and speed. You get to see images slightly faster, but the quality isn't the best.

(You can see this lesser quality by loading an image file from your hard drive into your Web browser. Then load the same image into a graphics program, and compare the images.)

Almost all Web browsers can save graphics files. You can either view the graphic separately, and then use a File menu Save function or you can right-click on the graphic and select "Save" on the menu that pops up. The graphic in question is saved in its current format. That is, if you are saving a GIF file from a Web page, it is saved as a GIF image. Web browsers do not convert graphics formats, nor do they allow you to resize or otherwise edit a graphic. These jobs are reserved for more specialized graphics applications.

EXPANDING YOUR GRAPHICS CAPABILITIES WITH OFFLINE HELPERS

Because your Web browser is not a dedicated graphics tool, you will want an offline helper or helpers to enable you to view, convert, and manipulate graphics files that you find on the Web—or that you want to put on a Web site.

If you have little experience with computer graphics, you may think of Windows Paint as a good graphics program. Paint's features, however, are very limited compared to other graphics applications. Paint can read only .BMP and .PCX files, and it saves images only in various flavors of .BMP. This limitation makes Paint useless when dealing with Web images because virtually all of them will be .GIF or .JPG.

You can get a utility that converts images to a number of different graphic formats. Then you can use Windows Paint's editing features, as limited as they sometimes are. But, why bother, when there are viewer programs you can use to view a program in its native file format?

FIGURE 6.1

The Image View 95 front end

Then, too, there are full-blown graphics editing programs for Windows that can handle all your display needs, and any editing or conversion chores you may have. Some of these programs are commercial, some are shareware, and some are free. In the following sections, we'll take a look at programs in each category.

Graphics Viewers

The basic requirements for a graphics (or file) viewer are simple enough: be able to load, display, and print graphics in any of the popular formats.

Beyond the basics, you want a graphics viewer that provides a quality image on your screen. Several graphics viewers are available that, although they can display graphics in any of several popular formats, do not provide a good rendering of an image. (For example, although good for other purposes, Apple's QuickTime viewer is a program with display quality that isn't good enough for many applications.)

You also want a viewer program that can do some basic display (and perhaps filing) alterations—resizing, saving as wallpaper, and so on.

The main application for file viewers, though, is to look at images. If you find an intriguing image online, a file viewer lets you examine it in greater detail and in different ways than a Web browser. In addition to the better quality displays provided by file viewers, there's the bonus of being able to look at an image in a different way—larger, smaller, and maybe even rotated or mirrored.

Among the better display programs are Image View 95 (**http://www.ewl. com/ImageView95**) and VuePrint (**http://www.hamrick.com/**), also available in a commercial, boxed version as PhotoPrint).

Image View 95, shown in Figure 6.1, is flexible in terms of sizing and other display options. It's also easy to scroll through all the images that you may have stored in a given directory, in two directions, using one-touch buttons—and a quick-menu selection that saves the current image as Windows wallpaper.

VuePrint (see Figure 6.2) is a multitalented viewer. It not only handles images in .GIF, .JPG, .BMP, .PCX and other popular formats, but also plays movies and sound files.

VuePrint's user interface is particularly easy to use. Zooming in and out is accomplished with one-key commands, as is moving to the next image in the current directory, and more. The program also handles cropping and can set up a slideshow of multiple images, varying at time intervals that you can set. VuePrint's particularly good for those who are new to using graphics.

You may also want to check out the CompuPic! Viewer (**http://www.photodex. com/cpic.htm**). This one has an interesting automatic cropping function, and can save files to disk in different sizes, among other features.

Graphics Editors

If you need to convert graphics between formats, you can get a utility to do it, but you are better off getting a graphics-editing program. A good editing program gives you a display tool, file conversion, and all the editing tools you need, which means that you won't have to string together several programs, and then open and close work files repeatedly. One decent graphics-editing program does it all.

Among the image-editing applications that Internet users may need, most involve converting an image for placement on a Web page. These

FIGURE 6.2

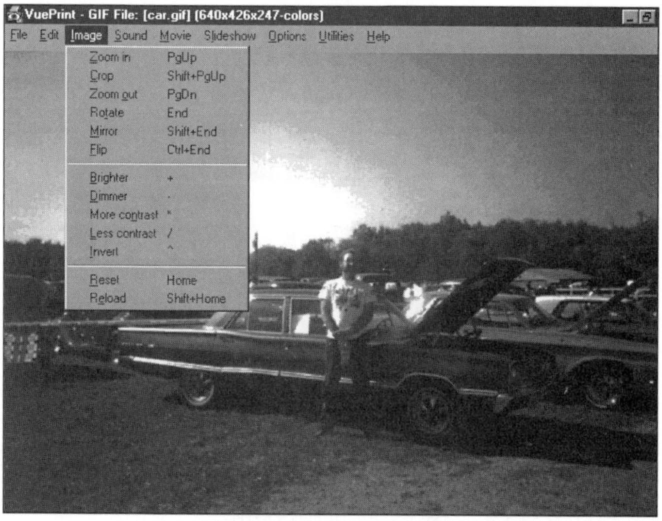

The VuePrint program

applications include cropping an image to emphasize a desired element, reducing the size of an image and its attendant file, changing colors, changing the file type, and altering other elements for aesthetic reasons.

If you purchased one of the graphics powerhouses like those sold by Aldus or Adobe, you have just about everything you need for any graphics work. Software in this category represents a substantial investment. Fortunately, commercial programs are not the only solution here. A shareware program may be sufficient for your needs, and at a quarter or less of the cost of a high-end commercial program.

FIGURE 6.3

The Paint Shop Pro 4 screen

Among the best of the shareware graphics-editing programs is Paint Shop Pro (**http://www.jasc.com/**). As far as capabilities are concerned, you can't do better in shareware graphics programs. Not far behind it is Graphic Workshop for Windows (**http://www.mindworkshop.com/alchemy/gww.html**).

Paint Shop Pro 4. Paint Shop Pro, currently in version 4 (see Figure 6.3), offers an amazing array of simple and complex image-editing tools for image creation, editing, viewing, and conversion.

There are so many features to Paint Shop Pro that there isn't room to list them all here. However, here's a quick rundown:

- Support for more than 30 image formats (including one-shot and batch conversion among the formats)

- Displays several images at once

- Provides sophisticated zoom operations (32 different in and out levels)

- Browse function for creating an on-screen catalog of a directory's files in the form of "thumbnail" images

- Flip and mirror functions, and image rotation

- Color alteration and enhancement, including "colorizing," color-to-gray scale, negative image, contrast, brightness, hue, shade and more

- Variable color palettes

- Resizing

- Histogram functions (A histogram is a graph of an image's color values. The range of colors is the horizontal axis, and a value for the relative distribution of color by pixels for each color along that range is plotted on the vertical axis. This makes identifying relative color densities in an image fairly simple.)

- Increase/decrease number of colors ("depth")

- Rapid browsing of directories and disks

- Scanner support

- Support for image processing plug-in and user-defined filters

- Flexible area selection, for copying, cutting, and coloring

- An array of tools for image creation and alteration, including paint brush, pen, pencil, marker, chalk, airbrush, and others

- Variable shape filling

- Cropping, and adding borders and frames

- Flexible capture capabilities

- User configuration for display of tools, and so on

- Numerous special effects, including deformation, embossed, shrink/stretch, blur, sharpen, and so on

That's the basic overview of Paint Shop Pro 4. There is a lot more, as I stated previously, but you can check it out for yourself when you download Paint Shop Pro 4. (Besides being available at the developer's Web site, you also can find it on AOL, CompuServe, and in other online service download areas.)

Graphic Workshop for Windows. The DOS version of this graphics program was one of my favorites. The Windows version also ranks high on my list.

As you see in Figure 6.4, Graphic Workshop has an up-front interface, with all its major commands on large buttons.

Graphic Workshop's capabilities are fairly similar to those of Paint Shop Pro, but with a different approach. Where

FIGURE 6.4

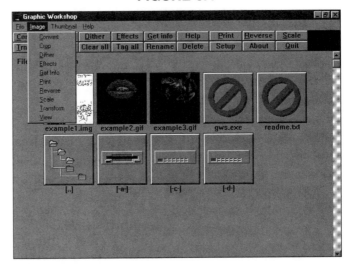

Graphic Workshop for Windows' visual-style user interface

Paint Shop Pro works by default from a File menu, Graphic Workshop lets you work from a "visual menu" of thumbnail images of all the graphics files in the current directory.

Overall, Graphic Workshop's a decent program, and whether or not you use it may depend on your preferences in user interfaces.

Now that you're familiar with the basics of computer graphics and some of the tools used in creating and modifying them, you may be inspired to try your hand at developing graphics for a Web site. That topic, and more, is covered in Chapter Nine. But first, we'll take a closer look at computer and Internet data formats in Chapter Seven.

PRODUCTS MENTIONED

▪ Graphics Viewers

CompuPic! Viewer
http://www.photodex.com/cpic.htm

Image View 95
http://www.ewl.com/ImageView95

VuePrint/PhotoView Plus
http://www.hamrick.com/

Apple QuickTime Image Viewer
http://quicktime.apple.com/

■ Graphics Editors

Adobe PageMaker
http://www.adobe.com/prodindex/pagemaker/main.html

Graphic Workshop for Windows
http://www.mindworkshop.com/alchemy/gww.html

Paint Shop Pro 4
http://www.jasc.com/

■ Books

Finding Images Online
http://www.onlineinc.com/pempress/images/

Computer/Internet Data Formats and Conversion

I n this chapter, you'll learn more about MIME data, binary data, sending binary files attached to E-mail, and retrieving binary files from newsgroups. This may seem confusing in some ways, but I believe I can clear up some of the confusion with a little background and some basic explanations as to exactly how computer data and files are structured, stored, and handled by your computer and the Internet.

If, however, you feel you don't need to understand the technical data in the first section, "COMPUTER DATA," feel free to jump ahead to "DATA & DATA TRANSFER ON THE INTERNET."

In Chapter One, you learned a little about data types—specifically, ASCII and binary data. This chapter expands on this knowledge, by explaining why programs, images, and other binary data files must be transmitted in an *encoded* form.

COMPUTER DATA

Computer *data* is machine-readable information of any kind. This information may consist of business or personal messages, text files (articles, contracts, jokes, politically incorrect tirades, documentation, reports, and so on), "lines" of a real-time conference, executable programs, graphic images, spreadsheet data files, database files, word processor and other program data files, and so on.

Inside your computer, the data is handled *representationally*, as *binary information* (more on this in the following section). Data may be entered in "real time" from a keyboard, retrieved from a storage device (a disk), generated by a program, or received via an interface from an external source. More commonly, data is typed, read from a disk file, output from a program, or received from a peripheral, such as a scanner or a modem.

The basic elements of data are *characters*—letters, numerals, symbols, and spaces.

Computers use numbers to represent characters—that is, a number between 0 and 128 represents a given character. The numbering system that computers use is known as the *binary* system.

Binary Information and Binary Numbers. To say that data is binary information (or, that it is in *binary data format*) means that each character a computer deals with is handled as a specific *binary number*. The numbers are transmitted internally and externally as varying electrical states, or *signals* of "off" (0) or "on" (1). Note that only 0s and 1s are used (as opposed to the numerals 0 through 9, which are used by the decimal system).

A *binary number* is a string of binary digits, such as "0001010" or "0100110." The values of the numerals, or *digits*, (0 and 1) are not used to determine the decimal value of a binary number: Rather, the values of the places marked by a 1 are summed. Each place has a set value. The first place on the *right* in a binary number has a value of 1, the second place a value of 2, the third place 4, the fourth place 8, fifth place 16, and so on. The value doubles for each successive place, moving from right to left.

Table 7.1 shows the decimal and binary numerals for 0 through 128, along with 256 and 512. Also, at the end of the table, you can see the place values for each of nine binary digits, and a sample binary value for the decimal 3.

TABLE 7.1
Binary Numbering System

Decimal	Binary	Decimal	Binary
0	00000	33	100001
1	00001	34	100010
2	00010	35	100011
3	00011	36	100100
4	00100	37	100101
5	00101	38	100110
6	00110	39	100111
7	00111	40	101000
8	01000	41	101001
9	01001	42	101010
10	01010	43	101011
11	01011	44	101100
12	01100	45	101101
13	01101	46	101110
14	01110	47	101111
15	01111	48	110000
16	10000	49	110001
17	10001	50	110010
18	10010	51	110011
19	10011	52	110100
20	10100	53	110101
21	10101	54	110110

Decimal	Binary	Decimal	Binary
22	10110	55	110111
23	10111	56	111000
24	11000	57	111001
25	11001	58	111010
26	11010	59	111011
27	11011	60	111100
28	11100	61	111101
29	11101	62	111110
30	11110	63	111111
31	11111	64	1000000
32	100000	...	
		128	10000000
		...	
		256	100000000
		...	
		512	1000000000
		(etc.)	

Place values:	256	128	64	32	16	8	4	2	1
Sample binary digit:	0	0	0	0	0	0	0	1	1
Decimal value:								2	+ 1 = 3

Again, the value of a binary number is determined by adding the values of the places that contain a 1. If a 0 exists in a place, this place's value is not counted. If you think this through, you can easily see that the binary number "11" is the same as the decimal number "3" (add the values of the places: 2 + 1 = 3). Similarly, the binary number 1010 is the same as the decimal number 10 (8 + 2 = 10). Nothing to it, right? (Keep this up and you'll be a binary math wizard in no time.)

There is a practical reason why computers use binary numbers to represent data. With only two states (0 or 1) to record, store, or transmit, data can be sent at extreme speeds. Also, errors are less likely; a transmitted value for a *bit* is either 0 or 1.

As for *how* computers know what is what in these strings of zeroes and ones they're constantly reading, moving, or storing, read on.

Bits and Bytes

Another word for the zeroes and ones that comprise a binary number is *bits*, which is verbal shorthand for *BInary digiT*, the smallest unit of computer data. A binary number—composed of several bits—that represents a computer character (sometimes called a data "word") is known as a *byte*. The letters, numbers, and symbols that compose computer data are represented by numbers known as bytes, which are composed of groups of bits.

The ASCII Table

If you've hung on this far, you are probably wondering how a computer knows which bytes represent which characters. You may also wonder why you need to know this. The truth is, you can use your computer and the Internet without understanding these technical details. But it is so much easier to troubleshoot, and deal with problems without panic, if you have a feel for what's going on in the background.

Besides, you may find this information interesting for its own sake.

As noted previously, a given binary number represents a given character. Something called the *ASCII character set* serves as a "Rosetta Stone" for translating binary numbers into characters.

You can find the full ASCII character set, which lists each character's binary value, the "English" character and/or the computer key the ASCII character represents, and the communications control character or function that the ASCII character generates, in Appendix D at the end of this book.

If you look at Appendix D, you will see that the first 32 numbers (0 through 31) represent control characters, many of which are used in transmitting data between computers and peripherals.

DATA & DATA TRANSFER ON THE INTERNET

Characters in the ASCII character set are referred to as *7-bit ASCII characters* because each character is composed of 7 bits. (That is, a group of 7 zeroes and ones.)

All modern computers use 7-bit ASCII characters, which is why they can communicate with one another over the Internet. Using the mutually agreed-upon code of the ASCII character set, they share a common language.

The Internet was designed to transmit 7-bit ASCII data, largely because this was the only standard in existence at the time the Internet was developing. Also, conventional modems and other computer communications hardware demanded 7-bit characters.

Decades later, this system continues to serve data communications needs, plus a number of control characters computers use to communicate with one another during the course of data transfer, but only if the data transmitted is composed of 7-bit characters. This means you can easily transmit textual data over the Internet and in E-mail because text messages and other documents are composed exclusively of the first 128 characters in the ASCII table; the letters, numerals, and symbols that your keyboard can produce on screen.

Unfortunately, much of modern computer data is also composed of *8-bit characters*.

8-Bit ("Binary") Data

As you may be aware, programs, graphic images, and most types of data files are not composed solely of text and control characters. (These data files include the native file formats used by most word processors, database programs, spreadsheets, and many other applications.)

These data files are in what is often referred to as *8-bit* or *binary data* format. (Again, we fall prey to confusing computer terminology; although *all* computer data is ostensibly binary in format, only data with 8-bit characters is "binary data.")

Binary data contains characters that come from the additional 128 characters (128 through 256) in the *extended ASCII character set*. The extended character set was devised for PCs to provide special graphics and control characters, among other characters. Other computers, such as the Macintosh, have their own extended character sets for the same reason.

These extended characters are represented by bytes that are 8 bits long. (If you write out the numbers 128 through 256 in binary form, you see why they are 8 bits in length. To write any number from 128 through 256 requires 8 binary digits.)

Binary Transmission of 8-Bit Data Over the Internet

Because computers on the Internet communicate using only 7-bit characters, it's easy to see that attempting to transmit 8-bit characters can foul things up.

Eight-bit characters being transmitted can be ignored, or they may be truncated and converted to 7-bit characters. Either way, data is corrupted. Also, data files of the type discussed here may contain certain 7-bit control characters that are intended to represent something else. The receiving system perceives these characters as commands, which totally garbles a transmission.

You can get around this incompatibility in two ways. First, *8-bit* or *binary transmission* protocols can be used to send 8-bit data in a symbolic form that can be transmitted over the Internet.

A *protocol* is another kind of mutually agreed-upon set of rules; in this instance, sending and receiving computers use a system that does not truncate or otherwise corrupt 8-bit data characters, which allows control characters that are a part of a data file to pass through just like any other character.

These protocols are limited to direct, real-time communication—typically, as a means of uploading or downloading a binary file, whether it's a file transmitted directly from a Web page (graphic or other binary file), or via Internet FTP (just about any kind of file).

This kind of file transmission is accomplished easily enough when computers communicate in real time because they can check for errors, adjust how data is sent, and/or re-send corrupted blocks of data. (This is why these kinds of protocols are often referred to as *error-checking protocols.*)

Obviously, this error-checking can be time-consuming. So, such intensive communications is impractical for common Internet applications, such as newsgroup and E-mail traffic—the sheer volume of these kinds of communication makes it impossible. Fortunately, these forms of communication involve only 7-bit ASCII data, and require no error checking and other accommodations in the way 8-bit binary data does.

As the Internet grew, however, the demand increased for transmitting binary 8-bit data via E-mail and newsgroups. Several means for encoding binary files for transmission as 7-bit ASCII data were developed for non-real-time communications, including newsgroups and E-mail. Today, one standard, MIME, prevails. But other techniques are still used to encode 8-bit files as 7-bit files.

MIME and Other Data Encoding Techniques

MIME, or *Multi-purpose Internet Mail Extensions*, is the standard for encoding binary data files. Your browser uses the MIME standard to determine what kinds of files it is receiving. (This is why it's a good idea to know a little bit about what MIME and other types of encoding. When you go to your Web browser's File Types setting, to tell it how to handle incoming data, you need to know what you're dealing with.)

There are several MIME file types, including audio, image, video, text, and application (executable programs).

Each has additional *subtypes* for specific data types or applications. There are, for example, subtypes for .GIF and .JPG images under the "image" type. There are also subtypes for handling data types for most major PC programs. (Look at the File Type listings in your browser's setup window; you will see many familiar programs listed under "MIME/Data Type.")

The MIME types and subtypes in part specify how a binary file is encoded. Your browser recognizes file types by the encoding technique used, and/or the filename extension of an incoming file. You also can define new data types, specifying the filename extension to identify a file type, and the application program needed to use it.

Learning Which MIME Type Is Which
It pays to spend a little time with your browser's MIME/File types listing, seeing what kinds of programs are dedicated to what kinds of files.

Open the list on your browser. (Netscape users: Select "<u>G</u>eneral Preferences..." on the <u>O</u>ptions menu, and press the "Helpers" tab. Explorer users: Select "<u>O</u>ptions..." on the <u>V</u>iew menu, then press the "Programs" tab, followed by the "<u>F</u>ile types..." button.) You will see a list of file types, along with a description for each type, and their extensions and the program used with them.

Some E-mail programs also let you do this. You can go so far as to embed lines in a message that start a given program. For example, you can put an URL in an E-mail message so that, when the recipient clicks it, the recipient's browser is launched. (This kind of feature is limited to a few top E-mail programs, such as Eudora, Pegasus, and BeyondMail.)

Again, MIME is the prevailing standard for any 8-bit file transfer, but other encoding techniques are used in sending E-mail and posting newsgroup messages. These techniques include *UUENCODE*, *Base 64*, and *BinHex*.

No matter which encoding process you use, 8-bit data characters are replaced by token 7-bit characters. Then they are transmitted as 7-bit messages. Special software handles the encoding and decoding.

If you send and receive binary files in or with Internet text messages, you need to know a bit about these MIME types. As you will learn, you do not necessarily need to know everything about encoding and decoding because your E-mail program may handle the encoding for you. But it helps to understand what happens in the background.

As noted, binary data is encoded by using token 7-bit characters to represent the actual 8-bit characters. A typical encoded file looks something like the data shown in Figure 7.1.

FIGURE 7.1

```
--PART.BOUNDARY.0.571.emout17.mail.aol.com.849482978
Content-ID: <0_571_849482978@emout17.mail.aol.com.75379>
Content-type: text/plain

This is a test with an attached file.  The headers above are for this
text message.  The headers below are for the Base 64-encoded file that
follows

--PART.BOUNDARY.0.571.emout17.mail.aol.com.849482978
Content-ID: <0_571_849482978@emout17.mail.aol.com.75380>
Content-type: application/octet-stream;
         name="SCHEDULE.DOC"
Content-Transfer-Encoding: base64
```

0M8R4KGxGuEAAAAAAAAAAAAAAAAAAAPgADAP7/CQAGAAAAAAAAAAAAABAAAAAQAAAAAA
AAAAEAAAAgAAAAEAAAD+////AAAAAAAAAD/////////////////////////////////
///
AAAAAAAAAAAAAAAAAWAAEBAQAAAAIAAAD/////AAAAAAAAAAAAAAAAAAAAAACAobvR
zNW7AYChu9HH1bsBAAAAAAAAAAAAAAAAAQAAP7///8DAAAABAAAAUAAAAGAAAABwAAAAgA
AAAJAAAACgAAAsAAAAMAAAADQAAAA4AAAAPAAAAEAAAABEAAAASAAAAEwAAABQAAAAVAAAA
FgAAABcAAAAYAAAAGQAAABoAAAAbAAAAABAAAAAeAAAAAAAAAAAsAAAAIgAACMA
AAAkAAAAJQAAACYAAAAnAAAAnAAAACkAAAAAckAAAAqAAAAKwAAAAP7///8tAAAALgAAAA
MQAAADIAAAAzAAAANAAAADUAAAA2AAAANwAAADgAAAA5AAAAOgAAAAPQAAAD4A
AAA/AAAAQAAAAEEAAABCAAAAQwAAAQwAAAEQAAABFAAAAARGAAAABIAAAASQAAAEoAAABLAAAA
zNW7AYChu9HH1bsBAAAAAAAAAAAAAAAAAQAAP7///8DAAAABAAAAUAAAAGAAAABwAAAAgA
AAAJAAAACgAAAsAAAAMAAAADQAAAA4AAAAPAAAAEAAAABEAAAASAAAAEwAAABQAAAAVAAAA

A portion of a Base 64-encoded message

FIGURE 7.2


```
This is a test, E-mailing a UUENCODED 8-bit file as a 7-bit
text file.

_=_
_=_ Part 001 of 001 of file sh.zip
_=_

begin 666 sh.zip
M4$L#!!0````(`%*V<B'E%Z)7J`<````>```,````4V-H961U;&4N9&]C[5E?
M;!M)&9^UDS;;9M/TX,I1.&X:VER/:U+;B9TV<#2.[32^Q+%E.XJ0(F!CC^/E
MUKN^W773/%T10N(A)QT22'<2$A3IT)W0(7'\>3F$^HPJ*#HJ<>@>BL0C2%"5
M!^!H^,WNVEZOT\0Y0'!1?^G/W\SL]^W\^V;FF^VM7QV_<_V')W]/?/@L"9+[
MVR(YY"D37-H8)B3@YN]0;V\WB[<?X@.%?X(#[ASV0?:#?,X/@Z);?@3R*#@(
M2F[90QP,Y(F./XM0DB(:I$$VR7YP`A[3?%>0%X@!N_R&\WC.J_O%F^+;-V^_
M)=AZ'W+**!))`_352)UFR1KY$]HM'2$#P]F=O"P>:*U=0NT'*)`E9(@VTA-GC
MT"M.NO7SM=-K_7R$7CWFI)U>,]1MD9P]%^JNMGZ<(((+`]V#^S@?5?^WZ6[_F
MX]Z4WF?-_9O/B7_]\WV![P'^]3\$\N;C""#'"9\#9SH_##Y*>)L(^0CX&/A1
MPL>(D(^!'P<?!S\!/@%2\!PX`GX2/`V>`4?!)\&SX%/@I\"GB=/.,<AQ\#P8
M`L-@!)P`)\$H&`.GP`0@17`:_#3X&?`9PL\V0BZ!,V`<G`438!),$<=I+X/S
M8!I\%EP@!W/?$]"KX!'7=WQKE\]71BD9NJE7++JB&V4:&P_1I%YJU)AFV7Z1
M*?!R%-G>P-/CS>?C,7+0XI0/$P]N=44;[[[*R,0-D;L>5H$'<,@7#[?7B1<O
M]G67=0'.NN616X-.\6Z2^^]/W7PODO?_ABN;Y7\<<GSR%V[^_<J@Y*SI?LG)
M>^4IR%'(WT#^W96_''+6U>,8KR+D\\><]<#;LQ.V?/7QU=^/W4#H:HD?_N?-
M&IIY_\CV^IX'2?][_/F@.S)^?&?0V<%>&W1VK+T\P/\^GK_H*?_O`.NK*C.5
MQL?IK*P]9TKA\`3-,%76&*.+^)6R5RM85>=H=I[2R6@H&I/.1L,33]%H9&(L
M%@M-2*FQFJRHTY1.12="H?'(5"0\4])K]8;)C"ML'$I;+^0I(RL-<R2H=0M
M6BA56;FA,DE:86LT9VZ6JKIYCA8L67V.&4C)6IGF#-Y\"_EI:5[?H):.(MVB
```


A UUENCODED MIME file

This file originally was Microsoft WORD for Windows text. I translated it to Base 64 encoding, using a helper program called Wincode. I then copied the resulting text file into an AOL E-mail message and sent it. (Figure 7.1 shows about one-tenth of the entire file.)

As you see, all the characters used are 7-bit ASCII. Based on the MIME file type and subtype ("application/octet-stream" in a message header) and the encoding type (also named in a message header), an unencoding program knows how to rebuild this group of 7-bit characters into an 8-bit binary file that exactly matches the original data file.

A UUENCODED binary file looks slightly different, with less header information, as shown in Figure 7.2.

I mentioned that I copied the file into an AOL E-mail message; you can as easily copy a file like this one into *any* E-mail system. And, you can enter a plain-English message to the recipient before the beginning of the encoded file without corrupting the data the encoded file contains.

Also, with some services such as AOL and certain dedicated Internet E-mail programs (such as BeyondMail, Eudora, or Pegasus), you can specify that the file be *attached* to an E-mail message. Figure 7.3 shows how this is done with Pegasus. Note that you can specify both the type of data (in this case, the Microsoft WORD document) and the type of encoding to use.

How an attached file comes through on the other end depends on whether you use an E-mail program that can handle encoding and decoding on its own, or a text-only E-mail program or system. I sent the example file shown in Figure 7.1 as an attached file from AOL to an ID on CompuServe. It came through as illustrated, with a brief text message that I typed preceding the encoded portion.

When I sent the UUENCODED message in Figure 7.2 to AOL and to a dedicated ISP, using Eudora, I received each as a separate file—the encoded portion of each message came through separate from the text message preceding it.

AOL's E-mail system recognizes MIME data in a message. Plus, it decodes the UUENCODED data and places it in a file that is downloaded separately from the text message that precedes it. The same features are true with a dedicated E-mail program such as Eudora.

As for how I handled the message that arrived in CompuServe mail (which does *not* separate MIME data), it was simple enough. I copied the entire message

FIGURE 7.3

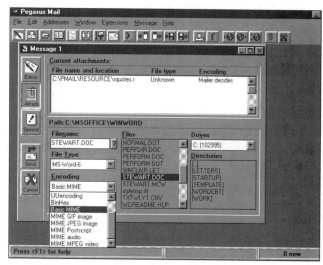

Preparing to send a binary document as an attached file with Pegasus, an E-mail program

to an open Notepad, and then saved it as a text file. Then I opened the file with an *unencoding program*, and the unencoding program saved it as its original file type—MS WORD—with the proper extension for that file type. Now, I can access the file with WORD just as I can access any other WORD file. The unencoding program sorted the encoded data within the message, and acted only on the encoded data.

Sending Files Larger Than the Limit

On some systems, there is a limit to the size of file you can send as a part of or attached to an E-mail message. (For example, CompuServe has a limit of 50,000 characters.) When using a system with a limit, one way around the problem is to use PKZIP or WinZip to compress the file.

If this doesn't do the trick, and you are dealing with a text or data file that can be sent in two segments, then easily reassembled at the other end, send the file in two parts.

UNENCODING/ENCODING PROGRAMS

Unless you are using an E-mail program or an online service that handles all encoding and unencoding of MIME data, you need a program to perform these tasks on your files.

The best Windows programs for handling MIME encoding and decoding are WinZip and Wincode. WinZip (discussed in Chapter Five, "Archiving Programs,") is the better of the two for the way I work. Its capabilities as a MIME utility are not really played up, but it is an extremely easy-to-use program, and you have the added bonus of WinZip's primary functions as an archive manager.

FIGURE 7.4

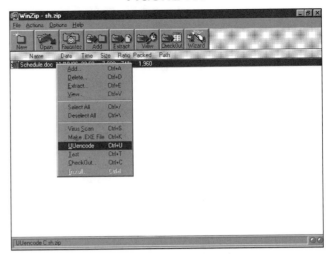

WinZip, shown as it encodes and unencodes MIME data

Wincode is a *dedicated program* (a program written for a single, defined purpose) that provides some worthwhile special features. It is, however, a little more difficult to use than WinZip. The following sections give you a quick rundown on each program so that you can decide which one will best serve your needs.

You may also find a program called Information Transfer Professional (XFERPRO) of interest. XFERPRO provides a fairly fast and easy tool for creating encoded files in Windows for sending text, programs, graphics, and other files via Internet E-mail. XFERPRO, a shareware product of Sabasoft, Inc., can be downloaded at Sabasoft's Web site (**http://www.sabasoft.com/**), or at the ZD Net Software Library (**http://www.zdnet.com/**).

Using WinZip with MIME Files

As described in Chapter Five, WinZip is the premier archive management tool. Because it already handles specialized encoding and decoding of ZIP and other kinds of archives, it is no surprise that WinZip also takes care of MIME format data.

In fact, I used WinZip to manually encode and unencode the messages in Figures 7.1 and 7.2. "Manually" is almost inappropriate because WinZip automates almost the entire process. I only tell it which files to work on, as shown in Figure 7.4.

To decode an encoded file, load the file, mark it, and tell WinZip to unencode it. WinZip goes to work, unencoding the file and displaying a list of the contents. Double-click the name of the file to unencode, and WinZip loads it into the application that can handle it. From here, you can edit and save the file as you desire.

Note that, although WinZip will open an encoded file under any name and any extension, WinZip doesn't recognize an encoded file unless you saved it with an extension commonly used with encoded files. These extensions are: .UU, .UUE, .XXE, .BNX, .B64, OR .HQX. Without one of those extensions, you will

FIGURE 7.5

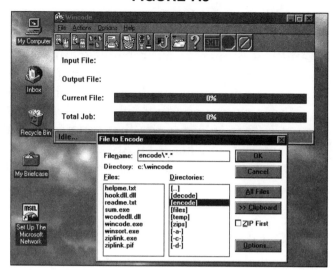

The Wincode front end

have to open the file manually. (Either type in the file's complete name, or tell WinZip to display all files in the directory—i.e., *.*.)

WinZip makes it similarly easy to encode a binary file. Simply create a new archive by using WinZip menu commands, place the desired file in it, then tell WinZip to encode the file. WinZip creates a text file similar to those shown in Figures 7.1 and 7.2. You can then copy this into a message and send it, as described previously.

Using Wincode

If you encode and decode a lot of MIME files, you may want to check out Wincode. Wincode offers several features to organize and simplify handling files.

Shown in Figure 7.5, Wincode has a business-like interface. All the major commands are available on buttons (with graphical symbols for labels), as well as on menus. In this respect, Wincode's user interface is more accessible than WinZip's.

Wincode organizes incoming and outgoing files into "Encoded" and "Decoded" subdirectories, and allows you to sort files in these work directories based on various criteria. Wincode also has a feature that *concatenates* (combines multiple files into one file). This feature is important where large binary files are transmitted in more than one part. (Multiple postings for one binary file is common in some of the "alt.binaries" Usenet newsgroups.)

Wincode is rather particular about filenames. You have to be careful, for example, about the names you give to files to be encoded because Wincode recognizes file types in part by their filename extensions. If you keep this in mind, Wincode is easy to use.

Handling Binary Files in Newsgroups

The examples I have given so far are of MIME files and E-mail. Binary files in Usenet newsgroups are handled much in the same way.

Most newsgroups carry only text, but some also provide binary files for transfer. These files require that you use special software, which "translates" files that contain token 7-bit ASCII characters into their original binary form. This tokenizing is necessary, of course, because 8-bit files cannot be carried in Usenet's text-only message format.

MIME-encoded newsgroup files are similar to E-mail files. As you see in Figure 7.6, they are not unlike encoded E-mail messages.

Decoding a MIME message from a newsgroup is a simple procedure: download it, and open the message with a program that can handle unencoding. Then save the unencoded file under an appropriate name. After doing so, you can use the file with the appropriate application.

DATA SECURITY AND DATA ENCRYPTION

There is great concern among Internet users about the vulnerability of transmitted data. As you know, data is transmitted over the Internet by being relayed through one and sometimes two or more computers. Because of this, there is the possibility of data in transit being viewed at any of the computers along the way. How likely this is to happen is difficult to say, but the possibility does exist.

You can deal with this potential vulnerability in several ways. The first and simplest method is to avoid sending sensitive data over the Internet—including credit card numbers. This

FIGURE 7.6

```
--------------50BC5E3027E5
Content-Type: image/gif
Content-Transfer-Encoding: base64
Content-Disposition: inline;
filename="KILB431.GIF"

R0lGODdhqwEbAfcAAAAAAIAAAACAAICAAAAAgIAAgACAg
ICAgMDAwP8AAAD/AP//AAAA//8A/wD//wAAEe7u7t3d3c
zMzLu7u6qqqpmZmYiIiHd3d2ZmZlVVVURERDMzMyIiIhE
REf//zP//mf//Zv//M///AP/M///MzP/Mmf/MZv/MM//M
AP+Z//+ZzP+Zmf+ZZv+ZM/+ZAP9m///9mzP9mmf9mZv9mM
/9mAP8z//8zzP8zzv8zM/8zAP8A//8AzP8Amf8AZv
8AM8z//8z/mz/mcz/Zsz/M8z/AMzM/8zMmczMZszMM8z
MAMyZ//8yZzMyZmcyZZsyZM8yZAMxm/8xmMxmmcxmZsxm
M8xmAMwz/8wzzMwzmcwZZswzM8wzAMwA/8wAZMwAmcwAZ
swAM5n//5n/zJn/mZn/Zpn/M5n/AJnM/5nMZnMZp
nMM5nMAJmZ/5mZzJmZZpmZM5mZAJlm/5lmzJlmmZlmZpl
mM5lmAJkz/5kzzJkzmZkzZpkzM5kzAJkA/5kAzJkAmZkA
ZpkAM2b//2b/zGb/mWb/Zmb/M2b/AGbM/2bMZbMMmWbMZ
mbMM2bMAGaZ/2aZzGaZmWaZZmaZM2aZAGZm/2ZmzGZmmW
ZmM2ZmAGYz/2YzzGYzmWYzZmYzM2YzAGYA/2YAzGYAmWY
AZmYAM2P//zP/zDP/mTP/ZjP/MzP/ADPM/zPMZPMmTPM
ZjPMZPMADOZ/zOZzDOZmTOZZjOZMzOZADNm/zNmzDNmm
TNmZjNmMzNmADMz/zMzzDMzmTMzZjMzMzMzADMA/zMADMAmT
```

A MIME-encoded message in a Usenet newsgroup

caution makes sense, even though the reported incidence of E-mail "spying" is low.

Other approaches you can take are to use browser and Internet data-security features and, with E-mail and other sensitive document transmissions, *data encryption*. These subjects are covered in the following sections.

Browser and Internet Data Security Features

As with other aspects of the Internet, security standards cover data encryption, and also keep data secure during transmission. Taking advantage of these features requires that the Web browser you use conforms to specific security standards. Both Netscape and Microsoft Internet Explorer conform to the prevailing security standards—Secure Socket Layer (SSL) and Private Communication (PCT).

Some of the most important security features are internal to Web browsers. These features include security certificates to authenticate your identity to a Web site, the warnings Netscape and Explorer offer when you start to send data to an unsecured Web site, and more. It's a good idea to leave these features active; even if they don't favorably affect your online activities now, there's a good chance they will in the future.

Web sites can also provide security, if your browser supports the security protocols these sites use. Web site security features include security certificates that guarantee that they are what they represent themselves to be, and that they are *secure sites*.

A secure site protects the routes used by data moving to it, so that credit card numbers or other sensitive data cannot be viewed *en route*. You still have to trust the person running the site, of course—it's analogous to giving your credit card number via voice phone over a line that is guaranteed not to be bugged. But secure sites provide some assurance that no one but you and the person to whom you are giving the sensitive information has your credit card information.

Data Encryption

Data encryption is similar to data encoding, although the intent is different. Rather than encode data to enable it to be transmitted, you encode data so it is not recognizable. The idea, of course, is to prevent the data from being understood and used by those who don't have the means of decoding it (described in the following section, "Data Decryption")—only those to whom you provide this means to decode the message can read it.

In practice, encryption is a process of *substitution*. An alternative value (a.k.a. *token*) is substituted for designated elements of a message or other data. This is typically done on the character level. For example, the letter "r" might be replaced by "m," and other characters similarly substituted for every character in the message.

This substitution is similar to what happens when a binary file is encrypted by using UUENCODE or any other protocol; one group of characters substituted for another group characters. The main difference here is that the goal is to make the data difficult to unscramble, except for those who have a means of *decrypting* it.

In theory, encrypted data cannot be read without a guide or reference to all the substitutions that have been made. However, a simple, non-varying pattern of character substitution is fairly easy to decode (for example, if "m" was always substituted for "r" and so on).

So, most encryption schemes vary the pattern of substitution enough so there is no recognizable pattern that can be used to decode the message.

Assuming encryption schemes or pattern(s) are too complex to be worked out, or "cracked," the only way you can read an encrypted message is with a *decryption program*, a guide to the encryption patterns used (often called a *key*), or the original encryption program.

Data Decryption

Data decryption is a process of reproducing data from an encoded message based on a known code or *cipher*. The code key to decrypting encrypted data is known, appropriately enough, as the *key*.

Simply described, a key is a reference or guide that can be used to decrypt encrypted data. In effect, a key tells the user (or with computer data, a decrypting program) which symbols represent which characters, and where and how. That is, the substitutions made by the encryption program.

Keys and Encryption Software

Encryption software usually performs both decryption and encryption functions. The receiver of encoded data usually must have both the decryption key and the software.

There are several approaches to encrypting and decrypting data. Some apply to "one-way" data transmission, such as when you send information from a Web site using a form on a Web page. Others apply strictly to E-mail.

One-Way Data Encryption. With one-way Internet data encryption, a program at the Web site encrypts data before it is transmitted. The recipient is the only person who has the key to deciphering the data. Therefore, the recipient is in control of both encryption and decryption.

E-mail Message Encryption. Encryption of E-mail is more "conventional" in that it requires that the sender encrypt a message, and that the receiver be able to decrypt it.

You do not, of course, want to send a decryption key with the encrypted message, and you probably don't want to send it separately, if there's a chance that it might be intercepted and used later to decrypt intercepted messages.

Fortunately, there is a solution. A system known as *public keys* and *private keys* was developed in the 1970s to allow encrypted messages to be sent without the sender needing to provide the recipient with a code key.

Therefore, unlike older computer and non-computer encryption schemes, the sender doesn't have the decryption key with the public/private key system.

The system uses a program (the public key) that encrypts data in a way that can be decrypted only by its counterpart, the private key. The public key can be used by anyone, but only the holder of the private key (the message recipient) can decrypt a message created with the public key.

This method works particularly well for someone who needs to receive encrypted E-mail messages from many people. Overall it works well in any situation where encryption is needed.

In practice, the sender needs only the recipient's public key. This setup enables the sender to use the program to encrypt a message in the required format. After it is encrypted, no one but the recipient can decode it because only the recipient has the private key.

Using encrypted E-mail files is analogous to sending a message in an envelope, as opposed to on a postcard. If this sounds like a good idea—something that anyone might use—read on.

Pretty Good Privacy. The header may seem facetious, but it is the name of the best public/private key encryption program going. Pretty Good Privacy is also the most-widely used program of its type.

Pretty Good Privacy, or PGP for short, is the work of Phillip Zimmerman, and is distributed as freeware.

In addition to creating public keys, PGP, of course, unencrypts messages from those who have a public key—provided the creator of the public key is the recipient. PGP also provides message authentication with *digital signatures*, also created by the PGP program.

A *digital signature* is a means of verifying the authenticity of an E-mail message. The message is first "hashed," which means each character is assigned a numeric value. Then a complex mathematical algorithm generates a string of numeric values that is almost impossible to duplicate or crack. The values are appended to the message, as the "digital signature," and stored by the system that generated them for later comparison if necessary.

(The U.S. Postal Service is using such a system as a means of providing "electronic postmarks" for E-mail with its new Postal Electronic Commerce Services, or Postal ECS.)

Public keys and signature files created with PGP are text files, and resemble the following block of characters:

```
ññ-BEGIN PGP PUBLIC KEY BLOCKññ-
Version: 2.6.2

foXwAAAQMjpgsAAAEDAMsiJK9Ah6VAXVfobv34chAeLeWxl
230LhBEskOAcO1nwbWugMgSs39/Oh7xLoU1G1ZvB7BRH8ZhvEBtcG2Ht5wPgw4m8FE7QcU
3l6eWd5IFNhbGVzIDxzYcrnOhBEskBzehBEsk29V f3QJfoXou39Y29VfobvtPg==
=wPgw
ññ-END PGP PUBLIC KEY BLOCKññ-
```

With PGP, you can create your own public key and distribute it to friends, associates, and others. One way to distribute your public key is to include it after your "signature" at the end of each message. (You can do this most efficiently by adding it to your "sig file," which is a user-definable block of text that many E-mail programs automatically place at the ends of outgoing messages.)

There also are public distribution servers for PGP public keys. Here, you can leave your public key for others, and obtain others' public keys. You can find one of these servers at this URL: **http://rs.internic.net/support/wwwpks/**.

To download PGP, go to this URL: **http://www.download.com/**.

PGP for PCs is a DOS application that works on files externally from the DOS command line. You type commands while running the program in DOS, directing it to act on a file you want to encrypt or decrypt.

If you prefer an easier interface than PGP for PCs, several DOS and Windows front ends are available for PGP. A list of these programs, with links, can be found at: **http://www.seattle-webworks.com/pgp/pgplinks.html**.

(This page also contains links to front ends for using PGP with Eudora, Pegasus, and other E-mail programs.)

TIP

If *all* of your correspondents use PGP, you can use it to protect against unwanted junk E-mail. If everyone who sends E-mail to you uses PGP to encrypt messages, you can simply reject any E-mail that comes through unscrambled.

For more information about data security, security standards, and what various companies are doing about security on the Internet, visit RSA Data Security's Web site, at: **http://www.rsa.com/**. This organization is responsible for designing and implementing most of the security standards in use on the Internet. (RSA Data Security also makes available a personal online/offline data security product called SecurPC.)

You may also want to check out the offerings of Aegis Star Corporation **(http://www.aegisstar.com/**). Aegis Star offers a wide range of business-message archiving and retrieval services.

PRODUCTS & SERVICES MENTIONED

The products and services we've discussed here are all available via the Internet. The following list shows you the URLs to use to download the various products, and/or get more information on a specific item.

▪ Encoding/Decoding Programs

Wincode
http://www.members.global2000.net/snappy/index.html

WinZip
http://www.winzip.com/

XFERPRO
http://www.sabasoft.com/

▪ Encryption Programs & Services

Aegis Star Corporation
http://www.aegisstar.com/

Pretty Good Privacy
http://www.download.com/

Pretty Good Privacy Front Ends
http://www.seattle-webworks.com/pgp/pgplinks.html

Public Key Distribution Server
http://rs.internic.net/support/wwwpks/

RSA, Inc.
http://www.rsa.com/

SecurPC
http://www.rsa.com/rsa/PRODUCTS/end_user.html

■ E-mail Programs

BeyondMail
http://www.coordinate.com

Eudora Pro
http://www.qualcomm.co

Pegasus
http://www.pegasus.usa.com

E-Mail and News Support Software

E-MAIL PROGRAMS

E-mail is without a doubt the number one Internet application. Whether for business, personal, or hobby reasons, each of us is "in touch" with dozens, scores, or even hundreds of others through E-mail. No statistics are available, but a safe assumption may be that a typical Internet E-mail user finds a dozen or more messages in his or her E-mail box each week. Some, including myself, have this much E-mail traffic—or more—every day.

Because E-mail has become as important as it now is, you may not be surprised to learn that a number of applications are available to help manage incoming and outgoing mail.

This is particularly true of Internet E-mail. In past years, commercial online services stored and handled your E-mail, with options such as online folders, file storage, forwarding and carbon copy capabilities, and more.

Nowadays, the aim of online services is to place as much of the service as possible on your computer, which speeds things along and reduces storage on remote systems. The same aim is true of ISPs. Of course, this is a trend with the Internet, anyway; even Web browsers keep much of Web page content on your computer, using disk caching.

Given this trend, it is natural that your computer also becomes an extension of the Internet in handling E-mail. This extension can be powerful and efficient, if you have the proper applications—which is the focus of this chapter. With today's E-mail management software, your system also enhances the Internet!

E-mail management programs can save you money if you use an ISP that bills on a per-minute basis. These programs move all E-mail activity—except for actually receiving and sending messages—offline, where no meter is running. Additionally, these programs handle message transmission much faster than you can if you have to physically open, load, and click to send or receive each message.

All the Myriad Features

E-mail managers enable you to do far more with your messages than is possible with most online E-mail systems. Just how much more is illustrated by the some of the features offered by the E-mail programs that this chapter examines.

Filing and Organizing. The most important features of E-Mail programs are filing and organizing capabilities. The better add-on E-mail products enable you store related messages in folders that you create. They also enable you to search messages by almost any criteria, including date ranges, subject, sender, and content. Filed messages are kept available for resending or forwarding and, of course, you can delete stored messages at will.

Now, we'll take a look at some important E-mail software features. In particular, address management features are an important element.

Address Book and Mailing Lists. Next on the list of important features is the *address book*. A good address book not only stores E-mail addresses, but also addresses messages, lets you send messages to more than one person without all the addresses showing (a.k.a. "Blind Carbon Copy"), and also is able to create and use mailing lists. A "smart" address book will also require that you enter only a portion of an addressee's real name (a.k.a. *alias* or *nickname*) to place it in a message's "To" field.

You can sort addresses by various means with a well-designed address book. Also, you should be able to create subgroups of selected addresses in your address book. Such subgroups are known as *mailing lists*, or *distribution lists*. You can use these subgroups as addresses—which means that you can direct a message to be sent to a number of people by entering only one address—the name of the group, or mailing list.

These features invite some people to compile large files with thousands of E-mail addresses. These people use these "bulk-mail" files to send unwanted commercial mail (commonly known as *spam*), but recipients can deal with spam by using a feature often incorporated into a program's filing system—*message filters*, which are discussed in the next section.

Message Filters. Message filters can block or reject E-mail from given addresses. If you find yourself on a spam mailing list and your software offers filtering, you can direct the filter to ignore and delete online messages from specific addresses or servers. Alternatively, you might tell the filter to ignore messages with certain keywords in the subject line.

Filters can be used for more than simply intercepting junk mail. Some applications' filters let you direct E-mail from given sources or E-mail having to do with specific topics to folders you create for them; your E-mail is sorted, before you see it, into groups for business, personal letters, and so on. Some filtering systems also handle copies of outgoing messages, filing them in the appropriate folders for future reference.

Encoding/Decoding/Sending Message Attachments. Message attachments are an increasingly important E-mail tool. As you know, attachments enable you to send binary files as well as large text files with an E-mail message. You can share data files by mail—graphics, programs, spreadsheet, word processor, or other files—in their native format.

Because transmission via Internet E-mail is limited to standard, 7-bit ASCII characters, binary files are transmitted in encoded form. They are converted to a symbolic ASCII form before sending, and must be converted again before they can be used.

Most E-mail software enables you to perform message attachments, but it is equally important that a program be able to encode and decode binary files. Ideally, an E-mail program should handle *all* major encoding formats. (To learn more about 7-bit and 8-bit ASCII characters, return to Chapter Seven, "Computer/Internet Data Formats and Conversion." And for a complete listing of ASCII characters, see Appendix D.)

Spell Checking. Some E-mail programs provide a spelling checker. With this convenient feature, you don't have to compose messages in a word processing program just to check your spelling. (And, if you abhor real-time spell-checking, in which words are checked as you type them, you may be happy to know that the spelling checkers in the products discussed in this chapter check a document *after* you finish it—not while you write it.)

Summing Up Features. Overall, E-mail managers are a powerful database management tool for incoming and outgoing E-mail. With the capabilities described here, you can do things with E-mail that you probably didn't know were possible.

Now, you will look at three popular Internet E-mail management programs. Then, you will check out the ultimate organizer for those who have multiple accounts on online services—a program that also has fairly sophisticated E-mail management features. Then, the chapter wraps up with a quick look at newsreader software.

Eudora Pro

Eudora Pro (named after Eudora Welty, the writer) is perhaps the world's most popular Internet E-mail manager. I see the Eudora name in more "X-sender:" E-mail headers than any other available program.

Intended to work with dedicated ISPs (but *not* online services, such as CompuServe or AOL in their current states), Eudora was designed from the ground up as an Internet E-mail management tool. A commercial program,

Eudora Pro offers full E-mail capabilities, with a lot of bells and whistles, including customized spell-checking, a full-featured address book, E-mail filtering, and a complete filing system.

The Eudora address book is particularly interesting and powerful. It enables you to create mailing lists and folders for related messages, and it has powerful search capabilities. (If you remember *anything* at all about a message you want to find in a Eudora folder, Eudora will find it.)

The filing system is powerful and features a sophisticated filtering system. You can tell the filter to search for phrases, words, or strings of characters in *any* message element—including To:, From:, Subject:, the carbon copy list, the Reply-To: field, the message itself, and/or any and all headers. And, you can use multiple filters, and store filter sets for later use.

Additionally, the filters can be set up to look for strings or words beginning or ending with a precise set of characters, thanks to the use of wildcards. You can use Eudora's Boolean logic to exclude or include messages with given filter terms.

The filters also handle *message disposition*—placing messages that meet filter criteria into appropriate folders—or deleting the messages. Finally, Eudora's filters operate on both outgoing and incoming messages.

The spell-checking system is particularly flexible—like *all* of Eudora's features. Figure 8.1 shows the Eudora interface and the spell-checker setup.

The Eudora manual and help system, although otherwise helpful, are light on the kinds of information that users need to set up the program to operate with a given ISP before logging on. Although some useful information is provided in a reference section, this information is not where it needs to be—up front, in the installation section. It would also help if setup information for major national ISPs were provided (for example, NETCOM and Mindspring). Questions as simple as how to enter an ISP as a POP (Point

FIGURE 8.1

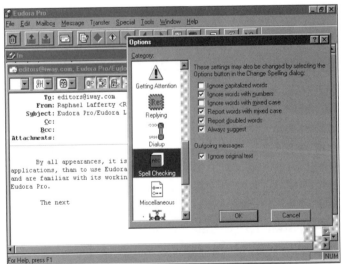

One of Eudora's flexible setup dialog boxes

of Presence) or SMTP (Simple Mail Transfer Protocol) provider really stump newer users.

Fortunately, so many people use Eudora that either asking your ISP's customer service representatives or scanning appropriate newsgroups gives you the needed information quickly. (The help system, incidentally, is context-sensitive.)

Message attachments—binary or not—are no problem for Eudora. Both BinHex and UUENCODE are supported. A *MAPI* (Messaging Application Program Interface) system allows you to attach files to messages from within Windows 95 programs.

To top off all these features, Eudora has the simplest user interface of any Internet E-mail management program. Menu selections, commands, and so on are just where you expect them. A simple user interface is almost a must for this kind of program, which requires quite a bit of learning. With Eudora, you can focus on learning the program's functions, rather than having to learn the designers' and programmers' philosophies on user interfaces. You also can customize the display to your tastes by font selection and other means.

Customizable options for nearly every program feature, including reply options and spell checking, round out a fine program. You also can change, exclude, or add *header elements*—a Reply—to an address, for example, different from your Sender address.

Aside from the problem of figuring out how to set up Eudora to operate with your ISP (which is somewhat endemic to all E-mail programs), Eudora probably is just the ticket for handling high-volume E-mail on a conventional ISP.

You can download a limited version (Eudora Light) at Qualcomm's Web site (**http://www.qualcomm.com**), but I recommend that you use the full-featured commercial version, Eudora Pro.

Pegasus Mail

Judging by what I see in E-mail headers, Pegasus is second in popularity only to Eudora among Internet users.

Created, published, and supported by a group in New Zealand, Pegasus is a shareware program that accommodates E-mail management on the Internet and on Novell networks. It has a number of interesting features—more features, in all, than any other E-mail manager reviewed here. In certain aspects, Pegasus is an over-achiever; it has features in some areas that few of us will use (for example, user-defined gateways for it to use other programs to collect mail, specialized plug-ins, and automatic polling for and announcement of new mail).

First, Pegasus has every E-mail feature that exists: header definition/altering, a complex and powerful filing system, message filters (wildcards supported), a spelling checker, mailing lists, support for all MIME and other encoding formats, a wide range of sort and search features for stored messages, folders within folders, customizable display, and nearly every other feature offered by your typical Internet E-mail manager.

Among the unique features Pegasus offers are message encryption, full support for all versions of NetWare MHS, and user-defined gateways for Fax and dial-up mail and other purposes.

Pegasus' help is context-sensitive, but at times spotty. Several special help files/topics add to the online help, taking it beyond the usual single searchable help file. Also, the program suffers from the same lack of information as Eudora in regard to what's required for a setup to work with a given ISP.

Pegasus also has a mail-merge facility that lets you embed fields in a template message, which then is customized from a mailing list. Up to 64 attachments can be made to a message, but although MIME formats are supported, MAPI is not.

Pegasus filters are powerful, using wildcards and multiple filter terms to search any message fields. The user interface is slightly more intimidating than Eudora's, and this complexity shows up in setting up filter search terms, as well as in the menu and command structure. However, most users who try it really like it—the interface can grow on you.

FIGURE 8.2

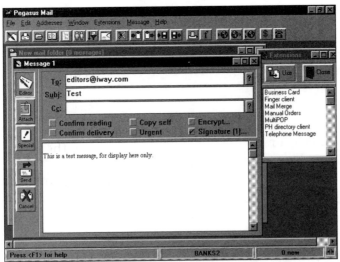

Pegasus offers an interface in which the most important commands are easy to select

The program makes good use of large buttons in its command interface. Figure 8.2 illustrates this use. In every operation, the most important commands related to the current activity are available at the click of a button.

Finally, you can customize nearly every area of Pegasus. This flexibility is a plus if you like to tinker and fine-tune a setup, and it's a must for some network users.

A plug-in manager is also present, encouraging software developers to create Pegasus add-ons. A few developers have written them. Their work is available for download at the Pegasus Web site: **http://www.pegasus.usa.com/ addons.htm**.

You can download the complete Pegasus package from the Web site, or from one of these sources:

Anonymous FTP: **ftp://risc.ua.edu/pub/network/pegasus**
or
http://www.pegasus.usa.com/ftp.htm

CompuServe: **GO NOVUSER** and search the software libraries using the keyword, **Pegasus**.

If you need some of the more esoteric E-mail features Pegasus offers, or if you need an E-mail manager for use with NetWare, Pegasus is a solid choice. Pegasus is recommended if you have unique or complex E-mail management requirements.

BeyondMail Personal Internet Edition

BeyondMail, a commercial program, is the Internet mail manager offered by Banyan Systems, who are known in the PC world for more than a few popular communications applications. BeyondMail is simpler to use, in terms of the relative number of features it offers, than either Eudora or Pegasus.

As with its competitors, BeyondMail offers a full suite of mail-management tools. You'll find an address book that handles mailing lists, a full-featured searchable filing system, customizable display elements, and spell checking. Similar to Pegasus, BeyondMail also handles message attachments and MIME encoding, but not MAPI.

A special feature lets you customize the text of messages, with selectable fonts, sizes, and colors. Of course, this flexibility requires E-mail software on the receiving end that can translate the special effects. Otherwise, the recipient sees only the text. You also can embed hypertext messages in E-mail messages. (This feature works when the recipient is using Netscape Navigator, Microsoft Internet Explorer, or Spyglass Mosaic, which BeyondMail will start if you press on a hypertext link containing an URL.)

Another BeyondMail feature of note is a *tickler file*. A tickler file lets you save a message until a specific date/time, at which point BeyondMail reminds you that it should be sent, and/or moves it to a designated folder. This works in concert with a to-do list.

Beyond the enriched-text and tickler features, BeyondMail isn't overly complex. Its filter (the "MailMinder" in the "Mail Clerk" system) scans only the "From" and "Subject" fields, and doesn't allow wildcards in specifying text or strings to look for. This simplification is echoed by most of BeyondMail's other elements and by the generally small number of features. This simplicity is a plus if you're new to Internet mail; you will neither be intimidated by a large number of features and options, nor will you waste time trying to figure out which features are used for a given task.

BeyondMail offers a multilevel message-filing system, and a nice-looking interface, as shown in Figure 8.3.

Although its user interface is more complex than Eudora Pro's, BeyondMail is simple enough that new users can get up and running quickly. The online help system could be better, but it should answer most of your questions.

If you're still feeling your way around the Internet or if you have a relatively small E-mail load, BeyondMail may be a good choice for learning about E-mail capabilities and managers. It's definitely worth a look.

E-Mail Connection (Between Online Services)

Not long ago, there were no Internet connections to carry E-mail between online services. To exchange E-mail with others who were on a system you didn't use, you had to open an account on that system, or vice-versa.

FIGURE 8.3

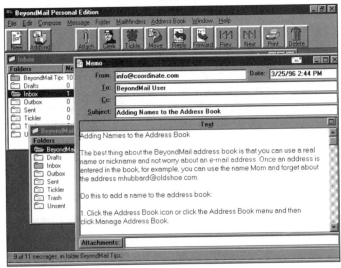

BeyondMail's user interface

Today, inter-system E-mail is a breeze. If you're on Prodigy, for example, and you want to send an E-mail message to friends who use NETCOM or DELPHI, it's no problem. You use the appropriate Internet addressing format, and your messages are on their way, as easily as you send internal mail.

Still, the commercial online services—AOL, BIX, CompuServe, DEL-PHI, Prodigy—offer far more than E-mail, (refer to Chapter Two, "Selecting a Browser and an ISP," for more information). Many of us have accounts on two or more online services. You may want to access content exclusive to certain services, or you might prefer one service's E-mail system, and another's chat rooms and Forums.

Maintaining multiple accounts, however, can be a pain. You have the chore of having to log on to several services to check your E-mail. You probably will have E-mail on each service because—given the choice—people tend to send E-mail to addresses on their host systems, rather than via the Internet.

Although this situation is manageable (offline reading and composition help, along with address books), it can become inconvenient. It's confusing at times, too, trying to remember who is on which service, and so on.

Enter just the tool to make all this easier: ConnectSoft's E-Mail Connection. A well-designed E-mail management tool, E-Mail Connection eliminates the need to start various terminal programs and online service front ends when you want to check your mail. After you configure E-Mail Connection for the services you use, it signs on and gets mail from any service(s) you specify—or from all of them. Configuring E-Mail Connection is simple, just provide account information (user name, password, and the phone number needed for connection).

The services E-Mail Connection can dial up and download E-mail from include: AOL, CompuServe, MCI Mail, the Prodigy Service, Internet service providers, and a few more esoteric systems, such as RadioMail.

E-Mail Connection also sends mail to the services that it can dial up and to a few others, such as AT&T Mail, EasyLink, and more via the Internet. In a few instances, it would seem that the program is lacking in not being able to check mail on some of these send-only services.

E-Mail Connection also sends and receives Faxes and handles SkyTel paging. No matter what destination you choose, E-Mail Connection sorts the address formats for you, which is a big help because so many services have rather odd addressing requirements.

Perhaps the greatest benefit of using E-Mail Connection is that all your mail goes to one place—E-Mail Connection's Inbox. From here, you can reply to mail as you read it—offline—and set up messages to be sent along with other messages that you may have just composed.

You can send and receive mail manually (you tell it "go," and it goes), or tell the program to do so at preset times. You can specify which service(s) are to be dialed up, and whether E-mail should be checked, sent, or both.

E-Mail Connection's user interface, shown in Figure 8.4, is straightforward. Major tasks are a button click or a Function keypress away. A vertical button/ menu bar at the left of E-Mail Connection's main screen enables you to get help,

FIGURE 8.4

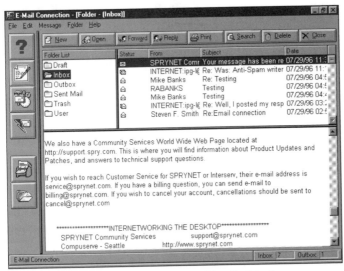

E-Mail Connection sports a friendly interface

compose mail, set up a host online service, send and receive mail, or access an address book or message folders without going through layers of selections. During reply or original message composition, easy-to-select options enable you quote a message, attach a file, keep a copy, get a receipt, and more.

The program's design avoids the "features and benefits" syndrome that ruins too many good software ideas. The designers could have put a lot more "functionality"—and made E-Mail Connection too complex and confusing—but they refrained. This conservative approach makes E-Mail Connection an easily used product that does exactly what you expect.

I would have loved to have had this kind of E-mail management software back in the mid-1980s, when I had accounts on nine online services. As billed, it truly can "send messages to anyone, anywhere, anytime." Obviously recommended for anyone with more than one online service account.

E-Mail Connection is a commercial program. For more information, visit the publisher's Web site at: **http://www.connectsoft.com**.

NEWSREADERS

Although the newsgroup interfaces created by some commercial online services are good tools (CompuServe's and—more so—AOL's, in particular), not everyone uses these online services. Also, whether or not you are satisfied with an available Usenet reader system depends on your individual tastes and needs.

Fortunately, there are choices in Usenet newsreader programs and, if you are a really intense, heavy-duty, and high-maintenance Usenet participant (or *lurker*), you may want to look into one of these programs. Newsreader programs are management programs for Usenet newsgroups messages. In this respect, these programs are similar to E-mail managers, and they share many of the same features.

The top newsreader programs are Free Agent and its commercial counterpart, Agent.

Free Agent and Agent

Forte, Incorporated's Free Agent is used by probably more people than any other newsreader. This acceptance has a lot to do with its features and functionality but, because it's free, keeps it ahead of its commercial version, Agent. (Agent is, as you'll soon see, a better choice.)

The Free Agent interface uses multiple *panes* (also "windows," or in Web parlance, "frames") to good effect. Figure 8.5 gives you an idea of how useful panes can be.

Any (or all) of these panes can be resized or maximized. This flexible feature enables you to easily track individual messages, threads, and newsgroups at large.

Foremost, Free Agent is a message *management* program, and in this job it excels. Among Free Agent's more outstanding features is the capability to go online, grab new headers in all selected groups, and display them as a "catalog" of new messages. If you mark the messages you want to read, Free Agent gets them for you.

(Alternatively, you can tell Free Agent to just log on and get all messages in selected newsgroups, but this is not the most efficient way to browse Usenet newsgroups. It's better to get only the message headers, or to restrict the messages you do get to everything after a very recent date. Newsgroups tend to pile up hundreds—or even thousands—of messages quickly.)

Free Agent can dial up independently to download and post messages, so it's your choice whether you want to log on with your ISP and/or browser, or just let Free Agent transfer your messages.

FIGURE 8.5

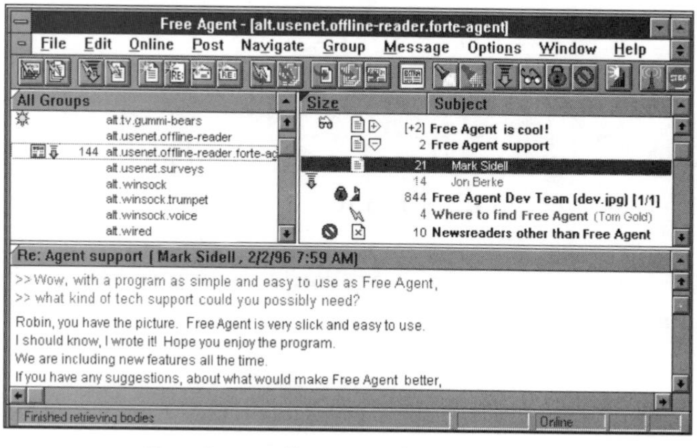

Free Agent offers pane-based viewing

After Free Agent downloads selected newsgroup messages, you can browse them in sequential (date/time) order. Special views and key commands act as strong message-browsing tools. Free Agent also follows *threads*, so you can track responses and comments on a given message without having to read unrelated messages.

You can search messages for specific words in the message subject or author's name. You also can search newsgroup titles in a similar fashion. (Messages, however, cannot be searched by content.)

Editing features make composing messages simple and, interestingly, you can send both E-mail and post newsgroup messages with Free Agent. (You cannot use Free Agent, however, to receive E-mail.)

If you need extended features, consider purchasing Agent, the full-featured commercial program from Forte. Beyond the features just described, Agent adds the following capabilities:

- Spelling checker for message composition

- User-defined folders for storing messages

- Filter lists that ignore Usenet messages based on subject, author, or message length

- A kind of "reversed filter" referred to as a Watch List, which watches for and retrieves messages based on subject, author, or message length

- Message sorting

- The ability to start your Web browser and go to an URL that is embedded in a message

- An address book

- The capability to receive E-mail (and unencode E-mail attachments)

- MAPI support and other enhancements that streamline and increase message reading, handling, storing, and searching

Obviously, the commercial version is the best route if you're seriously involved with newsgroup activities.

PRODUCTS MENTIONED

▪ E-Mail Programs

BeyondMail
http://www.coordinate.com

E-Mail Connection
http://www.connectsoft.com

Eudora Lite
and
Eudora Pro
http://www.qualcomm.com

Pegasus
http://pegasus.usa.com

Pegasus Add-Ons
http://www.pegasus.usa.com/addons.htm

▪ Newsreaders

Free Agent and Agent
http://www.forteinc.com/agent/index.htm

See also this Usenet newsgroup
alt.usenet.offline-reader

Help for Your Web Site

The simplest answer to the question of how to create or improve a Web site is "Hire someone else to do it." This approach is fine, if hiring out the work fits your time and budget constraints, and your work style. Whether or not you pay someone else to create your Web pages, you will benefit greatly from knowing a bit about how and what Web pages are, and the HTML and other tools used to create them.

This chapter gives you a quick look at basic considerations in choosing a Web site provider (which may be the ISP or online service that you now are using), and then moves on to helper applications and online utility services for creating, maintaining, and enhancing your Web site.

WHY DO YOU NEED A WEB SITE?

This is a good question for anyone to ask before setting up a Web site. Answering it will help you plan the design and target your potential audience.

There are many reasons to publish a Web site (including as a hobby—but we'll stick with the productive reasons). If you have a product to sell, you may want to put up an online brochure, with photos or other illustrations. This kind of "brochure" site is an excellent passive selling tool, and potential customers don't have to request information and then wait to receive it; they can see it *now*. (Of course, you have to make your brochure easy to find, but we'll discuss this later in this chapter, in the section, "Getting the Word Out: Publicizing Your Web Site.")

You might go a step farther and put an entire catalog online. Many vendors have done so with great success. An online catalog allows customers to shop or comparison-shop at their leisure.

Alternately, you can use what is known as an *autoresponder* at your site to E-mail information to those who request it. These tools are E-mail "robots" that are set up to send a specific text file to anyone who sends E-mail to them. (One company that provides autoresponders is JJ Electronic Plaza, at: **http://www.jjplaza.com**.)

You can also go all the way with a Web site and take orders online. (Even if you don't do so, you can at least provide a form or a "mailto:" link that interested parties can use to request more information. Also, be sure that you provide an address and telephone number to your contact page. This completeness of information adds a dimension of legitimacy to your business, and it doesn't restrict potential customers to using only E-mail as a means of communicating with you.)

Before you jump in with both feet, think about what you want your Web site to accomplish. Then, plan for what you need; for example, if you want to take orders online and accept credit cards, you need to be a credit card merchant, and you will need a way to make ordering secure at your site. (You can always restrict orders to E-mail if a secure server is impractical. Note that setting up secure servers, software, and customer-order forms are best left to experts.)

Web sites are good for *gathering* as well as providing information. If you plan on creating or offering a new product, you could get valuable input from potential customers browsing the Web—or from those already handling the product you're considering.

(You can find information and tutorials on creating Web page forms at some of the sites listed at the end of this chapter, under the section, "HTML Tutorials and References.")

Of course, you do want to have something to attract people to your Web site and its questionnaire; something beyond listings with the search engines, that is. This something may include interesting facts and graphics, or even a "thank you" gift that you can mail to those who respond to your questionnaire. This is particularly useful for ongoing questionnaires, where you can provide compilations of results as you go.

Educators will find questionnaires useful, as well. Quite often, putting up a questionnaire or a poll is an effective means of gathering a lot of information on a given topic fast. (Here's a tip: you can offer to share the information your questionnaire collects with those who respond.)

Interactive Web pages are another popular and useful application for Web sites, particularly those sites dedicated to educating youngsters. You can set up the online equivalent of flash card tests, or even the multipath stories where the reader chooses what the protagonist will do at critical junctions. A bulletin board-like setup can be used to let visitors contribute to ongoing stories. The possibilities are endless.

Again, ask yourself *why* you want to have a Web site. This will help you plan what you need to do and how to accomplish it.

WHERE TO GO? WEB SITE HOSTS

Before you think about creating a Web site, you have an important decision to make: where will your site be hosted?

If your requirements are basic, just about any online service or ISP will do—provided, that is, the ISP in question does Web site hosting; not all do.

If you won't need to "publish" a lot of large files and won't be using *CGI* (Common Gateway Interface) scripts, Java, or binary programs, your needs probably can be met by any provider that offers Web sites. All you need is a reasonable amount of file space to store your Web page files (all providers that do Web site hosting offer at least one megabyte), ready access via a local dial-up number, unlimited access for you and for Web site visitors, and E-mail—all at a reasonable price. An online service—AOL, CompuServe, or Prodigy, for example—can handle these kinds of requirements, and all provide tools to help you create your Web site.

Web Sites from the Outside Looking In

To get an idea of how much you can do with a Web site hosted by an online service or ISP, take a look at what's being done!

AOL, CompuServe, and Prodigy (the online service—*not* Prodigy Internet) make members' Web sites easy to access and search at these URLs:

http://members.aol.com

http://ourworld.compuserve.com

http://pages.prodigy.com

ISPs that offer Web site hosting often make their users' sites available. Here are the URLs for the user home page indexes for Concentric Network, Earthlink, Mindspring, Sprynet, and a local provider in southwestern Ohio, OneNet:

http://www.concentric.net/club/community.html

http://www.earthlink.net/company/business/

http://www.earthlink.net/company/free_web_pages.html

http://listuser.gte.net/ListUsers.html

http://www.mindspring.com/community/index.html

http://www.sprynet.com/ourworld/searchow/index.html

http://www.one.net/explore/clients/

You will find personal, small business, and corporate Web sites hosted by these providers.

So, if you already have an account on one of the online services, it might be a good idea to see what you can do with the tools available. I have set up several viable Web sites on CompuServe and AOL. (If you are already on AOL or CompuServe, I suggest building a basic Web site using their tools; this can be a valuable learning experience.)

You, however, may have more advanced requirements that can't be met by an online service. If so, you'll find it necessary to search a bit for a Web site provider that suits your needs. "Advanced requirements" include the following:

- *Site monitoring and information about traffic.* This includes how many times a specific page is accessed, with which page(s) visitors spent the most time, and even where visitors come from. This kind of information is available to the system administrator (from log files), and some services provide regular reports, at no charge or for a small fee. (There are, however, alternate sources for much of this information, as discussed in following sections of this chapter.)

- *Expanded file storage capacity for your Web pages and files.* Many ISPs and online services place a limit on the total size of the files that make up your Web site. CompuServe, for example, allows five megabytes of storage. (This amount is ample for a basic Web page, even enough for you to provide several files for download.) Other providers allow as much as 25 megabytes.

- *High limits (or no limits) on Web site traffic and downloads.* A high number of Web site visits, or "hits," and/or hundreds or thousands of downloads for one Web site tie up a significant percentage of a Web host's server resources. This means other sites and server functions are delayed or immobilized. Because of this, many providers place a limit on traffic, or charge extra for more than a certain number of hits or quantity of files downloaded per day or per month. You want a reasonable limit—several hundred hits per day, and at least 500K per day in data transfer (Web page files or downloads) at no extra charge.

- *The capability to run CGI scripts, use image maps, Java applets, Shockwave, and other advanced Web page support features.* Some of these features require program files and other binary storage on the server, which should be set up to provide it.

- *Free services.* These might include a counter that you can include on your home page (or any of your site's pages), basic demographic reports (days and hours when your site was most active, operating systems used by visitors, and so on), and/or other enhancements.

You also need to consider the following factors:

- *The ISP's Internet Connection.* The ISP's connections to the Internet should be a high-speed *T1* or *T3* connection. (For reference, a T1 line supports data connections as fast as 1,500,000 bits per second. This is nearly ten times as fast as an ISDN connection. A T3 connection is 45,000,000 bits per second!) This speed ensures that visitors to your Web site won't have to wait long for your pages to load into their browsers.

- *Ease of access.* If you deal with a local ISP, you will have local access numbers. A national ISP usually provides local number access via a packet-switching network (PSN). You need to know whether the PSN is owned/operated by the ISP (as is the case with most online services, NETCOM, and other ISPs). If it is the ISP's own PSN, you're in good shape. If the ISP uses a public PSN such as SprintNet or Tymnet, figure on busy signals, dropped connections, and slower response times during peak usage periods. Also, find out if the ISP charges extra for public PSN access. If 800-number access is provided, ask about the charges for this service.

- *Pricing.* Does the ISP charge a setup or activation fee? If so, see whether you can get a similar price, without the setup fee, elsewhere. Can you get a discount for paying several months' usage in advance?

- *Software.* Does the ISP provide the software you need to connect—dial-up and/or Winsock software for the SLIP/PPP connection to the Internet? You shouldn't need dial-up software with Windows 95, but you will need software for services that use proprietary software (NETCOM, for example, is one such service). This is not critical; you can find most other software you might need, such as Telnet and FTP clients, as shareware that is downloadable from the Web and online services. The same is true for Web browsers, but it's nice if the ISP provides some of these things, or a download area—although it's not absolutely necessary.

- *Value-added services.* These include extra-cost services such as providing you with your own domain name (**mycompany.com**, for example), consultation on Web site design, special applet programming, and so forth. Such services can greatly enhance your Web site.

- *Extras.* Many ISPs offer helpful tools and services for building Web sites. These tools range from proprietary software such as CompuServe's "Home Page Wizard," to ready-to-use counters for your Web site. Interactive search and real-time chat features are also possible. Some ISPs also offer support forums or newsgroups, and download pages with programs or links to download sites for programs that can be helpful to Web site builders. (An example of a page that offers download links can be found at: **http://www.sprynet.com/ourworld/tools/authortools.html**.)

You will usually find one or more pages that list prices for dial-up accounts as well as usual and special Web hosting services at an ISP's Web site. Figure 9.1 is an example of this kind of page:

NOTE: Strictly Business. Many ISPs distinguish between personal and business Web sites in pricing as well as services. The ISP you select may charge higher setup and monthly fees for a business site. Because of this, you may be tempted to tell the ISP that you want a personal account with a personal Web site, in order to save money.

There are several reasons for not doing this. First, you probably will be violating the ISP's terms of service. You will probably be found out if your site begins generating a large number of hits and/or downloads. If this happens, you will at the least be upgraded to a business account, and may have retroactive charges assessed. At worst, you will lose your account.

Second, if you sign up for a business account, you get more for your money. OneNet, for example, the ISP whose rates are shown in Figure 9.1, allows business customers to have 200 megabytes storage space for a Web site, as opposed to 25 megabytes for a personal Web site. Other benefits for business accounts may include access to special libraries of ready-to-use images and CGI scripts, multiple accounts, and more.

FIGURE 9.1

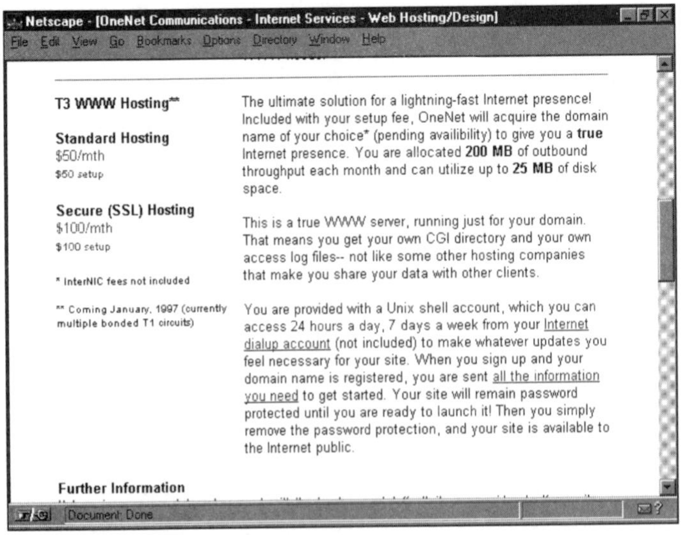

A typical price schedule for Web site hosting

Finally, certain value-added services are provided only if you have a business account. These include domain name service, help with Web page design, and more.

"Free" Web Sites: Are They Worth the Price?
Avoid the "free Web site" come-ons that turn up in your E-mail box. Many are bait-and-switch schemes. Most are multilevel marketing (MLM) scams that require that you sell *x* number of others on "free" Web sites each month, or be charged for your "free" site.

Still others require that you participate in selling some other kind of product, using MLM—and sign up a monthly quota of "downliners"—to get your free Web site. Of these, most limit your Web site to advertising the MLM product in question.

The providers in these schemes are often low-budget, and may disappear or dump your site at any time. Besides, no legitimate business wants to be associated with these providers.

For still more help in finding an ISP, check these sites:

iWORLD and Mecklermedia's searchable list of ISPs worldwide:
http://thelist.iworld.com

Another searchable list of ISPs worldwide:
http://www.celestin.com/pocia/

Do comparative price lists on ISPs. The preceding resources give you the URLs for ISPs in your area, as well as national and regional ISPs. Visit prospective ISPs, and start a list of comparisons.

Put Your Business in Your Web Site Name
For a relatively nominal fee, you can have your Web site hosted by *your company*. That is, you can buy a domain name that matches your business's name. If your company name is Hot Lumber, Inc., for example, you can set up as hotlumber.com.

This can add to your business image, and makes your Web site's URL easy to remember.

Most ISPs provide this service, known as *domain name service*. A small initial sign-up fee, and usually a reasonable monthly fee go along with the service.

For more information on domain names and registration, visit the New Domain Name Registration FAQ at: **http://rs.internic.net/domain-info/registration-FAQ.html**. To see whether a domain name you want is already taken, check with the Internic Domain Name Checker, at: **http://rs.internic.net/cgi-bin/whois**. (Internic is the organization responsible for issuing domain names on the Web.)

WEB SITE BASICS

If you've read Chapter One, you know that Web sites are collections of files. The files consist of any or all of the following:

- *HTML documents.* These are the heart of a Web site, presenting important textual information, and displaying or calling/activating other types of Web site files. This is the only kind of file that is absolutely required for a Web site.

- *Graphic image files.* Also known as "inline images," these files will usually have .JPG or .GIF extensions. Almost all Web sites offer such graphics. Also, JPG or GIF files are used to create the image maps that you see at so many Web sites. (See Chapter Six for useful information about graphic formats.)

- *Video and sound files.* (multimedia)

- *Program files.* This category includes CGI and binary program files, Java applets, and ActiveX controls. (Refer to Chapter Four for more information on Java and ActiveX.)

- *Files for download.* (While *all* files on the Internet can be downloaded, files in this category are usually large ZIP files and, for convenience, are offered on a separate page.)

In all instances, these files are created offline, and uploaded to a specified directory on the Web site host.

HTML Files

As noted, HTML (or Hypertext Markup Language) files are the heart of a Web site. They not only display text, but they also direct the manner in which the text displays—the fonts, the sizes, and special effects such as boldface and italics. Additionally, HTML files contain commands that display graphic, sound, video, and other kinds of files—including other HTML files.

As you can see, HTML files are responsible for everything that happens at a Web site. They serve as the "director" for the entire Web site, on a page-by-page basis.

HTML was designed as a means of marking up text pages to display various font styles and sizes, effects such as boldface, and to *link* a page to other pages on the Web. (These pages might be at the same site or elsewhere.)

NOTE: Links to Objects. Web page hyperlinks do not always lead to other Web pages. Sometimes the link is to an object. *The object may be another image, as is the case with* thumbnail images, *which are tiny versions of an online image provided to let you preview it before you download it or view it full-size. Other objects to which links lead include programs, downloads, applets, and even a defined location on the current Web page.*

In the few the years since its inception, a number of features were added to HTML, including accommodation for more file types, additional fonts and text effects, and so on. (HTML is now in version 3; version 4 looms on the horizon. And it is worth noting that most Web browsers are still "catching up" with version 3; therefore, you should use your browser to test any advanced HTML features you implement to make sure that they are supported.)

HTML's core is the coding system used to produce text effects, call other documents, and perform a number of other functions. It is safe to say that HTML is itself the core of the Web; without it, the Web could not exist.

HTML Coding. HTML is one of the simplest computer "languages" there is. Its few complexities lie in the wide range of commands.

HTML documents are plain-text (a.k.a. ASCII) files that you can create by using any text editor, including programs, such as Windows Notepad, and any word processor that allows you save files in plain text or ASCII format. There also are special HTML-editing programs, which are examined later in this chapter.

Figure 9.2 shows an HTML file in "raw" form.

Various formatting and other coding elements in an HTML document are indicated by *tags*. HTML tags use lesser than (**<**) and greater than (**>**)

FIGURE 9.2

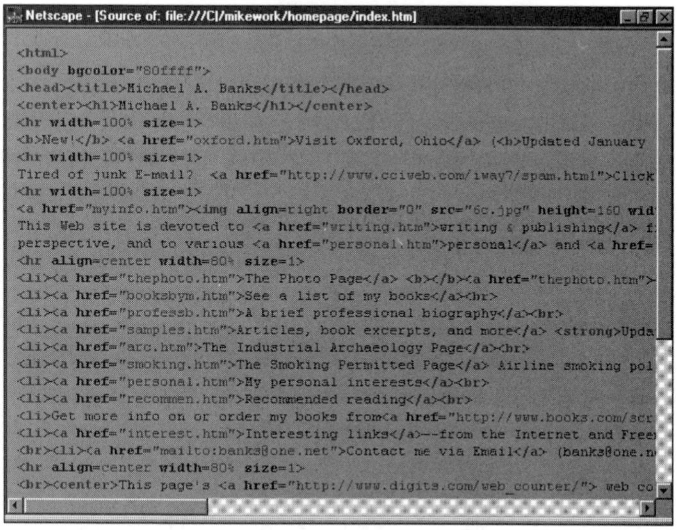

Typical HTML file

symbols, a.k.a. "angle brackets," to enclose and mark the beginnings and ends of commands.

Commands consist of simple text strings, most of which are *mnemonic*. (That is, they remind you of their meaning, as is the case with <b> for bold, <u> for underline, and <i> for italic.)

The majority of HTML commands are three letters or less. Here are some examples:

Command	Effect
b	**Boldface**
i	*Italics*
u	<u>Underline</u>

Command tags are usually paired. One tag turns "on" an effect, and the other switches it "off." The "off" tag usually is the same command as the "on" tag, but preceded by a front slash (/) within the angle brackets. Therefore, to make a word, phrase, sentence, or section of a document in boldface, you would precede it with **<b>** and follow it with **</b>**.

For example, this line:

This is an example of <b>boldface.</b>

would be displayed as:

This is an example of **boldface.**

Similarly, this line:

Here are examples of <u>underlining</u>, <i>italics</i>, and <b>boldface</b>, all in one sentence. And here are all three in one <u><i><b>word</u></i></b>.

would be displayed as:

Here are examples of <u>underlining</u>, *italics*, and **boldface**, all in one sentence. And here are all three in one ***<u>word</u>***.

Properly formatted tags are invisible when a browser displays a document.

Making Links. Beyond indicating how text is to be formatted for display, HTML tags are used to link one HTML page to another, with what are known as *anchors*. The linked page can be at the same site, or anywhere else on the Web. The code for a linking tag to a local page looks like this:

<a href="xxxx.html">Click here for more</a>

"xxxx.html" is the filename called when someone clicks on the link. The **a href=** is the anchor, which is the portion that tells a browser this is a link, and the characters within the quote marks define the link. The final "**>**" closes that part of the command.

(Note that this example link is for a file, xxxx.html, that is in the same directory as the page from which it is linked. If you have multiple directories at a site, it is necessary to include the directory information with the filename. For example, /otherdir/xxxx.html. The same is true of files located at other sites; these must be preceded by their sites' URLs.)

The link on the Web page would look like this:

<u>Click here for more.</u>

As well as being underlined, a line of text providing a link will usually appear in a different color than the surrounding text. (The color choice and whether or not hyperlinks are underlined are usually browser setup defaults and can be changed. After you use a link once, it changes color, so you know you have already used it.)

Everything following the anchor is underlined and is a part of the link, until the **</a>** (close anchor, or end of link). Links are underlined by default—a feature "built into" the link command. When you click any of the underlined text, the link is activated and the page named in the command is loaded. (The net effect here is that clicking the link causes a browser to send a command requesting the file named in the link.)

NOTE: .htm or .html? HTML files at some sites have the extension .htm while files at other sites use .html. With a PC, you will save files by using the .htm extension, but it doesn't matter either way, as long as you use the same extension for all HTML files at your Web site—and in all links within your Web site.

Most Web hosts allow you to use .htm or .html, as you prefer. A few require .html. Your ISP offers instructions as to which extension you must use for HTML files uploaded to your Web site. (Changing your uploaded .htm files to .html files usually is a matter of specifying that they use the latter extension on your Web server.)

External links must use .htm or .html, as appropriate. Some hosts require that you use one extension or the other. Also, some hosts are case-sensitive with respect to URLs.

Links to pages on other sites look like this:

**<a href="http://www.onlineinc.com/pempress/index.html">
Pemberton Press</a>**

The same thing happens here that happens with the local page link. The only difference is that, in clicking on this link, you are requesting a file on another server.

*NOTE: Default Web Site Files. If you included only **http://www.onlineinc.com** as the page request in the preceding example, a special file named index.html would have loaded. This file is actually the home page for the entire site.*

When you create a Web site, you will have one file named either index.html or homepage.html that serves as the default file that loads when someone enters your URL without an additional file request. This explains why, when you go to some sites, you see in your browser's location window an additional filename at the end of the URL you entered.

Creating Links with Images
If you're new to HTML coding, I'm sure you've wondered how to make an image link to another page or an image. Referred to as "clickable images," such links are fairly simple to make. Simply replace the link's text with an image source tag.
 For example, if you have the following link:

`<a href="photos.htm">Click here to view photos.</a>`

and you want to use an image for the link to the "photos.htm" page, you only need to replace the text "Click here to view photos." with an image source like the following:

`<a href="thephoto.htm"><img src="dogs.jpg"></a>`

The key is placing the image source in the middle of the anchor link.

Other HTML Tags. Here is a sampling of other important HTML tags:

**
** Forces a *break* (carriage return) at the end of a line. This is important if you want to separate elements of text.

<IMG SRC Defines the *image source* file for an inline image (Full usage: **<IMG SRC="example.gif">**). You can place an image tag in the middle of an anchor link to define the image as a link to a given URL.

<li> A *list item*. Used in an unordered list (definition follows), this creates bulleted items in a list.

<p></p> Marks the beginning and end of a *paragraph*. Without this command, carriage returns are stripped from blocks of text, resulting in a browser display that shows the text without line breaks, adding its own to make the text fit the screen. Also, more than one paragraph will be run-on into one long block of text. With this command, all carriage returns in the block of text defined by the tag are used.

<pre></pre> Text marked with this tag is regarded as *pre-formatted*, and displayed literally as you entered it, with all spaces, tabs, and carriage returns preserved. (Multiple blank spaces usually are reduced to one space.)

<ul></ul> An *unordered list*, which displays as a bulleted list. (Other types of lists are possible, included numbered lists.)

Learning HTML. Learning HTML is not difficult. Ask anyone who is proficient at HTML coding, and you will probably find that he or she learned most of what they know by jumping in and writing their own code—and by looking at the source code for Web pages around the Net.

I learned HTML in much the same way. I tried using various tags and, when I couldn't get them to work properly or didn't know the tags to use for a particular effect, I surfed for pages on the Web with the features I wanted, and viewed their source code. (To view a Web page's source with Netscape Navigator, select Document Source on the View menu. With Explorer, select Source on the View menu.) This surfing provided "live" examples of what I was trying to learn.

Of course, I did not steal others' code. I merely looked at the source code to see what commands were required to produce a specific effect. After I learned this, I did it on my own, my way.

Online References. I also used online references to HTML coding. One of the best is "A Beginner's Guide to HTML," which is located at:

http://www.ncsa.uiuc.edu/General/Internet/WWW/HTMLPrimer.html

Links to other HTML references can be found at these sites:
http://csugrad.cs.vt.edu/serversetup/htmldocsindex.html

http://www.kersur.net/~polyvis/html.html

"Testing, Testing..." Always test your HTML documents offline—the links, in particular—before placing them on your Web site. As with most things involving computers, HTML code must be precise because it will be interpreted literally. One missing **"** or **>** can render most of the links on a page useless, and make some of it unreadable.

You should also keep a "mirror copy" of all your site's pages in a directory on your hard drive. This allows for fast testing and integration of new pages, and gives you a backup in case something happens on the server.

You can preview your code and test links by using your favorite Web browser. Start the browser, and then open the file that contains the document you want to test. (With Navigator, select Open File on the File menu. With Explorer, select Open and the File menu and enter the file's name and location.)

Some results of bad coding will be immediately visible. For example, if you forgot to close an anchor link with **</a>**, everything on the page following that link will be underlined—the entire page will be one big link. This tells you about where the problem is located.

It is best to have the document open with an editor and with a browser at the same time. That way, you can fix a problem, save the document, and then reload it with the browser for immediate testing.

Graphic Images

Graphics are as ubiquitous as text on Web sites. Despite the fact that graphics can slow down a Web page's loading, they are expected—particularly at commercial sites.

As noted previously, graphic images used with Web pages will be .GIF or .JPG files just because these are graphic types that *all* browsers can display. They also tend to be more common and supported by more graphics programs than any other file type. (Chapter Six provides detailed information about these and other file types.)

Image Maps

Although image maps are, strictly speaking, simply .GIF or .JPG files, they differ from the typical online image enough that I should explain them here.

In concept, *image maps* are a means of organizing and making information accessible visually, as opposed to using text links. On this level, an image map is the next step beyond the single "clickable image" link discussed previously.

In practical terms, an image map is a graphic that is divided into regions—and each region is a link. For example, you might take an image of a map of the United States and divide the image into fifty regions. Each region would physically match a state. The URL for a given region would link to the URL of a page having to do with that state.

These are fairly simple, once you've created one. To that end, I will discuss an excellent image map creation tool later in this chapter.

Improve Your Image with Reduced File Sizes
There is one element that all image formats have in common: the greater an image's resolution (the more dots/pixels), the larger the file size. I mention this because file size is an important consideration when preparing files to include on a Web page. Larger files can take "forever" to load—or at least seem like it to someone with a slow connection. So, you may have to look at a tradeoff between file size and resolution—or will you?

Actually, it's possible to make an image's file smaller and retain resolution with the same solution. If you reduce the size of an image (number of pixels wide by number of pixels high), you reduce the file size. At the same time, the resolution of most images actually improves slightly.

Professional graphic editing programs such as Adobe Illustrator and Acrobat offer additional means of reducing file size without overly compromising image quality.

However you do it, use every option possible to reduce those image file sizes. This can make the difference between people returning to your site, or avoiding it. It also discourages people from turning off their graphic displays when they visit your site. This can be a vital consideration if you provide important information in your site's graphics.

Multimedia: Video and Sound Files

The basis of multimedia on the Web, video and sound files, are major components of some Web sites. Like graphic image files, video and sound files not only enhance your Web site, but they can also add content.

Note that they also slow down page loading; that's the tradeoff for moving up to multimedia. Also, visitors to your site will be required to have certain add-ons or plug-ins to use some multimedia files.

The major video and sound file formats are:

Video

.AVIMicrosoft Video Clip

.GLGRASP animation

.MPGMPEG video (also .MPE or .MPV)

Sound

.AIFAudio Interchange Format sound

.AUBasic PC sound (also .SND)

.RARealAudio (also .RAM)

.RMIMIDI audio sequence (also .MID)

.VOCAudio/voice

.WAVA PC sound file

Some video and sound files are offered as downloadable files, but more and more are set up to be displayed or run by Web browsers. (If you haven't set a program to run a particular type of file in your browser's settings when it encounters one of these files, you will be given two choices. You can name an application to use with the file, or you can download the file.)

If you offer such multimedia files at your Web site, you should make sure that visitors can find and/or download the appropriate applications. Place this information (usually in the form of a link) next to the data file, if you can. For example, if you offer RealAudio files, provide a link to RealAudio's Web site (**http://www.realaudio.com**).

CGI Script and Program Files

Program files that run on your server include CGI (Common Gateway Interface) files, and any other programs with which CGI scripts interact.

Sometimes mistaken for complete programs themselves, CGI scripts function as data interfaces for programs stored on a Web server. When certain types of data are received by a Web site, and/or certain pages or links are activated, a CGI script routes incoming data to a program (activating the program first). For example, when you sign up for an ISP, a CGI script prompts you for information, checks it, and then routes it to a specified program on the server.

Warning: Large Files!

A common courtesy found at the better Web sites is to let your visitors know the size of a multimedia file *before* they access it. A quick, parenthetical statement of file size (such as "4,903K") gives a visitor the opportunity to decide whether he or she wants to tie up a lot of time with the file. Visitors who go to check out a file and discover it is several megabytes in size often feel "ambushed" by such a time-consuming download.

It's also a good idea to provide alternate files, when possible. For example, .AVI video files are often smaller than .MPG files. Although the .AVI file may offer lesser quality, many visitors will prefer to access it. So, you can provide the same video in both versions (and note their file sizes with their descriptions). After they've viewed the file, they may return for the higher-quality .MPG file. Either way, many more people will view the video.

Programs that run on a server (called *Web-side* applications) may or may not use a CGI script; most do. Setting up these programs, and the CGI scripts that work with them, requires more technical knowledge than most people possess. If you plan to use Web-side applications, you should turn to a consultant or your ISP for advice (most offer Web design and creation services).

Programs that run on visitors' computers, referred to as *client-side* programs, are typically Java applets and ActiveX controls. Both must be transmitted to the client computer to operate, and some can be quite complex, as is the case with the Java-based IRC (Internet Relay Chat) program shown running in Figure 9.3.

As with server-side applications, creating successful client-side applications requires technical expertise. Again, it is recommended that you place these chores in the hands of experts. Unless, that is, you have the time to learn and experiment for yourself. Java and ActiveX programming *can* be self-taught.

Files for Download

A prominent feature of many Web sites is a collection of files for download. These may be data files, shareware, demo programs, or any other product or sample you can provide in a computer file.

FIGURE 9.3

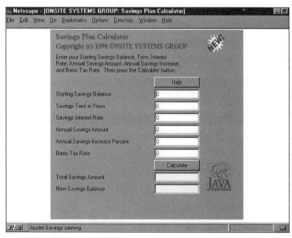

A Java-based client-side program in action

CHAPTER 9

Some sites are set up for FTP access of downloadable files, but the easiest way to make a file available for download is to provide a link to it in a Web page.

Such a link uses an *anchor*, described previously. If, for example, you want to provide a file named GETTHIS.ZIP for download, you would place the file in your Web site directory and create this anchor link:

<a href="getthis.zip.">Click here to download GetThis.</a>

which would appear on the Web page as:

Click here to download GetThis.

Alternatively, you might get a little more elegant and focus on one part of the string as the link, by writing the following code for the anchor link:

Click <a href="getthis.zip.">here</a> to download GetThis.

That code would result in a link that looks like this:

Click here to download GetThis.

As you know, any file type that is not included in your browser's setup results in your getting a prompt like the one shown in Figure 9.4.

In the case of an .EXE or .ZIP file, you click "Save File..." after which Netscape Navigator prompts you for the file's name and location.

If a program or other file is required to use the downloaded file, you must

FIGURE 9.4

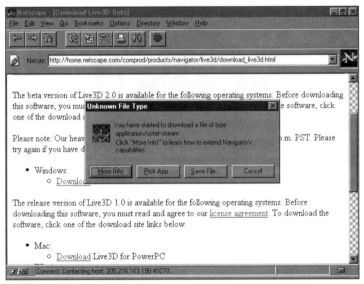

Browser query prompt for handling an unidentified file type

156 THE INTERNET UNPLUGGED

provide a link to enable a visitor to download what he or she needs. One file type that is found frequently at Web sites is .PDF (Portable Data Format). The Adobe Acrobat reader can be obtained at this URL: **http://www.adobe.com/prodindex/ acrobat/readstep.html**. This is, by the way, one of a number of offline helpers you really should have, but usually will not know about until you need it.

Finally, as with multimedia files, you should include the download file's size in the link or with its description.

Putting It on the Web

Assuming that you have created all the files you need, you have to upload them to your Web site.

If you use an online service as a Web site host, you are given a full or partial front end program to handle both Web site creation and uploading. These tools greatly simplify assembling your files and getting them onto the service's Web site server. However, some also place limitations on you. With CompuServe's Home Page Wizard, for example, you have to wait for the server to go through checking your online directory and other tasks before your files are uploaded. Also, unless you know how to work your way around its "features," you will not be able to create and upload pages with all the features you may want. (The CompuServe front end filters out many HTML formatting elements.) In contrast, you can upload pretty much anything you want to AOL's Web server—after you figure out how—but the upload procedure is a bit cumbersome and slow. In either case, you cannot use alternative means of uploading to the servers in question.

These limitations—and those associated with other online services' Web site front ends—are the result of the front ends being designed for beginners. The goal of the designs was to simplify things as much as possible. This unfortunately places limitations on Web sites created with them.

In contrast, building the Web site you want on most ISPs' servers is easy. (Provided you know how to create the kinds of pages and effects you want.) Any type of file you need can be uploaded, and—unlike CompuServe's front end—there is no editing or filtering of HTML documents. When it's time to upload, you either dial up with what is referred to as a "shell account," using a standard terminal program such as PROCOMM, or you use FTP to upload your files. In any case, you are required to provide your user ID and password before you can upload or delete files.

Most ISPs are UNIX-based, and provide you with a directory structure that looks a bit like the one shown in Figure 9.5.

FIGURE 9.5

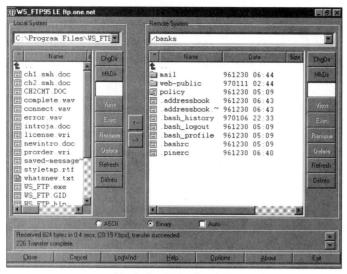

User directory structure

One directory is reserved for your Web site's files. (In Figure 9.5, this directory is named "web-public.") After you log on, you use the proper command to go to the directory, where you can upload, download, or delete files as you desire. (Your ISP will provide you with detailed instructions as to how to log on, find your directories, and so forth.)

For uploading files to your Web site, FTP is the best approach. Your browser probably can handle it; if not, there are several FTP client programs available. Most of these provide extra features that really simplify logging on and transferring. For example, WS_FTP, shown in use in Figure 9.5, automates sending your user ID and password, and moving to the appropriate directory.

This FTP client acts as a file manager, letting you mark multiple files for transfer, and view the server's files as if they were in a directory on your system. WS_FTP has other interesting features, but the automated logon and file management capabilities alone make it worth having. With this tool, you can test a new Web page online, edit it, and view it "live" again in literally seconds.

HTML HELPERS

As noted, you can create HTML documents with any text editor or word processor that can save files in 7-bit ASCII format. There are, however, special tools for creating HTML documents. Some tools are better than others, but all create usable HTML code.

Word Processors and HTML

With the growing popularity of the Web, it's not surprising that some word processors, such as WordPerfect, can create HTML documents complete with tags, based on conventional WYSIWYG ("what you see is what you get") on-screen formatting. That is, a word displayed in **bold** on-screen is saved as boldface by a word processor capable of converting on-screen text to HTML tags.

The WYSIWYG feature of this kind of a word processor is handy, but it doesn't quite duplicate the appearance of a Web page as displayed by a Web browser. Also, you can't display graphics or test links within the word processor. So, you still need to preview documents with a browser. Additionally, no word processor is capable of perfectly translating all formatting, nor of inserting all the effects you may want to use.

Still, if you are accustomed to working with a word processor, and a newer or special version of your program offers HTML formatting conversion, you may find using the word processor is a good way to get most of the HTML tags into your document. After you save the document, you can edit the resulting HTML document and add any additional tags manually. (Note: Your word processor may already do HTML file conversion of on-screen formatting. One way to check is to see if "HTML" is one of the file-type options available when you save a file. Double-check the file to see whether the word processor does indeed do conversions, or if it just calls any file saved in 7-bit ASCII an HTML file.)

More elaborate, non-system-specific tools are available. Among these are Microsoft WORD for Windows, versions 7 and higher, which convert font size and type, bolding, and other character and layout effects to HTML code when you save a document in HTML format. Corel's WordPerfect 7 and higher offers a similar feature.

Microsoft makes available a couple of add-ons for WORD that help make HTML documents. For WORD 95 users, there is the Microsoft Internet Assistant for WORD 95. Those who use Microsoft WORD 6 can download the Microsoft Internet Assistant for WORD 6.0. You can find both of these add-ons at this URL: **http://www.microsoft.com/msword/internet/ia/**.

Dedicated HTML Editors

You may find a dedicated HTML authoring/editing program to be more your style. For some, seeing the HTML code at will is the best way to work on an HTML document. (Even better, some HTML editors let you switch between or simultaneously view an HTML document and its appearance as displayed by a browser.)

HoTMetaL PRO. Among the more interesting of dedicated HTML editors is HoTMetaL PRO, a commercial program published by SoftQuad. This program is ideal for HTML beginners or more advanced Web designers.

FIGURE 9.6

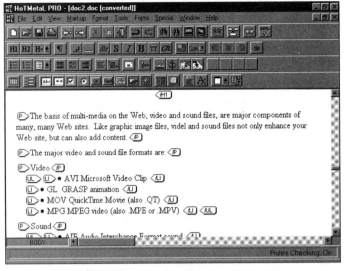

HoTMetaL PRO lets you mark up documents with a few mouse clicks

Shown in Figure 9.6, HoTMetaL PRO lets you insert tags for just about any formatting element you desire, quickly and unobtrusively. You can do this by selecting tags from a list, as in the figure, or switching to a mode that lets you edit the HTML document directly.

The prepared tags let you create your document from scratch quickly and easily. The latest HTML version is always supported (you get free updates to the program if you buy it), which means you can add any existing HTML feature to a document. This includes online forms (user ID/password dialogs, text fields, radio buttons, "send" buttons, and more)—usually the more difficult aspects of HTML coding. The program also supports tables, frames, Java applets, and ActiveX controls.

Templates let you build a document from a solid base, with various elements (including forms) already included.

Graphic manipulation is simple. An add-on application called MetalWorks is included with HoTMetaL PRO. With it, you can edit any element of an image. This makes resizing, creating "thumbnail" images, cropping, improving resolution, coloring, and so on a simple task. A small library of ready-to-use GIF images is provided.

After you edit an image to your satisfaction, you can turn it into an image map, using features built into MetalWorks.

HoTMetaL PRO also checks documents for HTML tag errors, showing you the location and nature of any it finds.

A spelling checker and thesaurus are built in—a welcome addition if you compose text for a Web page directly on the page (as opposed to writing and checking it with your word processor, then pasting it into the Web page).

HTML documents can be previewed by altering the display, or you can see a document "live" by using your browser.

HoTMetaL PRO also converts documents created by popular word processors into HTML documents—complete with HTML tags for text formatting and layout.

Good online Help, a Help-based tutorial, and an excellent manual (which includes background on technical topics) round out this excellent program. It's about average on disk space requirements; a typical installation requires around 15 megabytes.

You can download a working demo of HoTMetaL at SoftQuad's Web site: **http://www.softquad.com**. Recommended.

Corel's Web.Graphics Suite. Another useful HTML editor is a part of Corel's Web.Graphics Suite. Web.Graphics is more than just an HTML editor and Web page creator, it is also a graphics workshop (with thousands of clip-art images and fonts), a virtual reality studio, and more.

As shown in Figure 9.7, Web.Graphics' WEB.DESIGNER component gives you a view of your Web page as you edit it. HTML and other elements can be dropped in, after which you can edit their attributes (size, labels, and so on) with a few mouse clicks.

WEB.DESIGNER lets you switch rapidly between the document view (shown in Figure 9.7), and the source code, and edit either. The program also validates in-progress or completed pages, finding and identifying errors.

Customizable button bars and word processor-like controls round out this powerful tool. There's also a spell-checking feature. Word processor documents can be converted to HTML documents, too, and the learning curve isn't bad; you can be creating a Web page or page elements ten minutes after you install the program. The only real downside to the program is the fact that a full install requires nearly 40 megabytes on your hard disk.

As noted, Corel provides a suite of programs for Web designers in one package. The program

FIGURE 9.7

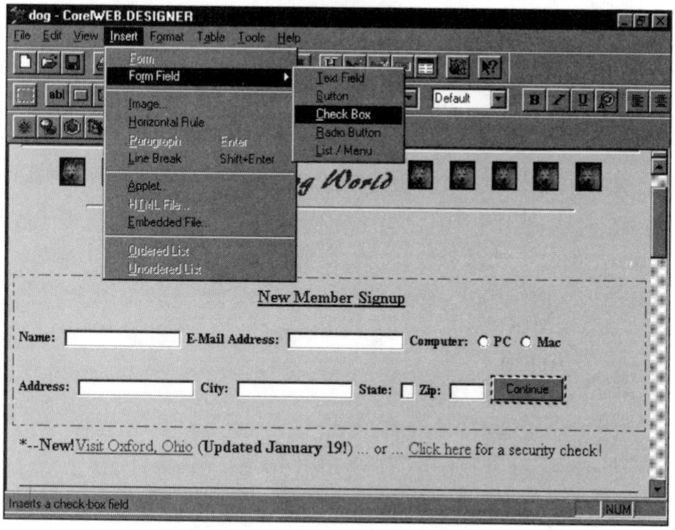

Corel's Web.Graphics' WEB.DESIGNER provides WYSIWYG editing

FIGURE 9.8

The WEB.DRAW component of Corel's Web. Graphics Suite can handle almost any graphic editing chore

package has far too many features and functions to cover here. However, I can say that this is probably the most comprehensive package going, with everything—including static and animated graphics, virtual reality artwork, and templates—you will need to create a professional Web site. Highly recommended. For more information, visit Corel's Web site at: **http://www. corel.com/**.

Links to additional tools for Web site building can be found at this URL: **http://www.w3.org/pub/WWW/Tools/**. A smaller, but better-organized list exists at: **http://www.uh.edu/www_resources/web_authoring.html**.

CREATING AND EDITING GRAPHICS

If you've spent much time with Windows Paint, you know that it's not the tool you need for creating and editing Web site graphics. Paint's drawing capabilities are fine for line art, and also more sophisticated art, if you have a good eye. But Paint's limited range of file formats and editing tools can leave you frustrated.

Fortunately, three programs are available that can easily give you all you need to create and fine-tune all your Web graphics. They are the WEB.DRAW component of Corel's Web.Graphics Suite; the powerful shareware standard, Paint Shop Pro; and for creating image maps, Boutell.Com's Mapedit.

Corel's WEB.DRAW

If you have Corel's Web.Graphics Suite, you have available a graphics-editing tool that will probably do everything you want. Shown in Figure 9.8, the WEB. DRAW component offers just about everything there is in editing—from sizing, to coloring and shading, to effects, and more.

WEB.DRAW also lets you create image maps. Finally, the Web. Graphics Suite comes with 7,500 ready-to-use graphics.

(Note that some servers require server-specific coding of image maps, in which case tools like this won't be useful.)

Paint Shop Pro

If your HTML editing needs are covered, but you need a good graphics editor, you could do worse than Paint Shop Pro. This venerable program, which has been around almost as long as Windows, is an ideal tool for fast edits, file conversions, screen captures, and colorizing.

As detailed in Chapter Six, Paint Shop Pro can handle all kinds of editing tasks. Its capabilities are particularly useful when you are resizing an image or for other reasons, you need to improve an image's viewing quality. (For a more complete overview of the program, see Chapter Six.)

Because it has so many applications, Paint Shop Pro should be on your system. You can download the program at this URL: **http://www.jasc.com/**.

Mapedit

Image maps are a great way to liven up your site. Rather than a scattered group of text links, an image map presents all links in a graphical fashion. This is often more efficient than text links, and it is certainly more attractive.

Image maps are a step beyond clickable graphics (discussed previously). An image map graphic is divided into regions, each of which is associated, or linked to, an URL or an object.

To make an image map, you need either knowledge of how to write the code for it (a cumbersome and tricky process), or a special tool. This sort of tool is provided with the Soft-Quad and Corel tools, which I discussed earlier. However, if you

FIGURE 9.9

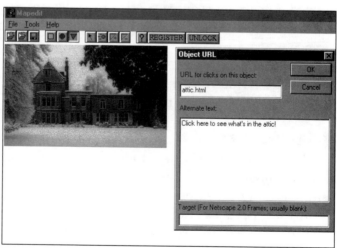

Mapedit simplifies the task of creating image maps

already use other tools for HTML creation or don't want to tie up hard drive space with those tools, you may want a dedicated image mapmaking tool.

The best offering in this category I have seen is a shareware program: Mapedit by Boutell.Com. This program will have you slicing up images in minutes. As shown in Figure 9.9, Mapedit's approach to creating an image map is fairly simple.

When you start Mapedit, it asks for the name of the HTML document for which you want to create an image map. When you provide the filename, Mapedit gives you a menu of all the images associated with the document. From this list you select an image to map.

The image you select is loaded, and you are ready to mark out the image map's regions and provide the URLs associated with each region.

The actual mapping, or marking of regions, is simple. Mapedit provides rectangle, triangle, and circle tools for outlining desired regions. There's also a special tool for odd-shaped regions.

After you outline a region, Mapedit asks for the URL to be linked to it, and other information.

In Figure 9.9, I used the triangle tool to outline the top of the house (the attic). When I completed that, Mapedit displayed a dialog in which I entered the URL for the link. The rest of the image would be mapped similarly.

Mapedit can create either client-side or server-side image maps. (A client-side map operates on the user's computer; a server-side map operates on the server.) Note that only newer versions of Web browsers (Navigator and Explorer version 3 and later) support client-side image maps. Server-side image maps may require special installation; consult the Mapedit documentation and check with your ISP regarding the installation of a server-side image map.

Fast and easy to use, Mapedit should serve all your needs. For more information or to download the program, visit this URL: **http://www.boutell. com/mapedit/**. Highly recommended.

KEEPING TRACK

After your Web site is published, you will want to have some idea of how many people visit it. This is easily accomplished by adding a counter to your site's home or index page. Your ISP may offer such a counter.

If your ISP doesn't offer a counter, other sources are available to which you can link. These are free for non-commercial or small commercial Web sites. Commercial sites getting a large number of hits are charged a very small fee for the use of the counters.

There are additional statistics that you can employ other than how many times someone visits your Web site. With the proper aids, you can learn everything from how many visitors use which kind of operating system and browser, to the peak days and hours for visitors, and the pages from which they came.

This section looks at online helpers for counting page visits and gathering statistics on the visitors to your site.

Counters

The most basic, and the most popular, statistic you can have is the number of browsers who visit a given Web page. Almost every site you visit has a counter, registering the number of "hits" or times the home or another page has been loaded by browsers.

For this reason, page counters are much in demand. They're provided by almost every ISP. If your ISP doesn't supply a counter, or if you want to place additional counters around your pages, you can turn to several resources. These services are provided at no charge, or for an extremely low fee (based on the number of hits you receive each month; usually two or three dollars).

Among the most popular of Web counters is the Web Counter Information Service. Located at **http://www.digits.com/**, this service offers both free and low-cost commercial counters. You can set up counters for as many pages as you want, and several options are available. As with ISP-offered counters, all you have to do is create a link to the counter on the page to be counted, using HTML code that Web Counter Information Service provides.

Visitor Demographics

If you need specific information about your Web site's visitors beyond the number of visits to a page, that's available, too. Your ISP may provide information from the system log for a fee, or at no charge to business customers.

If you want an alternate statistic source for your Web pages, or if your ISP doesn't provide statistics, you can turn to any of a number of services and tools that track all kinds of information about the visitors to your Web site. Among the better of these services is WebTracker. Linked to your page with a couple of lines of code and one of several icons, WebTracker provides a surprising number of statistics. Some of these are shown in the portion of a WebTracker online report in Figure 9.10.

The information available includes:
• Total number of visitors since inception

- Number of days in operation, and average number of hits per day

- The number and percentage of hits that are return visits

- Types of browsers used by visitors, with the number and percentage of total of each

- Operating systems used by visitors, with the number and percentage of total of each

- From which domain types visitors originate

- Hits by day of the week, and hour of the day

Each statistic is presented numerically and graphically, as shown in Figure 9.10. You also can provide access to a limited range of these statistics, in the same format, to visitors.

You can gather statistics on one or more pages of your Web site. You only need to sign up a page at the WebTracker site (**http://www.fxweb.holowww. com/tracker/index.shtml**), and then add the code provided to the page you want tracked. When you want to check statistics, you go to another URL and enter your ID and password.

WebTracker is a service of FXWeb Web Technologies. It is free for small, non-commercial sites. Larger sites are charged based on number of hits monthly.

Utility programs are also available that get statistics directly from your ISP's server logs. These are a bit tricky to install for beginners, but they can be set up to provide as much as (or more information than) a service like WebTracker.

FIGURE 9.10

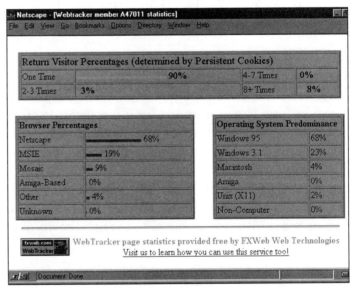

WebTracker tells you all about your site's visitors

Two such programs are WebTrends, by e.g. Software (**http://www.egsoftware. com/**) and Boutell.Com's Wusage (**http://www.boutell.com/wusage/**).

GETTING THE WORD OUT: PUBLICIZING YOUR SITE

The greatest Web site in the world is nothing without visitors. Therefore, you want to do everything possible to get the word out about your site.

You can spend a lot of time posting announcements of your site at online classified ad sites, on online service message boards, and in Usenet newsgroup topics *where such postings are permitted.* However, you will be wasting your time, for the most part. Such announcements are usually lost among quasi-commercial, drek-touting, multilevel marketing or get-rich-quick schemes. Those who do read them tend to class legitimate announcements with the scams that permeate public posting venues.

A more practical approach is to place information about your Web site with the places people go to find Web sites—with search engines.

The major search engines offer a means of adding your Web site to their listings, often using keywords that you provide. Most engines also add your pages' content to their indexes, so that your site can be found by both a search phrase and keywords.

Some of the major search engines to which you can add your listings include:

AltaVista	**http://altavista.digital.com/**
Excite	**http://www.excite.com/**
HotBot	**http://www.hotbot.com/**
Infoseek	**http://www.infoseek.com/**
Lycos	**http://www.lycos.com**
WebCrawler	**http://wc1.webcrawler.com/**
Yahoo!	**http://www.yahoo.com**

(Yahoo! is what is sometimes called a "hierarchical index" because it consists of entries arranged in various groups, or hierarchies, even though it is searchable.)

Check out a few of these to see what the submission procedures are.

There are a number of other search engines, but these are a good start. There also are directories galore, for business, personal, and special interest. In fact, there are several hundred of each, worldwide.

The idea of submitting information about your Web site so many places is a bit daunting. Fortunately, services exist that do this for you. Some of these services take information you provide one time and contact the search engines. Others help you compile the information required by each search engine, and pass it along.

Submit-It is one of the better—known submission services. Shown in part in Figure 9.11, the Submit-It submission form provides lots of flexibility, and submits to multiple Web sites for you.

FIGURE 9.11

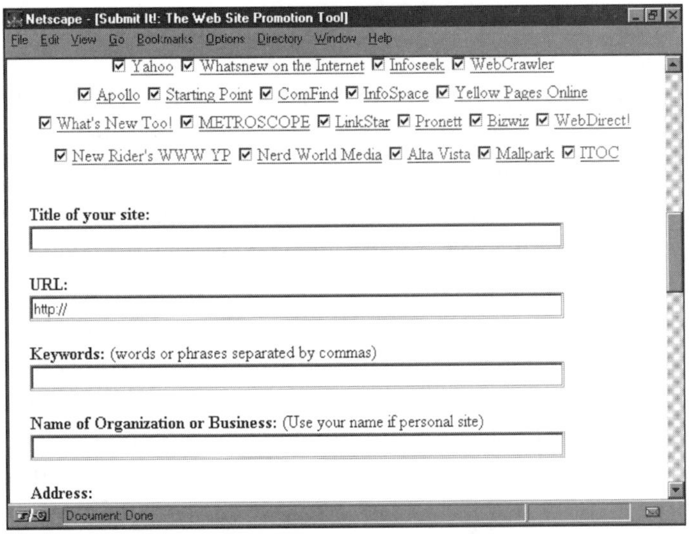

Submit-It publicizes your Web site to search engines and Internet directories

The Submit-It service is connected with some 300 search engines and directories worldwide, on a selective basis. The service is free for individuals and businesses, to a certain extent. To take full advantage of the service, you should register. Take a look at Submit-It for yourself at: **http://www.submit-it.com**.

An ancillary service provided by Submit-It is the Internet Link Exchange. Located at: **http://www.submit-it.com/sublink.htm**, the Internet Link Exchange is a free service that sets up members to display links for other members.

Another URL submission service is PostMaster. This fee-based service submits your site's information to more than 400 other sites. PostMaster is located at: **http://www.netcreations.com/postmaster/**.

Yet another fee-based Web site promotion service is WebPromote (**http://www.webpromote.com/**). This is a fairly effective, fee-based promotion service.

There are many more such services. For an extensive listing, visit this URL: **http://www.lehigh.net/zuzu/weblink.htm**, and click on "getting your Website seen."

Spam

Although it may seem to be an excellent idea, sending an announcement directly to thousands, hundreds of thousands, or millions of Internet users can be a complete disaster.

You will often find on the Web or in your E-mail box solicitations offering to sell you thousands of E-mail addresses. There also are offers by services to send your "commercial message" to thousands of "eager buyers."

Do not send out bulk E-mail, or have it sent for you! Do not send out unsolicited commercial E-mail, in bulk or otherwise!

Doing so is known as "spamming," and spam—the unsolicited commercial messages so often sent out—is the plague of the Internet.

If you do send spam to a mailing list, or have it sent for you, you will learn how unwanted and universally hated this kind of unsolicited commercial E-mail is. You will receive dozens, hundreds, or more E-mail messages. At the very least, these messages will demand that you stop E-mailing to the sender. Some will carry threats. Most will express anger, some with—and some without—profanity and vituperativeness.

A large number of recipients will complain to your ISP. This may result in you losing your Internet access account and Web hosting service. Some recipients may also decide to give your advertising back to you a thousand-fold, or more, by sending thousands of copies of your E-mail back to you. This will fill up your E-mail box, and maybe overload your ISP's resources.

Two or three expressions of interest—which is about all you can expect—are not worth all this grief. Those who sell the lists and mailing services will tell you that they send only to those who want commercial E-mail, and that you will have a guaranteed percentage of sales. At best, they are exaggerating; at worst, they are lying in order to sell their "product." I have on file dozens of comments from those who have tried selling legitimate products by spamming. They are unanimous in saying that they will never do it again. (Most of them were taken in by the promises of the list-sellers and mailers, and had no knowledge of "spam.")

The only people who make money from spamming are the list-sellers and mailers. You stand to lose time and maybe your Internet service and Web site; they stand to lose nothing.

If this isn't enough to convince you that bulk E-mail is a bad idea, consider this: well over 70 percent of bulk E-mail (based on a sample of 2,000 E-mail spams I have collected) are multilevel marketing schemes, or other scams. If you try to market a legitimate product using bulk E-mail, you will be lumped in with the con artists and scamsters. Which, of course, turns potential customers against you.

Other Online Helpers for Your Web Site

Besides counters and Web statistic reporting services, you may find several other useful sorts of services.

For openers, there are services that report to your visitors when pages at your site have been modified. This is a convenience appreciated by those who have a solid interest in your products or your site's topics. A service called "URL-Minder" (**http://www.netmind.com**) will send those who have signed up at your Web site an E-mail notice when you make changes to your pages. This is a free service.

For those who want to have their HTML coding tested, there's a service that does it online, for free. Visit "A Kinder, Gentler HTML Validator." This service validates documents by URL. Enter the URL in the form provided, wait a few seconds, and the Validator provides a full report on the HTML document on your screen. The URL for this service is: **http://ugweb.cs.ualberta. ca/~gerald/validate/**.

An interesting service is the GIF Wizard, at: **http://www.raspberryhill. com/gifwizard.html**. If you enter the URL and name of a GIF file on a page at your Web site, GIF Wizard will analyze the image and give you a complete report on optimizing the image for size.

While not a service, but definitely an online utility, the CyberSpyder Link Test can be used to check your site's links to make sure they are still valid. This is an important concern, since Web sites often appear and disappear rapidly, thus rendering links to them useless. A shareware program for Windows, the CyberSpyder Link Test is available for download at: **http://www.cyberspyder.com/cslnkts1.html**.

PRODUCTS & SERVICES MENTIONED

■ HTML Tutorials and References

A Beginner's Guide to HTML
http://www.ncsa.uiuc.edu/General/Internet/WWW/HTMLPrimer.html

Desktop Publishing & Web Design Links
http://www.lehigh.net/zuzu/weblink.htm

HTML Reference Index
http://csugrad.cs.vt.edu/serversetup/htmldocsindex.html

HTML Reference Documents Listing
http://www.kersur.net/~polyvis/html.html

Web Page Authoring Reference/Resource Listing
http://www.uh.edu/www_resources/web_authoring.html

World Wide Web and HTML Tools Listing
http://www.w3.org/pub/WWW/Tools/

■ HTML Creation/Editing Software

Corel's Web.Graphics Suite
http://www.corel.com/

HoTMetaL PRO
http://www.softquad.com

Microsoft Internet Assistant for WORD 95
http://www.microsoft.com/msword/internet/ia/

Microsoft Internet Assistant for WORD 6.0
http://www.microsoft.com/msword/internet/ia/

■ Graphics Software

Corel's WEB.DRAW
http://www.corel.com/

Mapedit
http://www.boutell.com/mapedit/

Paint Shop Pro
http://www.jasc.com/

■ Online Web Support Services

A Kinder, Gentler HTML Validator
http://ugweb.cs.ualberta.ca/~gerald/validate/

GIF Wizard
http://www.raspberryhill.com/gifwizard.html

URL-Minder
http://www.netmind.com

Web Counter Information Service
http://www.digits.com/

WebTracker
http://www.fxweb.holowww.com/tracker/index.shtml

■ Web Support Software

CyberSpyder Link Test Utility for Windows
http://www.cyberspyder.com/cslnkts1.html

JJ Electronic Plaza
http://www.jjplaza.com

WebTrends, by e.g. Software
http://www.egsoftware.com/

Wusage
http://www.boutell.com/wusage/

■ Search Engines

AltaVista
http://altavista.digital.com/

Excite
http://www.excite.com/

HotBot
http://www.hotbot.com/

Infoseek
http://www.infoseek.com/

Lycos
http://www.lycos.com

WebCrawler
http://wc1.webcrawler.com/

Yahoo!
http://www.yahoo.com

▪ Web Site Announcements and Publicizing

Desktop Publishing & Web Design Links
http://www.lehigh.net/zuzu/weblink.htm

Internet Link Exchange
http://www.submit-it.com/sublink.htm

PostMaster
http://www.netcreations.com/postmaster/

Submit-It
http://www.submit-it.com.

WebPromote
http://www.webpromote.com/

▪ ISPs and Example Web Sites

iWORLD and Mecklermedia's ISP List
http://thelist.iworld.com

Providers of Commercial Internet Access Listing
http://www.celestin.com/pocia/

■ Web Site Hosts
(For Viewing Sample Web Pages)

AOL
http://members.aol.com

CompuServe
http://ourworld.compuserve.com

Concentric Network
http://www.concentric.net/club/community.html

Earthlink (Personal)
http://www.earthlink.net/company/business/

Earthlink (Business)
http://www.earthlink.net/company/free_web_ pages.html

Mindspring
http://www.mindspring.com/community/index.html

Prodigy
http://pages.prodigy.com

Sprynet
http://www.sprynet.com/ourworld/searchow/index.html

OneNet
http://www.one.net/explore/clients/

Important Add-Ons and Plug-Ins

As you learned in Chapter Four, plug-ins and add-ons are special kinds of utilities that expand or enhance a Web browser's capabilities. In this chapter, you will look at some plug-ins and add-ons in specific categories. You'll also find a list of must-have plug-ins and files.

BOOKMARK AND NAVIGATION HELPERS

Anyone who has been surfing the Web for more than a few months is familiar with the problems associated with bookmarks. The list of bookmarks displayed by your browser seems to grow endlessly. You can organize related links in folders, but even this can become cumbersome after you have added a few dozen links to your bookmark file. Before long, opening your bookmark list within your browser is like opening another poorly organized database.

As you might imagine, others have experienced the same problem, and there are some solutions available.

Putting It Online

A natural, if not obvious, solution for many has been to put their bookmarks on the Web. There's certainly enough room at your Web site to put up a page that contains all your bookmarks.

But, maybe you don't want your bookmark file there, and have to go through uploading a new page every time you add a bookmark. If this is the case, you'll be interested to know that there are some free Internet services that handle your bookmarks for you.

These services not only make your lists available on the Web, they also create lists for you. Two that I'll examine here are from Netscape and Microsoft, in support of their respective browsers. Another is an independent service.

Netscape's PowerStart Page. If you went through Netscape's online registration, you may have seen the Netscape PowerStart page. As shown in Figure 10.1, it neatly organizes links by category.

There are more categories and links on the page than are shown here; to reach other categories, you simply scroll up or down.

Links on the PowerStart page are a combination of those taken from lists provided by Netscape, and those you provide. Links are added on a special setup page, where you can add options such as a calendar and a notepad.

To check this out in more detail, visit this URL: **http://personal.netscape.com/custom/index.html**.

FIGURE 10.1

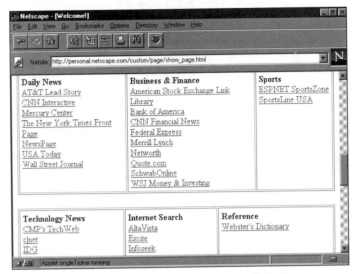

Netscape's PowerStart page organizes links for you

Microsoft Custom Page. Microsoft offers a service called "Microsoft Custom Page" based on the Microsoft Network. At first glance, the service seems to be similar to that offered by Netscape. However, it is little more than an advertising vehicle, and using the multiple pages of links it provides is bulky and cumbersome. Setup is equally difficult.

If you want to judge it for yourself, you can check out the Microsoft Custom Page service at: **http://www.msn.com/custom/workspace.htm**.

Do-It-Yourself with itList. If you find the Netscape or Microsoft pages impractical for whatever reason, take a look at the itList service. Billed as "The Web's First Online Bookmark Manager," the service is free.

After setting up your list with a password, you see a list similar to that shown in Figure 10.2.

You can add or remove bookmarks using tools at the site. (Your bookmark list is password-protected.) Or, you can send additions to your list via "E-mail." itList's automated system takes care of putting them on your page.

The only possible drawback here is the fact that anyone can view an itList user's bookmarks.

itList is located at: **http://www.itlist.com/**.

FIGURE 10.2

The itList service puts your bookmarks online

FIGURE 10.3

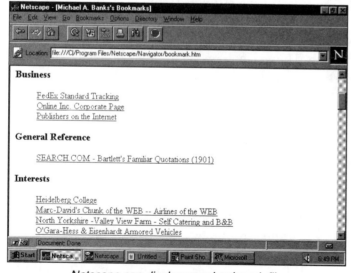

Netscape can display your bookmark file

Drawbacks to Keeping Your Bookmarks Online

There are a couple of potential drawbacks to having your bookmarks online. The main one is that, if the Internet's a bit slow, you may have to wait for your bookmark page to load. The other drawback is that you may run into a situation when an overloaded server, or a server that's down, will keep you from getting your bookmarks.

If either of these concern you and you use Netscape, you might consider this simplified approach: load Netscape's bookmark file. (It is an HTML file.)

Select Open File on your browser's File menu, and load the file, BOOKMARK.HTM. You should see something similar to the display shown in Figure 10.3.

As with an online bookmark page, you can load this any time you want—and fast. Better still, set the bookmark file as your "home page." On Netscape's Options menu, select General Preferences. Click on the Appearances tab. You will see a field labeled "Browser Starts

With." Enter **file:///C1/** followed by the location of your bookmark file.

(Note that the "Browser Starts With" selection cannot be changed in some free versions of Netscape that are widely distributed, such as the one available for download from CompuServe. Your best bet for full functionality is to either buy Netscape in a

FIGURE 10.4

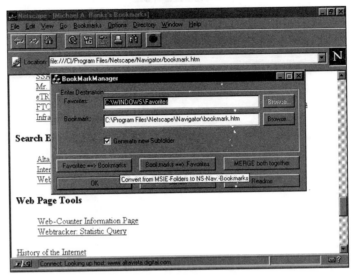

Bookmark Manager

package at your software store or download it from the Netscape Web site.)

With Explorer, select Options on the View menu, and press the Navigation tab. In the text box labeled "Address:" type **file:///C1/**, followed by the location of your bookmark file. (Be sure to enter this line correctly, exactly as shown, or you'll get an error message, and be locked out of changing this option.)

Now, whenever you press the "Home" icon on the toolbar or select Home on the Go menu, your bookmark page will load.

Bookmark Conversions

If you are switching from Netscape to Explorer, or vice-versa, you'll want to get a program that converts bookmark files between the two formats. These programs are also useful if you use both Netscape and Explorer, and need both browsers to use the same bookmarks.

These conversion programs are similar in form, but one of the better programs in terms of function is Bookmark Manager, shown in Figure 10.4.

Bookmark Manager, a shareware program, simplifies conversion between Netscape and Explorer bookmark files. As you can see in Figure 10.4, all you have to do is press a couple of buttons, and the job's done. (The default file locations are already entered for you.) This one is available at: **http://ourworld. compuserve.com/homepages/Edgar_Hofer/bookmm.htm**; or at: **http:// www.alberts.com/authorpages/00013289/bookmm.htm**. The program is available in both English and German.

SOUND AND AUDIO HELPERS

Most people associate 3-D images and video with "multimedia." However, sound—in the form of music, voices, and audio—seems to be the most prevalent element of multimedia on the Web. This is not surprising when you consider how quickly sound is delivered from the Web, compared to video. The faster speed is due to smaller files. Efficient technology also plays a part, such as "streaming audio," which is used to play sounds as the files are delivered.

RealAudio

RealAudio is the *de-facto* standard for voice delivery on the Net. It is used by sites that deliver a lot of speech content, such as MSNBC (**http://www.msnbc.com**). It's also the application of choice for the increasing number of radio stations that offer Internet broadcasts. (For a listing of Internet radio broadcasts and "events," see: **http://www.timecast.com/**.)

As detailed in Chapter Four, RealAudio is pretty much a plug-and-go application. After you've downloaded and installed it, you don't need to do anything else. When you click on a link or come to a site that offers sound clips, your browser starts the RealAudio player and loads the incoming sound. (You can save a clip after it has played. RealAudio files are remarkably small.)

RealAudio can be downloaded and demoed at: **http://www.realaudio.com**. Note that, as is the case with many other popular and free applications, customer service is not very satisfactory.

TrueSpeech

TrueSpeech is a plug-in for Netscape Navigator. (Microsoft's Internet Explorer has partial TrueSpeech capability built in—*if* it encounters TrueSpeech files in .WAV format, it can play the files.) TrueSpeech is designed to play sound clips created with TrueSpeech encoder.

TrueSpeech is getting quite a bit of support from the Net, although it still trails behind RealAudio in number of sites that support it.

You can check out the TrueSpeech and the free TrueSpeech encoder at: **http://www.dspg.com/internet.htm**.

CUSTOM NEWS FEEDS

One of the newest technologies of the Internet is that of intelligent agents. The most intriguing of these agents is PointCast.

PointCast

PointCast, about which you will hear quite a bit online and off, is a leading-edge application. Designed to bring multimedia news to Internet browsers, the

PointCast network (**http://www.pointcast.com/**) and its required software are provided free of charge.

Actually, PointCast is more than a news source; it also provides weather, market reports, and quite a bit of other information, all neatly categorized and presented as shown in Figure 10.5.

Supported by advertising, the PointCast Network has an astounding range of offerings. Among other services, it offers:

- Accuweather reports and maps

- CNN Headline News

- Reuters news

- Content from newspapers such as the *Los Angeles Times*, *Boston Globe*, and others.

- Information and articles from *Time*, *People*, and *Money* magazines

There's quite a bit more, of course, and PointCast seems to add more every week.

Obviously, the content is there, but getting at it can be time-consuming. I found that daily updates can take an hour—or much longer. At this point, PointCast is a service that requires you to have the latest in hardware and very fast links to the Internet. I recommend PointCast *only* if you have a fast Pentium, a fast modem, and a fast connection.

(In the corporate world of fast modems, fast connections, and distribution on fast LANs, PointCast *does* achieve what it sets out

FIGURE 10.5

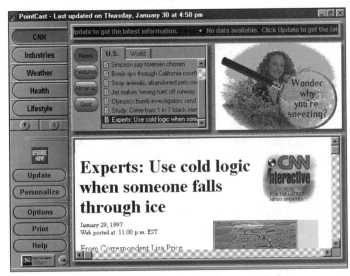

The PointCast Network brings needed information to your computer

to do. However, the rest of the world will have to wait until available technology catches up with a good idea.)

VIDEO HELPERS

Video on the Web is in its infancy. Links are often too slow to support the technology, and the Web has too much traffic to be able to count on consistent quality in real-time video. So, it is almost inevitable that there will be pauses, delays, and loss of synchronization during many real-time video transmissions.

Developers continue working on improvements to software designed to operate with existing technology. So, Web video may one day fulfill its promise—given improvements in Internet bandwidth as well as video software technology.

That aside, let's look at what is available now.

QuickTime

The Apple QuickTime plug-in for PCs is one of the *de-facto* standards for computer video. It enjoys a high degree of popularity, largely because it has been accepted by many as a multimedia standard.

QuickTime is a true multimedia tool. It performs these functions:
* Displays still images from disk files or embedded in Web pages (The resolution isn't always the best.)

* Loads and plays sound, music, and MIDI from disk files

* Plays sound and music files embedded in Web pages

* Displays video, with or without sound, from disk files

* Displays video, with or without sound, embedded in Web pages

As shown in Figure 10.6, QuickTime's movie player provides a nice

FIGURE 10.6

The QuickTime Multimedia Player is extremely flexible

background and virtual controls. Depending on the file it is displaying, it may be resized.

QuickTime can handle video files created in its own format, **.MOV**, and **.MPEG** files. More than 20,000 Web sites use QuickTime video. QuickTime's audio and video capabilities are also used on hundreds of commercial CD-ROM products.

To download QuickTime, visit this URL: **http://quicktime.apple.com/**.

Shockwave Director

Shockwave is probably the most popular multimedia application on the Web. It is used by CNN, Discovery Channel Online, Warner Brothers Records, General Motors, Kodak, and thousands of other Web sites to deliver streaming audio/music, streaming video, small-scale animations, and multimedia combinations thereof.

Shockwave comes in several components, each of which handles a different aspect of multimedia. Shockwave Director is the video end (with audio), and is probably the Shockwave application you will most frequently need. (It is a very popular front end for online games.) However, it is a good idea to get the entire Shockwave package.

For more information about Shockwave—and to download the program— visit Macromedia's Web site at: **http://www.macromedia.com**.

VDOLive

VDOLive is a real-time video application that holds a lot of potential. It is picking up some strong followers, including the American Film Institute and various recording companies (who are putting performer video/sound clips online). Shown in Figure 10.7, VDOLive offers simple controls, via a menu displayed by right-clicking the mouse.

FIGURE 10.7

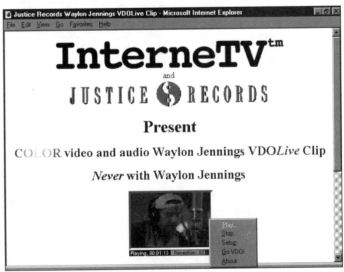

VDOLive at work

VDOLive is particularly good with streaming video—that is, managing sound and video in real time.

For more information and to download VDOLive, go to: **http://www .vdolive.com/**.

DOCUMENT HELP

For many years, the only practical way to make text available to others online was in the form of 7-bit ASCII files. This text could be shared by anyone who could get online, no matter what sort of computer they used.

Some people wanted to provide their documents to others, complete with formatting. These folks uploaded their files in their word processors' native formats. This attempt was a disaster; only those who used the same word processor and the same kind of computer as the uploader could access and successfully view that kind of file as the uploader intended it to look.

Obviously, there was a need for a document format that retained formatting and everyone could share.

Adobe Acrobat PDF Reader

This need was met by PDF (Portable Document Format). Interestingly, PDF has remained a consistent standard—a rarity in computing. There are hundreds of thousands of PDF files (distinguished by the extension **.PDF**) on the Web.

The PDF format was originated by Adobe (**http://www.adobe .com**). PDF files are created with Adobe Acrobat, a commercial program available for almost all computer systems. PDF files can be read by using a free program, Adobe Acrobat Reader.

Figure 10.8 shows a portion of a PDF document as viewed with the Adobe Acrobat Reader.

FIGURE 10.8

Adobe's free Acrobat Reader displays PDF documents, complete with formatting

The free Adobe Acrobat Reader allows you to view and print PDF files. When you install the Acrobat Reader, it automatically adds a plug-in for Netscape Navigator, and an ActiveX control for Internet Explorer.

The Acrobat Reader lets you browse and navigate documents with the scroll bars, or by page number, section, or other means. You can view the document in page-layout mode, while simultaneously displaying specific pages, as shown in Figure 10.8. A zoom feature lets you magnify or reduce the view of the document on your screen.

To learn more about the Adobe Acrobat PDF Reader, and to download it, go to: **http://www.adobe.com/prodindex/acrobat/readstep.html**.

ABSOLUTE MUST-HAVES

Of all the plug-ins and add-ons discussed in this book, and of those you will see on the Net, there are fewer than a dozen that can be considered absolute must-haves.

Files and programs that require these programs are prevalent throughout the Web. Do yourself a favor and download the required programs and files. These programs are:

Adobe Acrobat Reader
http://www.adobe.com/prodindex/acrobat/readstep.html

PKZIP and PKZIP for Windows
http://www.pkware.com/download.html

QuickTime
http://quicktime.apple.com/sw/

RealAudio
http://www.realaudio.com/hpproducts/player/index.html

Shockwave Director
http://www.macromedia.com/shockwave/download/

Visual Basic Runtimes
http://www.softseek.com/Utilities/VBRUN_Files/index.html

http://www.fys.ruu.nl/~beljaars/download.html

http://www.execnet. com/filelibs/l397p001.html

WinZip
http://www.winzip.com/

Again, applications for these programs and files are common throughout the Web. You need them almost anywhere you find sound, video, formatted documents, files for download, or programs written in the Visual Basic language.

PLUG-IN AND ACTIVEX CONTROL INFORMATION

For still more information on plug-ins and ActiveX controls, refer to Chapter Four and also visit these starting points on the Web:

ActiveX Controls
http://www.microsoft.com/ie/ie3/activex.htm

BrowserWatch ActiveX Arena
http://browserwatch.iworld.com/activex.html

BrowserWatch Plug-In Plaza
http://browserwatch.iworld.com/plug-in.html

Netscape Plug-Ins and Components
**http://home.netscape.com/comprod/mirror/navcomponents_
download.html**

SOFTWARE AND INFORMATION SOURCES

■ Plug-Ins and Add-Ons

Adobe Acrobat PDF Reader
http://www.adobe.com/prodindex/acrobat/readstep.html

Bookmark Manager
http://ourworld.compuserve.com/homepages/Edgar_Hofer/bookmm.htm

http://www.alberts.com/authorpages/00013289/bookmm.htm

PointCast
http://www.pointcast.com/

RealAudio
http://www.realaudio.com

http://www.timecast.com/

TrueSpeech
http://www.dspg.com/internet.htm

QuickTime
http://quicktime.apple.com/

Shockwave Director
http://www.macromedia.com

VDOLive
http://www.vdolive.com/

■ Browser-Related Services

itList
http://www.itlist.com/

Microsoft Custom Page
http://www.msn.com/custom/workspace.htm

Netscape's PowerStart Page
http://personal.netscape.com/custom/index.html

Getting Help
from the Internet

A s you know, the Internet is not a static resource. Internet elements like Usenet present an interactive venue. The same is true of many Web sites. Programs can be run on host computers to collect, organize, and do anything else with information that you can do on your desktop (and if you are a cell-phone/modem-toting road warrior, your laptop) PC.

Thanks to these capabilities, the Internet's resources have been turned to more than simply presenting information. The Internet can be used to find information—and provide help with using its many features.

In this chapter, you will examine some useful Web sites that help you with using the Internet. Some sites are information resources about the Internet, while others help you find the kind of general or specific information that you need.

FINDING INFORMATION ON THE INTERNET

The World Wide Web is the most evident—and the richest—of the Internet's knowledge repositories. Web pages host electronic versions of reference works, virtual museums of history and culture, current news, maps, essays, and much more. The Web is richly laden with photos, text, and even multimedia information resources that, in certain respects, rival some of the best libraries in the world.

Public discussion forums, including Usenet newsgroups and bulletin boards on commercial online services, also serve as information repositories and at times sources of information-on-demand. Professional online services, such as Dow Jones News/Retrieval, and Knight-Ridder's DIALOG, are available for the more advanced law, science, and business researchers.

In sum, the Internet's collective components offer the knowledge of millions of experts and researchers. To say that the quantity of information stored on tens of millions of Web pages is staggering is an understatement. It is a true treasure-trove, but getting at the treasure can be troublesome.

One problem is, how do you access all of this information? Far from being a well-organized library, with card catalogs and information neatly sorted, the Internet is an anarchy, with information scattered hither and yon, without form or order.

So, how do you go about finding specific information? How, for example, can you find information on Muslim life in the 19th-century Russian Empire? Who do you ask? Is there a Web site for it? If so, what is the address? How can you know whether this information even exists?

The answer to this question—and the key to finding almost anything on the Internet—is the "Search engine."

Search Tools for the Web

Search engines are as close to card catalogs or indices as you will find on the Web. Search engines use sophisticated software to catalog tens of millions of Web pages worldwide. Frequently updated, the catalogs are placed at your disposal in searchable format.

Search engines exist as Web sites. Visit one, and you will find a form into which you can enter a "query." Figure 11.1 shows this kind of form. (This is AltaVista, located at: **http://altavista.digital.com/**.)

The search engine uses your query to assemble a list of Web pages that meet the criteria specified by your query. (Several of the results of a search can be seen in Figure 11.1.)

The listing is actually a temporary custom menu in hypertext format. You select items (URLs) on it by clicking on them. Most search engines offer you a choice of how items in a list are displayed—with terse or verbose explanations, or in context.

FIGURE 11.1

Search Terms and Searches. The entire search process begins with your query. Do not let the term "query" mislead you. You can't usually just type a question; you have to tell the search engine to find what you want by using *keywords* or *phrases*. These textual elements are also known as *search terms*.

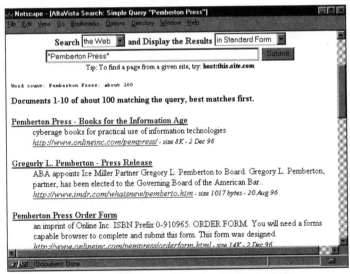

The AltaVista search form and results list

A *keyword* is a word associated with the information you want to find. Just as you enter a last name when you want to find someone in a name-and-address database, you enter an associated word when searching for information on a certain topic.

For example, a keyword for finding information on Muslim life in the 19th-Century Russian Empire would be "Muslim." However, if you enter this in a search engine's query form, you will see a listing with something on the order of 40,000 Web pages, which is obviously too many pages to wade through. You want to do something to *narrow* your search.

Narrowing a search reduces the number of "hits" a query returns. It is accomplished by limiting the range of the search. This can be done by specifying an additional keyword.

If you are lucky, there will be an unusual word, such as "mitochondria," associated with your subject. Using this kind of word for a search term will return a list of very few documents.

Content and Summary Searches. Before I show you how to narrow a search, it may help for you to know what is happening in the background during a search.

Most Internet search engines look for the information you request based on the actual content of Web pages. Therefore, if you query a search engine with a keyword, you are asking it to show you all Web pages that contain the keyword. A word such as "Muslim" will return a list of all kinds of Web pages—current events, news, religious essays, personal resumes, and just about any document that you might expect to contain the word.

Although, strictly speaking, this kind of search is a *content search*, it might be considered a "subject search." This search is very broad, and in effect turns up anything to do with a subject. Your search can be refined, as you learn in the following section, to yield very precise results.

A few search engines index Web pages and/or Web sites are based on criteria created by those who operate them. A summary of a given document or site is created and this, rather than the document itself, is searched. Or, a set of keywords attached to the summary is used in a search.

This kind of search is called a *summary search*, which is sometimes faster than a complete content search. However, results depend on the accuracy and relevancy of concept keywords attached to the document, or words included in the summary. Summary searches are not always useful if you are seeking a specific phrase. Also, you will have to put a little more effort into a summary search, trying to second-guess what words a summary writer may have considered appropriate.

Narrowing a Search. Knowing that a search engine looks at the entire content of every Web page it catalogs, you have a better idea of how to narrow, or refine, your search. To limit the number of hits, you have to get specific. So, you add a couple of keywords. In this case, maybe "Russian" and "19th." These keywords tell the search engine that you want to see *only* Web pages that contain the words "Muslim," "Russian," and "19th." This narrows the search, and returns fewer Web pages, few enough that you can go through a listing manually and find what you want.

If you still didn't find what you want with a narrowed search, you might *widen* or *expand* the search by removing one of the keywords. Or, you might try an entirely new set of keywords.

Note that each search engine operates a little differently. There are variations in how you enter multiple keywords. For example, one of the most comprehensive and powerful search engines on the Web, AltaVista (refer to Figure 11.1), requires that you enter multiple keywords like this:

+Muslim +Russian +19th

This example shows how you tell AltaVista that you want to see all Web pages that contain "Muslim" AND "Russian" AND "19th"—also known as an *AND search*. Without the **+** signs, AltaVista interprets this request as, "Show me all Web pages that contain ANY of these words." (That is, "Muslim" OR "Russian" OR "19th.") This approach—called an *OR search*—would give you a list of a few hundred thousand Web pages—obviously, not what you want.

Another search engine may require only that you enter multiple keywords separated by spaces to perform an AND search. Requirements for entering search terms vary from one search engine to another. Each search engine offers details about how to enter search terms for specific results. Read them!

A few search engines offer advanced versions of the AND/OR searches, employing *Boolean logic*. With them, you can specify operators, such as AND, OR, and even NOT, to include documents that have a given phrase, but which do not have a given word in addition.

Scored Results. Some search engines, such as Lycos (**http://www.lycos.com**) shown in Figure 11.2, cannot easily do AND searches, and will interpret by default a multiple keyword entry as an OR search. However, search engines that operate in this manner usually give you a "scored" list of results (also called *relevancy ranking*). This means Web pages that contain all three words are listed first, those with two of the three words second, and so on.

Search Controls. Only a few search engines have buttons or selections to specify an AND or OR search with multiple keywords. A search engine known as "HotBot" (Figure 11.3) is one of these kinds of engines.

Search Phrases. With many search engines, you can use phrases as search terms. This technique is useful when you are searching for documents based on a phrase that they ought to contain. (Note that you may find this disappointing; not everyone thinks in the same way, and the phrase that you think should be in any document about a given topic actually may be in none, but it is worth a try.) Enter something like "Muslim life in the 19th-Century Russian Empire," and you will see a list of all Web pages that contain that

FIGURE 11.2

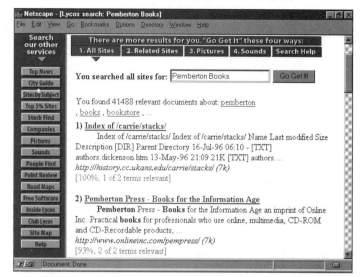

A "scored" listing of search results, created by Lycos

FIGURE 11.3

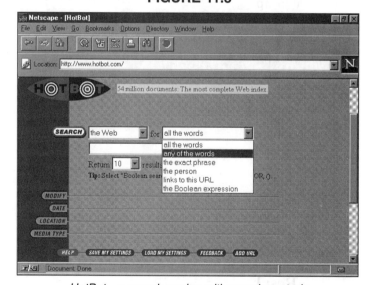

HotBot—a search engine with search controls

literal phrase—all of those words, in that specific order.

(For the curious: there really is a Web site devoted to this somewhat obscure topic. The URL is: **http://www.uoknor.edu/cybermuslim/russia/rus_home. html**.)

A final flourish that some search engines offer is the capability to narrow searches by making selections on a form. These additions allow you to specify an AND or an OR search, and to limit your search to a certain category of Web pages. Excite, Infoseek, and Deja News, among others, offer these kinds of controls.

FIGURE 11.4

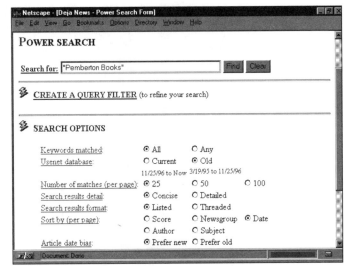

Deja News, a Usenet search tool

Major Search Engines

There are several hundred search engines on the Web. Many are redundant—they offer the same data as other similar engines. So, here is a list of the major search engines. The following list shows the most popular and effective search tools on the Web:

AltaVista
http://altavista.digital.com/

C:NET's Search.Com
http://www.search.com

Excite
http://www.excite.com/

HotBot
http://www.hotbot.com/

Infoseek
http://www.infoseek.com/

Lycos
http://www.lycos.com

WebCrawler
http://wc1.webcrawler.com/

Yahoo!
http://www.yahoo.com

(NOTE: Yahoo! is actually an index of Web sites. Rather than searching the content of pages based on a keyword or phrase, Yahoo! presents lists of pages organized by topic and subtopic.)

Several of these search engines—Excite, HotBot, Infoseek, Lycos, and Yahoo!—let you do general subject searches by browsing categories of Web pages, each of which has subcategories. Thus, a government category may offer "State" and "Federal" subcategories, with each of these offering additional subcategories. Imagine this structure as an inverted pyramid approach to manual searching.

Note that many of these search engines can be directed to search either Web pages, or Usenet newsgroups. AltaVista, Excite, Infoseek, and Yahoo! offer this option. A few can even be directed to search reviews or current news for your keyword or phrase.

Specialized Search Engines

There are a large number of specialized search engines, many of which are actually just specialized databases. These are devoted to specific subject areas, such as chemistry, medical, and history. There are far too many to list here, but you can get several lists of specialized search engines using AltaVista. Go to: **http://altavista.digital.com/**, and enter this search term, including the quotes:

"Specialized Search Engines"

Doing so results in a list of several dozen specialized search engines.

Searching Usenet Newsgroups

Usenet newsgroups are an interesting source of information (and often entertainment) on just about any subject. The ratio of useless posts and chatter to useful information in newsgroups is rather high, but it is possible to isolate relevant messages or threads, and, therefore, get useful information—or find people who have the information you need.

There are nearly 20,000 newsgroup topics. (For a current listing of newsgroups visit this URL: **http://www.yahoo.com/news/usenet**.) The sheer size of the list obviously implies an impossible job, if you had to search newsgroups manually.

As noted previously, several search engines can be directed to search Usenet newsgroups. These engines are invaluable when you want to examine current (or past) discussions on a given topic. The same search rules apply with regard to search terms as when you are searching the Web. A good search tool for newsgroups is Deja News, shown in Figure 11.4.

Located at: **http://www.dejanews.com/forms/dnq.html**, this search engine is tied to an archive of current and past postings in nearly every newsgroup in existence. The archive database is searchable by keyword or phrase, with push buttons that let you specify whether current or old Usenet postings are searched, the order in which results are displayed, and so on.

FIGURE 11.5

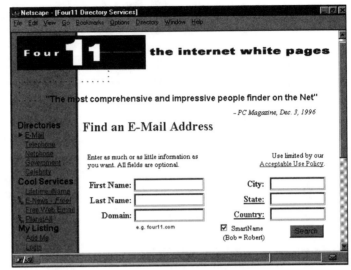

Four11.Com finds E-mail addresses based on names

The Deja News database currently has newsgroup postings back to 1994. It eventually will contain virtually every posting since Usenet's inception in 1979.

Finding People. As you might expect, there are several ways to locate people online. If you are on a consumer online service such as AOL, CompuServe, DELPHI, or Prodigy, you will find searchable member directories. These directories let you search on varying criteria ranging from name, city and state, country, hobbies, interests, and so forth. Inclusion in these directories is voluntary on the part of the consumer online service members.

The Internet has no member directory. However, you can find an E-mail address or ID for someone who you know is online. You also can figure out who is behind an online ID (that is, to do a "reverse lookup" on the ID).

Most "people information" on the Internet is available at Web sites hosting directories. Some sites contain postal address and telephone numbers as well as E-mail addresses.

Perhaps the best-known of E-mail address resources is Four11.Com (located at: **http://www.four11.com**). As shown in Figure 11.5, it consists of a simple form for entering the information you know. Four11's database presents a list of all E-mail addresses that meet the search criteria that you enter.

You can do the reverse at Internet Address Finder (**http://www.iaf.net**). Give this search tool an E-mail address, and it provides you with the owner's name and other info—provided that information is in its database. IAF also searches for E-mail addresses based on real names.

If the E-mail address for which you want to find a name is not at one of the commercial online services, you may be able to find the name using a utility known as "finger." Finger is a program built into most Web servers, which provides information about a given E-mail address.

There are Web interfaces for finger at: **http://www.magibox.net/~unabest/ finger/index.html** and **http://cs.indiana.edu/finger/gateway**. Just enter the E-mail address (*xxxx@xxx*.com). If the finger program is enabled by the ISP and there is user information available, you will see it. (At the very least, the information available should be the user's real name.) Note that not all ISPs are finger enabled, nor are most consumer online services.

Other E-mail search tools include:

PeopleFinder
http://www.peoplesite.com/indexnf.html

Lycos PeopleFind
http://www.lycos.com/pplfnder.html

Switchboard
http://www.switchboard.com/

WhoWhere? E-mail Addresses
http://www.whowhere.com/

Yahoo Individual White Page Reference
http://www.yahoo.com/Reference/White_Pages/Individuals/

If you want to be comprehensive when searching for someone, you might try the All-in-One Search Page (**http://www.albany.net/allinone/all1user. html**). This tool combines several of the people finders just mentioned, along with several more.

Finding Businesses Online. As with people finders, there are several business locators online, which allow you to search for businesses by category. (Note that these are not "people" finders.) The most common of these are "online Yellow Pages."

Among other locations, yellow pages can be found at:

AT&T 800 Directory
http://www.tollfree.att.net/dir800/

Companies Online
http://www.companiesonline.com

EUROPAGES
http://www.europages.com/home-en.html

Switchboard
http://www.switchboard.com/

Yahoo! (Select "Yellow Pages" on the menu.)
http://www.yahoo.com/

YellowNet
http://www.yellownet.com/

Caveat. Not all information you find on the Internet is accurate. Many Web sites are established by people who have a personal agenda, or for whatever other reasons slant information in a certain direction. This slanting may consist of omitting information, presenting opinion as fact because of personal beliefs, or lying outright.

This phenomenon isn't limited to Web sites created by individuals or fringe groups. Even news reports from "legitimate" sources are often slanted. More factual information, posted by "experts," organizations such as museums or colleges, or whomever, should also be viewed with just a pinch of skepticism.

Also, some well-meaning individuals may post partially false or incomplete information because they are not as informed as they should be on a given subject.

My advice is simple: if the information seems inconsistent, check it against one or more other sources.

I'm not saying that most information online is suspect. Only a portion of online information is misleading or untrue. However, because there is no requirement for fact-checking or accuracy online, you should always verify the validity of online information.

Do not assume that everything on the Internet is accurate. Approach it pragmatically as a series of databases, commentary, and expert sources, and you will find the Internet to be a valuable research resource.

ONLINE REFERENCES

The best place to go for detailed help with the Internet is often the Internet itself. You can also find help with using specific applications—like your Web browser—online.

Hypertext, the language of the Web, is an excellent tool for presenting tutorials, reference works, and just about any other information that uses examples and refers to other information sources. What might be a footnote, an appendix item, or another document entirely in a book is only a mouse-click away on the Web. Many references are searchable, as well. (And remember: you can always use your browser's search function to look for specific text on any page you're currently viewing. Select "Search" on the Edit menu to open the search dialog box.)

Therefore, online references are well worth checking out and—in some cases—adding to your bookmark list. This goes for Internet-related topics and others.

We'll take a quick look at some of the better examples of these kinds of references here.

FINDING ONLINE REFERENCES & GUIDES

Your first exposure to online help may well involve your browser. Both Netscape and Microsoft offer extensive online help for those who use their products.

As noted in Chapter Two, Netscape has seen fit to put the entire manual for their browser at their Web site. Located at Netscape's Web site, it is available by selecting Handbook on Netscape's Help menu.

Online help for Microsoft's Internet Explorer is available at: **http://www. microsoft.com/iesupport/**. Selecting Online Support on Explorer's Help menu gets you there.

The list of online references and other resources is almost unending, and the amount of information that is available online is surprising, especially when you consider that so much of it is or might be copyrighted, and perhaps sold in another form. Many lists are provided by organizations, or by companies as a promotional vehicle.

You can find a large number of general references on the Internet. For example, the ninth (1901) edition of *Bartlett's Familiar Quotations* is online at: **http://www.columbia.edu/acis/bartleby/bartlett/**. This searchable first edition is out of copyright and is an interesting resource.

Encyclopedic references are available in plenty. The CIA's World Factbook (**http://www.odci.gov/cia/publications/95fact/index.html**) offers a compendium of information about politics, societies, cultures, geography, and other aspects of the nations of the world. The Encyclopedia Smithsonian (**http://www.si.edu/resource/faq/start.htm**) is a marvelous science and natural history reference.

The list goes on. There are dictionaries, almanacs, and many other general references.

Getting more specific, the eclectic mix of references on the Internet also includes:

A listing of Chambers of Commerce nationwide
http://chamber-of-commerce.com/

A Yellow-Page listing of businesses that are online, provided by Dun & Bradstreet
http://www.companiesonline.com/

The most comprehensive listing of book publishers' Web sites on the Internet
http://www.faxon.com/Internet/publishers/pubs.html

The Thomas Register
http://www.thomasregister.com/

Federal Express package tracking
http://www.fedex.com/track_it.html

A daily Web stock report for 300 NYSE stocks
http://www.stockmaster.com/

Some of these sites are free, while some carry charges.

The list is virtually endless—and constantly changing. To locate more current and manageable lists of online references, use search engines.

FIGURE 11.6

An online menu of reference resources created by WebCrawler

Using Search Engines to Access Online References

Search engines are useful for locating online references by category. Usually, you can enter the topic with which you need help, and you get a list of possible sources. However, this can be time-consuming, unless you can narrow the search sufficiently to make manual browsing practical.

For example, you can enter the search term, "online encyclopedias" at AltaVista or WebCrawler (**http://wc1.webcrawler.com**) to see a list of online encyclopedias.

A better approach is to use the browsable lists offered by certain search engines. At WebCrawler, you will find a selection tagged "Reference." Click on it, and you go to: **http://wc2.webcrawler.com/select/ref.new.html**, where you see a submenu listing these topics:

Business	Maps
Computers	Phone Books
Consumer Guides	Quotations
Dictionaries	Research
E-mail Addresses	Science
Encyclopedias	Travel
Government	TV Schedules
Health	Web Search
History	ZIP & Area Codes

Each of these links leads to another menu of specific sites. Select a site, and you get a review and a link to the site in question. As shown in Figure 11.6, the menu is compact and simple to use.

Similar menus of reference information can be found at:

Excite (business references)
http://www.excite.com/Reviews/Business/?a-Rb-t

Infoseek (small business reference directory)
http://www.infoseek.com/Business/Small_business?tid=484

Lycos
http://a2z.lycos.com/News_and_Information/Reference_Information/

Yahoo!
http://www.yahoo.com/Reference/

SELECTED INTERNET REFERENCES AND GUIDES

These Internet-related online references will be of particular interest if you are learning about the Internet, browsers, plug-ins and add-ons, and creating Web sites.

■ Using the Internet

EEF's Extended Guide to the Internet
http://www.eff.org/papers/eegtti/eegtti.html

InterNIC Information and Education Resources
http://rs.internic.net/nic-support/

Online Internet Course from Oberlin College
http://www-ts.cs.oberlin.edu/wt95/wt95home.html

Realizing the Full Potential of the Web
http://www.w3.org/pub/www/

Using the Internet for Competitive Intelligence
http://www.cio.com/CIO/arch_0695_cicolumn.html

■ Using Web Browsers

Getting Started with Netscape
http://www-acs.ucsd.edu/using-mosaic.html

QuickTutors 95
http://www.windows95.com/deals/index.html

Using Netscape
http://www.pipex.co.za/solo/netscape.html

Using the Microsoft Internet Explorer
http://www.gsmdata.com/msie.htm

Using Web Browsers
http://www.traverse.com/TCCInfo/TCCNews/web.html

■ Plug-Ins, Controls, and Add-On Programs

ACTIVEX.COM
http://www.activex.com/library/mult.html

Best Netscape Plug-Ins
http://www.earthcon.com/plugins/

Internet ActiveX Controls FAQ
http://www.microsoft.co.jp/visual/icp/jp/icpmain/icpfaq.htm

Netscape Plug-Ins and Add-Ons
http://www.mydesktop.com/update/netscape.html

ZD Net Software Library—Netscape Plug-Ins Toolkit
http://www.hotfiles.com/toolkits/tksd099a.html

■ Creating Web Sites

HTML Validation Resources
http://www.devry-phx.edu/webresrc/webmstry/langval.htm

HTML References
http://union.ncsa.uiuc.edu/HyperNews/get/www/html/lang.html

Multimedia & Clip Art
http://www.itec.sfsu.edu/multimedia/multimedia.html

Tips & Techniques for Better Inline Graphics
http://voodoo.denveronline.com/New/GrDsF.html

WEB SITES MENTIONED

■ General Search Engines

AltaVista
http://altavista.digital.com/

C:NET's Search.Com
http://www.search.com

Excite
http://www.excite.com/

HotBot
http://www.hotbot.com/

Infoseek
http://www.infoseek.com/

Lycos
http://www.lycos.com

WebCrawler
http://wc1.webcrawler.com/

Yahoo!
http://www.yahoo.com

■ Specialized Search Engines

All-in-One Search Page
http://www.albany.net/allinone/all1user.html

AT&T 800 Directory
http://www.tollfree.att.net/dir800/

Companies Online
http://www.companiesonline.com

Deja News
http://www.dejanews.com/forms/dnq.html

EUROPAGES
http://www.europages.com/home-en.html

Four11.Com
http://www.four11.com

Internet Address Finder
http://www.iaf.net

Lycos PeopleFind
http://www.lycos.com/pplfnder.html

PeopleFinder
http://www.peoplesite.com/indexnf.html

Switchboard
http://www.switchboard.com/

WhoWhere? E-mail Addresses
http://www.whowhere.com/

Yahoo Individual White Page Reference
http://www.yahoo.com/Reference/White_Pages/Individuals/

Yahoo's Usenet Newsgroup Listings
http://www.yahoo.com/news/usenet

YellowNet
http://www.yellownet.com/

▪ Web Interface Sites for Finger

http://www.magibox.net/~unabest/finger/index.html
http://cs.indiana.edu/finger/gateway

▪ Web Sites of Interest

Bartlett's Familiar Quotations
http://www.columbia.edu/acis/bartleby/bartlett/

Book Publishers on the Internet
http://www.faxon.com/Internet/publishers/pubs.html

CIA World Factbook
http://www.odci.gov/cia/publications/95fact/index.html

Chambers of Commerce Listing
http://chamber-of-commerce.com/

Dun & Bradstreet/Lycos Listing of Businesses Online
http://www.companiesonline.com/

The Encyclopedia Smithsonian
http://www.si.edu/resource/faq/start.htm

Excite Business Reference Listing
http://www.excite.com/Reviews/Business/?a-Rb-t

Federal Express package tracking
http://www.fedex.com/track_it.html

Infoseek Small Business Reference Directory
http://www.infoseek.com/Business/Small_business?tid=484

Lycos Business Reference Listing
http://a2z.lycos.com/News_and_Information/Reference_Information/

The Thomas Register
http://www.thomasregister.com/

Web Stock Report
http://www.stockmaster.com/

WebCrawler Business Database Listing
http://wc2.webcrawler.com/select/ref.new.html

Yahoo Business Reference Listing
http://www.yahoo.com/Reference/

Glossary of Terms

A

ActiveX controls. Mini-applications designed for use with Microsoft's Internet Explorer. These controls can be embedded in and/or called by Web page. A program that runs within or outside your browser to perform a task or handle a specific type of data.

Add-on. A program that runs within or outside your browser to perform a task or handle a specific type of data.

Address. (See *URL*.)

Applet. A small, usually free, mini-program transmitted from a Web site to your PC, and run on your PC. Java programs are examples of applets.

Archive. A file that contains one or more other files, usually in a compressed form.

Archiving software. A special kind of utility software required to place files into an archive. The same program—or, in a few cases, an accompanying program—is needed to remove or "unpack" files from an archive; an excellent file management tool; serves as a way to speed up and organize downloads.

ARPANET. Acronym for *A*dvanced *R*esearch *P*rojects *A*gency *Net*work, created in 1969 by ARPA. This wide area network was the prototype for the Internet.

ASCII. Acronym for *A*merican *S*tandard *C*ode for *I*nformation *I*nterchange. ASCII is commonly used to refer to text files (as in ASCII files) that are composed of characters that are only 7 bits in length. (The Internet was originally designed to handle only ASCII text.)

Attachment. A file sent with an E-mail message. Most often, a binary file that has been UUENCODED to 7-bit data so that it can be sent via the Internet.

B

Bandwidth. A measure of frequency that is expressed either in hertz or in bits per second, which indicates the "width" or amount of information that a channel can handle. Higher frequency denotes a higher bandwidth.

Beta software. Software that has been (usually mostly) completed by the developer(s) but before a commercial release that still needs testing in "the real world." Beta software is distributed free of charge to many users, who then try the program and report to the developer any operational shortcomings or "bugs" that they find.

Binary data. Commonly used to refer to 8-bit data of the type that comprises program and many data files. 8-bit data characters are typically non-printable.

Bit. (*BI*nary digi*T*). The smallest element of computer data. A bit is either a binary 1 or a binary 0 (zero).

Bit-mapped graphics. Pixel-based graphics; graphics that are generated by turning on and/or altering the intensity and color of specific screen elements called *pixels*.

Bits per second (bps). In online communications with PCs, the measurement of the speed at which modems and serial ports can transmit and receive data in bits. (See *Bit*.)

BMP. *B*it-*m*apped graphics. A PC image format.

Bookmark. A recorded URL, or Web page address, that can be used to direct a browser to retrieve the page at that address. As a way to record your favorite places on the Web, bookmarks are usually stored in bookmark files and are accessed as menu items or as HTML documents.

Boolean search. A search method that uses logical operators (such as AND, OR, and NOT) in a database. Many Internet search engines use Boolean operators to help you find (or eliminate) specific information on the Web.

Browser. A program whose functions include navigating the World Wide Web, loading and displaying HTML documents and graphics, and handling associated tasks. (Also known as a Web browser.)

Browser-side. Occurring, taking place, or running on a user's Web browser program. Also, Client-side.

Byte. A computer data character, a byte is composed of either 7 or 8 *bits*.

C

Cache. An area in memory (or on disk) that keeps frequently used program information or data readily available. Most Web browsers have a disk cache feature that you can customize to keep recently accessed Web pages available on your hard drive.

CERN. European Organization for Nuclear Research (the acronym is in French); where the World Wide Web was created.

CGA. *C*olor *G*raphics *A*rray. A CGA display might have a resolution of 320 by 200.

CGI. Acronym for *C*ommon *G*ateway *I*nterface. CGI acts as an interface between Web pages and programs running on a host machine, funneling information between the program and the Web page.

Cipher. A secret method of representing information to ensure computer security. *Data decryption* is a process of reproducing data from an encoded message based on known code or cipher.

Clickable image. A graphic image that is also designed to be a hyperlink.

Client. A program that performs a function on behalf of another program. For example, WS_FTP is an FTP client.

Compression software. Archiving software; an excellent file management tool; serves as a way to speed up and organize downloads.

Concatenates. Combines multiple files into one file.

Cookies. Information that some Web sites store on your disk, and which others can retrieve later. You can use this feature to help identify you to a Web site, as well as to gather information about your Web activities, and more.

D

Data decryption. A process of reproducing data from an encoded message based on a known code or *cipher*. The code key to decrypting encrypted data is known, appropriately enough, as the *key*.

Data encryption. Data is encoded so it is not recognizable. This prevents data from being understood and used by those who don't have the means of decoding it; only those to whom you provide the means to decode the message can read it.

Data resources. Consist of millions of data, text, and program files stored on tens of thousands of computers on the Internet worldwide.

Default home page. On the World Wide Web, the document that first appears when you start your Web browser or click the "Home" button. Usually, the home page of the creator of your browser. Most browsers allow you to easily modify this setting.

Demoware. A popular approach to marketing anything by putting a product in the hands of the consumer.

Density. The number of pixels per row and column, which can be used to calculate the number of pixels per square screen inch.

Digitizing. The process of converting the analog data provided by a scanner (or a digital camera) into a digital representation of the image.

Dithering. A process whereby colors are converted to shades of gray.

DNS. *D*omain *N*ame *S*ervice. DNS is a protocol used by computers on the Internet to translate IP addresses.

Document. On the Web, an HTML *page*. Less often, an image or program file associated with an HTML page.

Domain name. On the Internet, the system used to identify specific Internet computer sites (such as bigblue.isu.indiana.edu or www.compuserve.com).

E

EGA. *E*nhanced *G*raphics *A*rray. An EGA display usually offers 4-color resolutions of 640 by 350 and 16-color resolutions of 640 by 200 from a 64-color palette.

Electronic mail.   Messages sent and received via computers over networks, including the Internet. Also known as E-mail.

Encode.   With computer data on the Internet, to create a file that is composed of 7-bit data that represents 8-bit data.

EPS.   *E*ncapsulated *P*ostScript. EPS files are often rather large because they carry information for printing.

F

FAQ.   A list of *F*requently *A*sked *Q*uestions on a given subject, along with answers. FAQs are a common means of providing information needed by those new to the Internet. On Usenet, documents that are posted on a regular basis that answer commonly asked questions about the newsgroup. Use the information in FAQs to avoid mistakes that would label you as a "newbie" (a user who knows little or nothing about this part of the Internet).

Finger.   A program on some ISPs' systems that provides information about a specified user of that system.

Flame.   In Usenet and E-mail, a message that uses threatening, aggressive, rude, or obscene remarks.

Forum.   On an online service, an area devoted to a group or special interest, usually consisting of a message board and download area, and sometimes including other features like realtime conferencing.

Frames.   The ability to display several more or less mini-Web pages within one page.

Freeware.   Software that is distributed free of charge.

Front end.   Describes a visual interface used to access information in a database or menu-driven multimedia program.

FTP.   Acronym for *F*ile *T*ransfer *P*rotocol. A protocol that enables file transfer over the Internet.

G

GIF.   *G*raphics *I*nterchange *F*ormat. Originally popularized on CompuServe, GIF is one of the two most common graphical image formats on the Web.

H

Helper program.   (See *Add-on.*)

Histogram.   A graph of an image's color values. The range of colors is the horizontal axis, and a value for the relative distribution of color by pixels for each color along that range is plotted on the vertical axis. This makes identifying relative color densities in an image fairly simple.

Hit. A slang term that refers to a visit to a Web page that registers on a counter. A page getting "100 hits per day" is registering 100 visits per day on its counter.

Home page. Often used to refer to a *Web site*, a home page is, strictly speaking, the first or index page at a Web site. A home page is the first HTML document you see when you go to a Web site.

Host. A computer connected directly to the Internet; usually one that serves as a site for Web pages.

HTML. *H*yper*T*ext *M*arkup *L*anguage. A system of *tags* in text documents that produces special text effects and formatting (fonts, boldface, etc.). HTML tags also call graphics and other documents for display, among other functions.

HTTP. *H*yper*t*ext *T*ransport *P*rotocol. The standard for the URL (Universal Resource Locator) for every page on the Web. The http address prefix directs a Web browser to look for an HTML document or other file on the World Wide Web (as opposed to on its computer's disk drive).

Hyperlink. Within an HTML document, a link to another document, or to a different portion of the same document.

Hypertext. A document (or segment thereof) that contains links to other documents; another name for an HTML document.

I

Image map. A graphic image that is divided into zones or regions, and each zone is linked to a different URL, image, or other object.

Index page. (See *Home page*.)

Inline image. A graphic image displayed by a Web page.

Internet. The term is most often used to refer to the World Wide Web; but the Internet is composed of many elements: the Web, Usenet newsgroups, the computers that host Web pages and other Internet resources, and the links, hardware, and software that make it function and tie it all together.

Intranet. The use of a dedicated file server running TCP/IP in a local area network to provide HTML documents and other files that are accessed by clients using a Web browser as their interface.

IP Address. *I*nternet *P*rotocol *A*ddress. A numeric 32-bit "address" that contains information necessary to identify a specific network and machine on the Internet.

IRC. Short for *I*nternet *R*elay *C*hat, IRC is real-time conversation of the "type and read" variety. IRC also refers to the software used in real-time conferencing.

ISP. *I*nternet *S*ervice *P*rovider. An ISP provides connection to the Internet. An ISP may be a consumer online service or an independent service provider, but the term usually is reserved for independent ISPs.

J

Java. A specialized programming language for use with Web pages. A Java program is an *applet* that is transmitted to and run on a computer that requests its Web page.

JPG. Also, JPEG. A popular graphic image format created by the **J**oint **P**hoto **E**xpert **G**roup. JPG is enjoying growing popularity on the Web.

K

Key. A reference or guide that can be used to decrypt encrypted data. In effect, a key tells the user (or with computer data, a decrypting program) which symbols represent which characters, and where and how; that is, the substitutions made by the encryption program.

Keyword. A word (or sometimes, a phrase) used in a database search as a search criterion.

Kiosk mode. A Web browser's capability that can remove the browser's "front end" (the menus, scroll bars, toolbar, and so on) to show only the Web page as a full-screen document. Mosaic, for example, has this feature.

L

LAN. **L**ocal **A**rea **N**etwork.

Library Software. Archiving software; an excellent file management tool; serves as a way to speed up and organize downloads.

Link. A hypertext link in a Web page.

Lurk. To read the information found in a newsgroup, but choosing to never contribute to the group.

M

MAPI. **M**essaging **A**pplication **P**rogram **I**nterface. This system allows you to attach files to messages from within other Windows 95 programs.

MIDI. **M**usical **I**nstrument **D**igital **I**nterface. A protocol for the interchange of musical information between computers, musical instruments, and synthesizers.

MILNET. **MIL**itary **NET**work.

MIME. **M**ultipurpose **I**nternet **M**ail **E**xtensions. This is a standard for encoding programs, data files, and multimedia data for transfer on the Web.

N

NCSA. **N**ational **C**enter for **S**upercomputing **A**pplications. A research center at the University of Illinois at Champaign-Urbana where NSCA Mosaic, the first of the graphical Web browsers, was created.

Network. Multiple computers, interlinked and sharing resources.

Newbie. In Usenet, a new user who is easily identified by making mistakes that have already been answered in available FAQs (Frequently Asked Questions).

Newsgroup. A conference that is located in the Usenet area of the Internet.

O

Online information service. A dial-up computer service that exists independently of the Internet, but may be connected to the Internet. The most popular commercial online services—all of which also serve as ISPs—are America Online, CompuServe, DELPHI, and Prodigy.

P

Packet switching. A means of sending data in small packets, over variable routes. This was the basis of the original Internet, and of today's packet-switching networks.

Page. Collectively, an HTML document and its supporting files (images, text, and so on); also, Web page.

PCT. *P*rivate *C*ommunica*t*ion.

PD. *P*ublic *D*omain.

PDF. *P*ortable *D*ata *F*ormat. Created by Adobe Acrobat.

Pixel. Short for picture element. The smallest element of an image on a display device.

Plug-ins. Programs added to your Web browser to expand or enhance its capabilities. A plug-in is run by the browser to handle a specific type of data transmitted by a Web page.

POP. *P*oint *of* *P*resence.

PPP. *P*oint-to-*P*oint *P*rotocol. An Internet standard, PPP provides router-to-router and host-to-network connections over synchronous (real-time) and asynchronous (non-real-time) circuits.

Protocol. A set of rules whereby computers communicate. TCP/IP is an example of a protocol.

R

RealAudio. A real-time audio player.

Real time. The time during which data processing occurs. The time that data is received and results returned is so quick that the process seems instantaneous

Remote terminal. A device connected to a computer by direct lines or telephone lines.

Resolution. On a display device, the relative quality of a graphic image, based on its density (the number of pixels per square inch), and the contrast between colors in the image.

S

Scanning. The process of "reading" an image (photo, drawing, painting, or a printed page) from paper for storage in a computer file, using a device known as a scanner. A scanner can reproduce, depending on its features, color or monochrome/gray scale.

Search engine. Essentially, any program that searches a database containing information about thousands of Web pages. When queried for information, the search engine presents a list of Web pages that meets the query's search criteria.

Search term. (See *Keyword*.)

Self-extracting archives. These special types of archives are .EXE or .COM files that, when run, unpack the files they contain.

Server. A computer that provides resources to other computers. On the Internet, usually any host for HTML documents and other files that are available to anyone else on the Internet. Also, the computer on which a given set of resources (such as the pages that make up a Web site) are stored and which, upon your browser's request, sends you HTML documents.

Server-side. Occurring, taking place, or running on a Web server.

Shareware. Software that is distributed on a free-trial basis.

Site. (See *Web site*.)

SLIP. *S*ingle *L*ine *I*nternet *P*rotocol.

SMTP. *S*imple *M*ail *T*ransfer *P*rotocol. The Internet standard protocol for transferring electronic mail messages from one computer to another.

Spam. In E-mail, unsolicited commercial messages.

Spawning. Knowing *when* to run add-ons (also known as plug-ins and helper applications) programs.

Spider. A program that searches the Internet for possible information sources such as Web pages and FTP sites. The results of these searches are placed into a database that Internet users then can explore with a search engine, such as the World Wide Web Worm or WebCrawler.

SSL. *S*ecure *S*ocket *L*ayer. A protocol for passing private, encrypted information over the Internet.

SVGA. *S*uper *VGA*. SVGA display supports images of 800 by 600 pixels, or even 1,024 by 768 pixels.

T

Tags. Term for the codes used in *HTML* documents that indicate text is to be used as special elements, such as lists, heads, hypertext, and so on. HTML tags are enclosed in greater-than/lesser-than symbols <>.

TCP/IP. Transmission Control Protocol/Internet Protocol. It refers to a set of rules by which computers linked to the Internet communicate and handle the data they're carrying.

Telnet. A protocol whereby anyone connected to the Internet can connect with a specific computer on the Internet.

Threads. Messages that are linked, by subtopic and/or a chain of posts and replies.

Tickler file. A tickler file lets you save a message until a specific date/time, at which point BeyondMail reminds you that it should be sent, and/or moves it to a designated folder. This works in concert with a to-do list.

Tymnet. A packet-switching network.

U

UNIX. An early computer operating system that still has its adherents today.

URL. Short for *U*niform *R*esource *L*ocator, an URL is a Web "address," such as www.sprynet.com, used to navigate to a specific Web site or page, and to identify a specific Web page.

Usenet newsgroups. A system of bulletin board-like areas on the Internet that are used for public discussion, and sometimes sharing encoded data files.

Utility. A specialized program that helps or enhances another program. Java applets, ActiveX Controls, and PKZIP are examples of utilities.

UUENCODED. A data or program file (8-bit files) encoded in such a way as to be transmittable as 7-bit ASCII file.

V

VGA. *V*ariable *G*raphics *A*rray. A high-resolution video display standard for personal computers. VGA displays images at 640 pixels horizontally by 480 pixels vertically.

Visual Basic. A powerful, visually-oriented programming language, introduced by Microsoft, for creating applications in Windows.

W

Web. Verbal shorthand for the World Wide Web. Sometimes called the WWW or "the Net," the Web is a globe-spanning hypertext network that is home to millions of Web pages, in the form of HTML documents and their supporting files. The Web is the graphical portion of the Internet.

Web counter. Tracks and displays the number of people who have accessed a Web page.

Web page. (See *Page.*)

Web site. A specific set of related and interconnected documents hosted on a computer connected to the Internet. Collectively, these are referred to as a Web site.

World Wide Web (WWW). See *Web.*

WYSIWYG. *W*hat *You* *S*ee *I*s *W*hat *You* *G*et.

br

Support Software and Web Site Listing

SOFTWARE

■ Archiving Software

ARC
http://www.shadow.net/~seaware/

ARJ
http://www.dunkel.de/ARJ/

LHA
http://www.shareware.com

LHARC
http://www.shareware.com

PKZIP/PKUNZIP and PKZIP for Windows
http://www.pkware.com

UNSIT/UNSTUFF
http://www.shareware.com

WinZip
http://www.winzip.com/

ZABTOOLS
http://w3.one.net/~banks/zabtools.htm

■ Audio, Video, and Multimedia Software

PointCast Network
http://www.pointcast.com/

QuickTime for Windows
http://quicktime.apple.com/

RealAudio
http://www.realaudio.com

http://www.timecast.com/

Shockwave Director
http://www.macromedia.com

TrueSpeech
http://www.dspg.com/internet.htm

VDOLive
http://www.vdolive.com/

▪ Browsers

Getting Started with Netscape
http://www-acs.ucsd.edu/using-mosaic.html

Microsoft Internet Explorer
http://www.microsoft.com/ie/download

NCSA Mosaic
http://www.ncsa.uiuc.edu/SDG/Software/WinMosaic/index.html

Netscape
http://home.netscape.com

PROCOMM PLUS for Windows (Web Zeppelin)
http://www.procomm.com

Using Netscape
http://www.pipex.co.za/solo/netscape.html

Using the Microsoft Internet Explorer
http://www.gsmdata.com/msie.htm

Using Web Browsers
http://www.traverse.com/TCCInfo/TCCNews/web.html

■ Document Display Software

Adobe Acrobat PDF File Reader (for Windows 95)
http://www.adobe.com/prodindex/acrobat/win95dnld.html

■ E-Mail Programs

BeyondMail
http://www.coordinate.com

E-Mail Connection
http://www.connectsoft.com

Eudora Lite and Eudora Pro
http://www.qualcomm.com

Pegasus
http://www.pegasus.usa.com

Pegasus Add-Ons
http://www.pegasus.usa.com/addons.htm

■ Encoding/Decoding Programs

Wincode
http://www.members.global2000.net/snappy/index.html

WinZip
http://www.winzip.com/

XFERPRO
http://www.sabasoft.com/

http://www.zdnet.com/

■ Encryption Programs & Services

Pretty Good Privacy
http://www.download.com/

Pretty Good Privacy Front Ends
http://www.seattle-webworks.com/pgp/pgplinks.html

Public Key Distribution Server
http://rs.internic.net/support/wwwpks/

RSA, Inc.
http://www.rsa.com/

SecurPC
http://www.rsa.com/rsa/PRODUCTS/end_user.html

■ Graphics Software

Adobe Pagemaker
http://www.adobe.com/prodindex/pagemaker/main.html

CompuPic! Viewer
http://www.photodex.com/cpic.htm

Corel's WEB.DRAW
http://www.corel.com/

Graphic Workshop for Windows
http://www.mindworkshop.com/alchemy/gww.html

Image View 95
http://www.ewl.com/ImageView95

Mapedit
http://www.boutell.com/mapedit/

Paint Shop Pro 4
http://www.jasc.com/

QuickTime Image Viewer
http://quicktime.apple.com/

VuePrint/PhotoView Plus
http://www.hamrick.com/

■ HTML Creation/Editing Software

Corel's Web.Graphics Suite
http://www.corel.com/

HoTMetaL PRO
http://www.softquad.com

Microsoft Internet Assistant for WORD 95
http://www.microsoft.com/msword/internet/ia/

Microsoft Internet Assistant for WORD 6.0
http://www.microsoft.com/msword/internet/ia/

■ Newsreaders

Free Agent and Agent
http://www.forteinc.com/agent/index.htm

See also this Usenet newsgroup:
alt.usenet.offline-reader

■ Web Site Support Software

CyberSpyder Link Test Utility for Windows
http://www.cyberspyder.com/cslnkts1.html

WebTrends, by e.g. Software
http://www.egsoftware.com/

Wusage
http://www.boutell.com/wusage/

SHAREWARE DOWNLOAD SITES

CNET Online's searchable PC shareware site, with browsable categories, feature stories, and more
http://www.download.com

Another CNET Online site—a shareware repository (reviews and downloads—browse or search)
http://www.shareware.com

Jumbo Shareware and Freeware Download Site
http://www.jumbo.com

Windows95.com Shareware Collection
http://www.windows95.com/apps/

ZDNet's Software Library
http://www.hotfiles.com/

ADD-ON & PLUG-IN INFO AND DOWNLOAD SITES

▪ Download Links & Info for Plug-Ins and Helper Apps in General

Each of these sites has information and links on plug-ins and/or helper applications for Netscape and Explorer:

I-World Internet News
http://www.iworld.com/

Plug-In Plaza
http://browserwatch.iworld.com/plug-in.html

Plug-Ins Today
http://www.hitznet.com/isocket/

"Recommended Plug-In Resources" (Links)
http://www.intouch.bc.ca/internetstore/utilities/plugins.html

■ Netscape Navigator Add-Ons

These URLs are all at Netscape's Web site. They offer extensive information on available plug-ins and helper apps, plus general background and technical information on add-on components.

Best Netscape Plug-Ins
http://www.earthcon.com/plugins/

Download Netscape Navigator Components
**http://home.netscape.com/comprod/mirror/navcomponents_
download.html**

Inline Plug-Ins Page
**http://home.netscape.com/comprod/products/navigator/version_2.0/
plugins/index.html**

Netscape Helper Applications
http://home.netscape.com/assist/helper_apps/

Netscape Plug-Ins and Add-Ons
http://www.mydesktop.com/update/netscape.html

ZD Net Software Library—Netscape Plug-Ins Toolkit
http://www.hotfiles.com/toolkits/tksd099a.html

■ Microsoft Internet Explorer Add-Ons

These URLs comprise "information central" for ActiveX controls for Explorer.

ActiveX Controls
http://www.microsoft.com/ie/download/ieadd.htm

http://www.microsoft.com/activex/controls/

http://www.mninc.com/tools/

ACTIVEX.COM
http://www.activex.com/library/mult.html

ActiveX Downloads and Info
http://www.activex.com

BrowserWatch ActiveX Arena
http://browserwatch.iworld.com/activex.html

General Info on ActiveX
http://www.microsoft.com/ie/ie3/activex.htm

Internet ActiveX Controls FAQ
http://www.microsoft.co.jp/visual/icp/jp/icpmain/icpfaq.htm

■ Java Info and Links

Gamelon Official Directory Site for Java
http://www.gamelan.com/

Netscape's Java Page
http://www.netscape.com/comprod/products/navigator/version_2.0/java_applets/index.html

Sun Microsystems' Java Page
http://java.sun.com/

Some Sites that Use Java:

CNET Online
http://www.cnet.com

EarthWeb
http://www.earthweb.com/java/

ServoNet's Java Site
http://java.servonet.com/

ONLINE HTML REFERENCES AND GUIDES

A Beginner's Guide to HTML
http://www.ncsa.uiuc.edu/General/Internet/WWW/HTMLPrimer.html

Desktop Publishing & Web Design Links
http://www.lehigh.net/zuzu/weblink.htm

HTML Reference Documents Listing
http://www.kersur.net/~polyvis/html.html

HTML Reference Index
http://csugrad.cs.vt.edu/serversetup/htmldocsindex.html

HTML References
http://union.ncsa.uiuc.edu/HyperNews/get/www/html/lang.html

HTML Validation Resources
http://www.devry-phx.edu/webresrc/webmstry/langval.htm

The NCSA Beginner's Guide to HTML
http://www.ncsa.uiuc.edu/General/Internet/WWW/HTMLPrimer.html

Tips & Techniques for Better Inline Graphics
http://voodoo.denveronline.com/New/GrDsF.html

Web Page Authoring Reference/Resource Listing
http://www.uh.edu/www_resources/web_authoring.html

World Wide Web and HTML Tools Listing
http://www.w3.org/pub/WWW/Tools/

ONLINE WEB SITE SUPPORT SERVICES

▪ General

GIF Wizard
http://www.raspberryhill.com/gifwizard.html

itList
http://www.itlist.com/

A Kinder, Gentler HTML Validator
http://ugweb.cs.ualberta.ca/~gerald/validate/

Microsoft Custom Page
http://www.msn.com/custom/workspace.htm

Multimedia & Clip Art
http://www.itec.sfsu.edu/multimedia/multimedia.html

Netscape's PowerStart Page
http://personal.netscape.com/custom/index.html

Public Key Distribution Server
http://rs.internic.net/support/wwwpks/

URL-Minder
http://www.netmind.com

Web Counter Information Service
http://www.digits.com/

WebTracker
http://www.fxweb.holowww.com/tracker/index.shtml

▪ Web Site Announcements and Publicizing

Desktop Publishing & Web Design Links
http://www.lehigh.net/zuzu/weblink.htm

Internet Link Exchange
http://www.submit-it.com/sublink.htm

PostMaster
http://www.netcreations.com/postmaster/

Submit-It
http://www.submit-it.com

WebPromote
http://www.webpromote.com/

SEARCH ENGINES

▪ General Search Engines

AltaVista
http://altavista.digital.com/

C:Net's Search.Com
http://www.search.com

Excite
http://www.excite.com/

HotBot
http://www.hotbot.com/

Infoseek
http://www.infoseek.com/

Lycos
http://www.lycos.com

WebCrawler
http://wc1.webcrawler.com/

Yahoo!
http://www.yahoo.com

■ Specialized Search Engines

All-in-One Search Page
http://www.albany.net/allinone/all1user.html

AT&T 800 Directory
http://www.tollfree.att.net/dir800/

Companies Online
http://www.companiesonline.com

Deja News
http://www.dejanews.com/forms/dnq.html

EUROPAGES
http://www.europages.com/home-en.html

finger Interfaces
http://www.magibox.net/~unabest/finger/index.html

http://cs.indiana.edu/finger/gateway

Four11.Com
http://www.four11.com

Internet Address Finder
http://www.iaf.net

Lycos PeopleFind
http://www.lycos.com/pplfndr.html

PeopleFinder
http://www.peoplesite.com/indexnf.html

Switchboard
http://www.switchboard.com/

WhoWhere? E-mail Addresses
http://www.whowhere.com/

Yahoo Individual White Page Reference
http://www.yahoo.com/Reference/White_Pages/Individuals/

YellowNet
http://www.yellownet.com/

MISCELLANY

AutoDesk MapGuide
http://www.mapguide.com

Bookmark Manager
http://ourworld.compuserve.com/homepages/Edgar_Hofer/bookmm.htm

Cooper + Peters Java Word Processor Applet
http://www.cooper-peters.com/cpwp.html

Corel Office for Java
http://www.corel.com/

U.S. Naval Observatory Master Clock
http://tycho.usno.navy.mil:80/what.html

http://www.onlineinc.com

Visual Basic Runtimes
http://www.softseek.com/Utilities/VBRUN_Files/index.html

http://www.fys.ruu.nl/~beljaars/download.html

http://www.execnet.com/filelibs/l397p001.html

Visual Basic Script
http://musicm.mcgill.ca/~simone/HTTP/webvb.html

INTERNET SERVICE PROVIDERS & ONLINE SERVICES

■ ISP Listings

iWORLD and Mecklermedia's ISP List
http://thelist.iworld.com

Providers of Commercial Internet Access Listing
http://www.celestin.com/pocia/

■ Independent ISPs

Earthlink
http://www.earthlink.com

GNN
http://www.gnn.com

Mindspring
http://www.mindspring.com

NETCOM
http://www.netcom.com

OneNet
http://www.one.net

SpryNet
http://www.sprynet.com

■ Online Services

America Online
http://www.aol.com

CompuServe
http://www.compuserve.com

DELPHI Internet Services
http://www.delphi.com

The Microsoft Network
http://www.msn.com

Prodigy
http://www.prodigy.com

■ Selected Web Site Hosts

AOL
http://members.aol.com

CompuServe
http://ourworld.compuserve.com

Concentric Network
http://www.concentric.net/club/community.html

Earthlink (Personal)
http://www.earthlink.net/company/business/

Earthlink (Business)
http://www.earthlink.net/company/free_web_pages.html

Mindspring
http://www.mindspring.com/community/index.html

OneNet
http://www.one.net/explore/clients/

Prodigy
http://pages.prodigy.com

Sprynet
http://www.sprynet.com/ourworld/searchow/index.html

SELECTED ONLINE REFERENCES

Bartlett's Familiar Quotations
http://www.columbia.edu/acis/bartleby/bartlett/

Book Publishers on the Internet
http://www.faxon.com/Internet/publishers/pubs.html

Chambers of Commerce Listing
http://chamber-of-commerce.com/

CIA World Factbook
http://www.odci.gov/cia/publications/95fact/index.html

Dun & Bradstreet/Lycos Listing of Businesses Online
http://www.companiesonline.com/

The Encyclopedia Smithsonian
http://www.si.edu/resource/faq/start.htm

Excite Business Reference Listing
http://www.excite.com/Reviews/Business/?a-Rb-t

Federal Express package tracking
http://www.fedex.com/track_it.html

Infoseek Small Business Reference Directory
http://www.infoseek.com/Business/Small_business?tid=484

Lycos Business Reference Listing
http://a2z.lycos.com/News_and_Information/Reference_Information/

Public Key Distribution Server
http://rs.internic.net/support/wwwpks/

The Thomas Register
http://www.thomasregister.com/

Usenet Newsgroup Listing
http://www.yahoo.com/news/usenet

Web Stock Report
http://www.stockmaster.com/

WebCrawler Business Database Listing
http://wc2.webcrawler.com/select/ref.new.html

Yahoo Business Reference Listing
http://www.yahoo.com/Reference/

"MUST-HAVE" PLUG-INS, ADD-ONS, AND UTILITIES

Adobe Acrobat Reader
http://www.adobe.com/prodindex/acrobat/readstep.html

PKZIP and PKZIP for Windows
http://www.pkware.com/download.html

QuickTime
http://quicktime.apple.com/sw/

RealAudio
http://www.realaudio.com/hpproducts/player/index.html

Shockwave Director
http://www.macromedia.com/shockwave/download/

Visual Basic Runtime DLL Files
http://www.softseek.com/Utilities/VBRUN_Files/index.htm

http://www.fys.ruu.nl/~beljaars/download.html

http://www.execnet. com/filelibs/l397p001.html

WinZip
http://www.winzip.com/

For More Information

MAGAZINES

DATABASE
Online Inc.
http://www.onlineinc.com/database

EMedia Professional
Online Inc.
http://www.onlineinc.com/emedia

NetGuide Magazine
CMP Media Inc.
http://techweb.cmp.com/ng/home/

ONLINE
Online Inc.
http://www.onlineinc.com/onlinemag

BOOKS

Finding Images Online: ONLINE USER's *Guide to Image Searching in Cyberspace*, by Paula Berinstein
Pemberton Press
http://www.onlineinc.com/pempress/images/

Internet Power WEB, by Neil Daly & Peter Bowen
Pacific HiTech
http://www.pht.com/index2.html

The Modem Reference, by Michael A. Banks
Brady Books
http://www.bradybooks.com/

Naked in Cyberspace: How to Find Personal Information Online, by Carole A. Lane
Pemberton Press
http://www.onlineinc.com/pempress/naked

One-Stop CompuServe for Windows, by Michael A. Banks
MIS:Press
http://www.mispress.com/

The Online 100: ONLINE *Magazine's Field Guide to the 100 Most Important
Online Databases,* by Mick O'Leary
Pemberton Press
http://www.onlineinc.com/pempress/ol100

The Online Deskbook: ONLINE *Magazine's Essential Desk Reference for
Online and Internet Searchers*, by Mary Ellen Bates
Pemberton Press
http://www.onlineinc.com/pempress/deskbook

*Secrets of the Super Net Searchers: The Reflections, Revelations, and Hard-
Won Wisdom of 35 of the World's Top Internet Researchers*, by Reva Basch
Pemberton Press
http://www.onlineinc.com/pempress/super

ONLINE INTERNET REFERENCES

EEF's Extended Guide to the Internet
http://www.eff.org/papers/eegtti/eegtti.html

InterNIC Information and Education Resources
http://rs.internic.net/nic-support/

Online Internet Course from Oberlin College
http://www-ts.cs.oberlin.edu/wt95/wt95home.html

Realizing the Full Potential of the Web
http://www.w3.org/pub/www/

Using the Internet for Competitive Intelligence
http://www.cio.com/CIO/arch_0695_cicolumn.html

The ASCII Table

The following table shows the ASCII (American Standard Code for Information Interchange) table. This table is broken down into each character's (or function's) decimal value, binary value, and the communications control, character or function that each character/key represents. Note that the first 32 numbers (0 through 31) represent control characters, many of which are used in transmitting data between computers and peripherals.

7-BIT "STANDARD" ASCII CHARACTER SET

Decimal Value	Binary Value	Character and/or Key	Communications Control Character/Function
0	000000	^@	NUL(nothing)
1	000001	^A	SOH (Start Of Heading)
2	000010	^B	STX (Start Of Text)
3	000011	^C	ETX (End Of Text)
4	000100	^D	EOT (End Of Transmission)
5	000101	^E	ENQ (Enquiry)
6	000110	^F	ACK (Acknowledge)
7	000111	^G	BEL (Bell)
8	001000	^H	BS (Backspace)
9	001001	^I	HT (Horizontal Tab)
10	001010	^J	LF (Line Feed)
11	001011	^K	VT (Vertical Tab)
12	001100	^L	FF (Form Feed)
13	001101	^M	CR (Carriage Return)
14	001110	^N	SO (Shift Out)
15	001111	^O	SI (Shift In)
16	010000	^P	DLE (Data Link Escape)
17	010001	^Q	DC1 (Device Control 1)
18	010010	^R	DC2 (Device Control 2)
19	010011	^S	DC3 (Device Control 3)
20	010100	^T	DC4 (Device Control 4)
21	010101	^U	NAK (Negative Acknowledge)
22	010110	^V	SYN (Synchronous Idle)
23	010111	^W	ETB (End of Transmission Block)
24	011000	^X	CAN (Cancel)
25	011001	^Y	EM (End of Medium)
26	011010	^Z	SUB (Substitute)
27	011011	^[	ESC (Escape)
28	011100	^\	FS (File Separator)
29	011101	^]	GS (Group Separator)
30	011110	^^	RS (Record Separator)

Decimal Value	Binary Value	Character and/or Key	Communications Control Character/Function
31	011111	^_	US (Unit Separator)
32	100000	space	
33	100001	!	
34	100010	"	
35	100011	#	
36	100100	$	
37	100101	%	
38	100110	&	
39	100111	'	
40	101000	(	
41	101001	)	
42	101010	*	
43	101011	+	
44	101100	,	
45	101101	-	
46	101110	.	
47	101111	/	
48	110000	0	
49	110001	1	
50	110010	2	
51	110011	3	
52	110100	4	
53	110101	5	
54	110110	6	
55	110111	7	
56	111000	8	
57	111001	9	
58	111010	:	
59	111011	;	
60	111100	<	
61	111101	=	
62	111110	>	
63	111111	?	
64	1000000	@	
65	1000001	A	
66	1000010	B	
67	1000011	C	
68	1000100	D	
69	1000101	E	
70	1000110	F	
71	1000111	G	
72	1001000	H	
73	1001001	I	
74	1001010	J	
75	1001011	K	
76	1001100	L	
77	1001101	M	
78	1001110	N	
79	1001111	O	
80	1010000	P	
81	1010001	Q	
82	1010010	R	

Decimal Value	Binary Value	Character and/or Key	Communications Control Character/Function
83	1010011	S	
84	1010100	T	
85	1010101	U	
86	1010110	V	
87	1010111	W	
88	1011000	X	
89	1011001	Y	
90	1011010	Z	
91	1011011	[	
92	1011100	\	
93	1011101	]	
94	1011110	^	
95	1011111	_	
96	1100000	`	
97	1100001	a	
98	1100010	b	
99	1100011	c	
100	1100100	d	
101	1100101	e	
102	1100110	f	
103	1100111	g	
104	1101000	h	
105	1101001	i	
106	1101010	j	
107	1101011	k	
108	1101100	l	
109	1101101	m	
110	1101110	n	
111	1101111	o	
112	1110000	p	
113	1110001	q	
114	1110010	r	
115	1110011	s	
116	1110100	t	
117	1110101	u	
118	1110110	v	
119	1110111	w	
120	1111000	x	
121	1111001	y	
122	1111010	z	
123	1111011	{	
124	1111100			
125	1111101	}	
126	1111110	~	
127	1111111	DELETE (Character delete or time delay)	

Index

D

E

F

G

H